LAURENCE LERNER

YOU CAN'T SAY THAT!

ENGLISH USAGE TODAY

GEORGIAN PRESS

Georgian Press (Jersey) Limited
Pirouet House
Union Street
St Helier
Jersey JE4 8ZQ
Channel Islands

www.georgianpress.co.uk

The moral right of the author has been asserted.

First published in 2007 by Georgian Press (Jersey) Limited

ISBN 978-1-873630-55-6

Produced by AMR Design Ltd (www.amrdesign.com)

Printed and bound in Great Britain by Halstan & Co Ltd

GEORGIAN PRESS

YOU CAN'T SAY THAT!

Laurence Lerner, born in Cape Town but long resident in England, is a retired professor of English and an (almost) retired poet: he has published ten volumes of poetry, including his *Selected Poems* in 1984 and *Rembrandt's Mirror* in 1987. He has taught in universities all over the world (including 22 years at the University of Sussex), and described some of his experiences in *Wandering Professor*, published in 1999. His other books include three novels and seven volumes of literary criticism. He is a Fellow of the Royal Society of Literature. Unable to break the habit of teaching, he now teaches senior citizens and other adults who just love literature and don't want to sit exams or get a diploma.

He is married to a biologist (also retired). They live in Lewes and have four sons and seven grandchildren scattered around the country.

To Werner Sedlak – in friendship.

Contents

Preface

There are plenty of books on English usage that tell you what to say and what not to say. Arranged like dictionaries, they are written like commands. This book, in contrast, is written to be read. Its aim is not simply to tell you what's right and what's wrong, but to discuss the issues involved, and so put you in a position to make your own informed decision. Do you want to be seen as a fuddy-duddy linguistic diehard, or a trendy radical? Are you more afraid of being mocked for ignorance or of being laughed at for pedantry? Such decisions are yours to make, and this book sets out to help you.

After a couple of opening flurries in Chapters 1 and 2, airing some topical issues and contrasting the two basic ways usage can be discussed (prescriptive and descriptive), the book moves steadily through the main issues concerning English usage. Chapter 3 establishes a central truth about all language – that it is constantly changing – and explores some of the consequences of this for English usage today. Chapter 4 deals with changes caused by space, not time, and discusses the relation of Standard English to the varieties that depart from it. Chapter 5 is about grammar: what it is and whether we need it, and points out some of the most colourful elements of English grammar. Meaning is central to language, and in discussing meaning Chapter 6 naturally deals with dictionaries, and what they can and can't tell us. Chapter 7 looks at language as a social activity, and explores how the social situation leaves its mark on the language we use: it concludes with a discussion of the language of computing, of emails and chat rooms, and the effect this is having on Standard English. One element in the social dimension of language is the need we often feel not to state things too bluntly, so Chapter 8 deals with euphemism: how and when we avoid terms that might give offence or sound too blunt. In our age of changing social relations and the shifting of taboos, the words and expressions that can give offence seem to be more numerous than ever before, and stepping carefully around them has given rise to the need for (and the objections to) political correctness: this is the subject of Chapter 9. The last two chapters deal with less controversial matters: Chapter 10 with the importance for English of our two contrasting sources of vocabulary, Anglo-Saxon and Latin; and the final chapter with the consequences of English becoming a world language.

A Note of Thanks

... to those who have helped me with this book. To my friends Derek Oldfield and Werner Sedlak who read it all and made many helpful contributions; to my grandchildren Robin and Deborah who helped greatly with the section on Netspeak; to my publisher Judith Brown who was unfailing in support and suggestions; and above all to my meticulous and unremitting editor Lyn Strutt, who scrutinised every sentence, sometimes drove me mad, and has certainly left the book much better than she found it.

CHAPTER ONE

Trendy or Diehard?

Hopefully, you are going to buy this book. Assuming, that is, you haven't already bought it.

So there we are, in the very first sentence of a book about English usage, committing an error. For I have plenty of friends – and so perhaps do you – who would not hesitate to complain that this use of *hopefully* is wrong. If you say *Hopefully, he'll arrive in time to catch the train*, or *Hopefully, it won't rain tomorrow*, dozens of people will hasten to tell you, helpfully or regretfully (or triumphantly), that you're wrong. You can catch a train eagerly, or reluctantly, or hopefully, they'll say, and that means you're full of hope. But, they will point out, you didn't mean that the person catching the train is hopeful, you meant that we are; and they will explain that in this case you ought to say *We hope he'll arrive in time*. And then they might add something rueful or indignant about declining standards, and shake their heads at what the world is coming to.

Are our helpful (or rueful or triumphant) friends right? Not altogether. Placed at the beginning of the sentence like that, *hopefully* doesn't mean that he'll arrive full of hope. It doesn't apply to the person arriving, it applies to the whole sentence. It is perfectly normal usage in English for an adverb to modify a whole sentence. We say *Frankly, you ought not to do that*, or *Unfortunately, the rules do not allow that option*, or *Interestingly, three different candidates made the same mistake*. We do not mean that you ought not to do it frankly (but may do it in secret); nor do we mean that the rules are unfortunate or that the candidates were interesting. We mean, rather, that the whole remark is being uttered frankly, that the fact conveyed by the whole statement is unfortunate, that the whole statement is interesting.

Your friends may not be convinced. They may have strong feelings about what they see as the misuse of *hopefully*. The reason their feelings are so strong is that the example is, for them, part of a larger tendency: the tendency of the language to get more and more sloppy, of young people to speak more and more carelessly – all of this is part of the way the world is going to the dogs. Well, the world is (of course) always going to the dogs, just as the world is always improving: some things get worse, others get better. Our children probably know less history than our parents did, but have better computer skills. Our great-grandparents had a much richer vocabulary for agricultural processes or theological niceties than we have, but a much poorer vocabulary for social movements or science. The argument between the believers in progress and the believers in decline will never be settled, because both are right, but in different areas. A little book on English usage can hardly tackle the huge question of progress or decline in our civilisation, but there are some things we can point out.

One is that changes in the meanings of words (something, as we shall see, which is going on all the time) can very easily be taken as evidence that thought, or civilisation, as a whole is declining. Take, for instance, the word *refute*. This means 'disprove': *I refuted his argument* means 'I succeeded in showing it was wrong.' But, as is often pointed out, the word is now frequently used with the meaning 'reject'. *I refute what he is saying*, says the indignant politician, oblivious of the fact that it is for others to judge whether his objections succeed in refuting it or not; what he means is 'I deny, or reject, what he is saying.' If we look up the word in *Chambers Dictionary* we find 'to disprove, loosely to deny', a neat illustration of the dual function of dictionaries: to tell us what is correct, and to tell us what the usage is. Chambers clearly feels we ought to know that alongside the established meaning, 'disprove', there is a looser usage which has grown up. What no one can say is whether this looser usage will become so widespread that future dictionaries will define *refute* as 'to disprove; to deny'. It may happen, or the loose meaning may die out. More interestingly still, if we look up *refute* in the *Oxford English Dictionary*, which tells us about the history of the word, we find that the earliest meaning given (but qualified as 'obsolete' and 'rare') is to 'refuse or reject' – not quite the modern loose meaning but very similar.

All this is a common enough state of affairs: a new meaning grows up, first as a loose usage, and then (possibly, we cannot predict) may become accepted. And while it is happening, there will be indignant protests. *That shows*, the protesters will say, *how standards of thought are declining: the young* (or *our politicians*, or *the media*) *can't even distinguish between denying something and actually refuting it*. Is that true? If we ask our refuting politician, or a young person, or a journalist, about the difference between denying and disproving an argument, they will have no difficulty in explaining it. They all have the word *disprove* in their vocabulary, and in contexts where this meaning is crucial, such as science, we are in any case likely to use a slightly more technical term. Scientific hypotheses can be refuted, but they are more likely to be *disproved* or *invalidated* – even, if things are left still uncertain, *disconfirmed*. Change in usage does not necessarily mean decline in thinking.

Occasionally, however, it does: as we see from the case of *disinterested*. Since the seventeenth century, this has meant 'impartial, unprejudiced, because not governed by one's own self-interest'. It derives, not from the meaning of *interesting* as opposed to *dull* or *boring*, but from the meaning of *interest* as in *He has an interest in the business* – that is, he has money invested in it, or *He is an interested party in this inquiry* – that is, he stands to gain (often financially) from the outcome. We expect judges to pass disinterested judgements, because we expect them to be honest and to declare themselves ineligible if they have an interest (in the material sense) in the outcome. Recently, however, *disinterested* has more and more come to be used with the same meaning as *uninterested*. This is now so widespread, especially in the spoken language, that it may inevitably come to be the normal meaning – though if you use the word correctly, if you say *I'm quite disinterested, I don't stand to gain anything by the outcome*, you will still be understood. (Meanings that are dying out often remain alive for a while in passive use, so there is no difficulty in using the word correctly oneself.) The case here is not quite the same as with *refute*, since there really is no other word with the exact shade of meaning as *disinterested*: it occupies a space that joins together the idea of being impartial (referring to your state of mind) with that of having nothing to gain (referring to your material circumstances). That is why it is a good idea to go on using it correctly.

It has a valuable meaning, which it would be a pity to lose, and the more we can lengthen its life the richer the language will be – though my prediction is that we shall lose it in the end.

I quoted *Chambers Dictionary* on *refute*, and now have to add that I used the 1983 edition; when we turn to the latest (2003) edition, we find that the qualification 'loosely' has been dropped, and the word is defined simply as 'to disprove, to deny'. On *disinterested*, the meaning 'uninterested' was already included in 1983, with the comment 'revived from obsolescence' – an accurate summary, showing us that the meaning was once current, then almost died out, and is now once more acceptable (though the 'correct' meaning is given first and made more prominent). This tells us two things. First, that dictionaries cannot pretend that the language is standing still: they recognise and record the reality of change, on which Chapter 3 will have much to say. And second, on both these words Chambers gives some support to the trendies against the diehards.

Back for a moment to the helpful friends who are so anxious to correct you. What corrections are they most likely to make? I can predict with some confidence that *hopefully* will be one of their favourite examples. Objecting to this use of *hopefully* is very fashionable, and fashion rules, not only in determining what mistakes people make, but also in determining what usages are denounced as mistakes by the diehards. To show this we need only move back a few generations. For many years, the standard work on common mistakes in usage was H. W. Fowler's *A Dictionary of Modern English Usage*, first published in 1926. You will not find in it any mention of *hopefully*, and all it has to say about *refute* concerns the pronunciation of *refutable* and whether there is such a word as *refutal*. But you will find all sorts of other fascinating issues discussed: whether to say *analyst* or *analyser* (Fowler claims the latter is correct); *pacifist* or *pacificist* (he reluctantly concedes that the former, though 'barbarous', has taken too strong a hold to be dislodged); *accompanist* or *accompanyist* (he prefers the latter); and whether to say *basic principle* (he regards *basic* as an unnecessary upstart, driving out 'fundamental, with its 500-year tradition'). So next time you are inclined to say that as a pacifist your basic principle is non-violence, whatever the analysts of strategy may claim, you can reflect that conservatives today may object only to the sentiments, but conservatives in 1926 would have objected equally to the usage. Hopefully, they'd let you get away with it today.

CHAPTER TWO

Describing and Prescribing

If we want to use English correctly, don't we need to know what the rules are? For there must, surely, be rules.

Well, yes and no. There are rules, but it's very difficult to know what they are. In fact, this brings us up against the hottest argument among those who write about language: that between prescription and description. For many centuries, the purpose of studying language was to tell people how to speak or write correctly, and grammar books and dictionaries were concerned with establishing rules and correcting mistakes. The French began it: the Académie française, founded in 1635, is probably the most famous institution for the prescriptive study of language. Its main concern from the very beginning was to give rules to the French language, and to clean it of 'the impurities it has contracted in the mouths of the common people, from the jargon of the lawyers, from the misusages of ignorant courtiers, and the abuses of the pulpit'. There has never been a similar academy in England, though strenuous efforts were made to set one up. In 1712 Jonathan Swift published *A Proposal for Correcting, Improving and Ascertaining the English Tongue,* in the form of a letter to the then chief minister, which urged that a 'judicious choice' should be made of 'such persons as are generally allowed to be best qualified for such a work' and that they be given the task of 'fixing our language for ever. For I am of opinion, it is better a language should not be wholly perfect than that it should be perpetually changing.' Swift mentions two main processes of corruption that he wishes to see halted: the use of 'cant words' (what we would today call slang) and (a surprisingly trivial detail, but he seems to have cared greatly about it) the 'perpetual disposition to shorten our words by retrenching the vowels', pronouncing *disturbed* and *rebuked* as two syllables instead of three. The proposal was too crudely prescriptive even for such a prescriptive age, and no such academy was ever founded in England. Samuel Johnson (himself something of a prescriptivist) made two unanswerable criticisms of it: that there would soon be disagreements among the members of such an academy, and that 'every man would have been willing and many would have been proud' to disobey its decrees.

This was a long time ago, and much has changed. Today lawyers and preachers have been replaced by journalists and politicians as the offending professions – though those who get most of the blame are still 'the common people'. And the prescribers are still active. The most famous of them in twentieth-century England were the brothers H. W. and F. G. Fowler – we've already encountered H. W. Fowler's *A Dictionary of Modern English Usage*. When it appeared in 1926, it was welcomed by all the enthusiasts of prescription. One reviewer thought it 'may still be successful in checking the all-too-rapid advance of illiteracies such as *alright* among the nominally educated', while another took the opportunity to attack those who needed such a book, calling them 'the dwellers in the wilderness, the regular sinners against all canons of grammar, clarity and taste'. But we saw in the previous chapter that many of the Fowlers' complaints now sound merely quaint. And the Académie française has never had much success in halting change, just as the French government today has had little success in its efforts to halt the flow of English words into the French language.

With the rise of modern linguistics came a very different idea of the purpose of studying language: that rather than telling people what to say, it should find out what they actually do say. That it should not prescribe, but describe. That, after all, is the purpose of science: biologists studying animal behaviour and psychologists studying human behaviour do not write about how birds or chimpanzees, children or schizophrenics, ought to behave, but try and find out how they actually do. And if linguistics is a science, should it not do the same?

Here is an example of how the descriptive linguist (in this case Professor T. F. Mitchell) looks at English. Let us say you know a charming young woman decorator. You will not call her a *young charming woman decorator*, though you might call her *a young and charming woman decorator*; and you will certainly not call her *a charming woman young decorator* or *a woman young charming decorator*. There appears to be a rule governing the order of the three adjectives which we all obey without any difficulty, though we may not know what it is. The linguist tries to find out what it is, and suggests, for instance, that we think of *woman decorator* as a kind of compound term, not joined closely enough to become a single word, but still thought of as words belonging together and so not to be separated; he may propose a term (*coalescing* in this case) to describe that relationship between two words. Finding this out (and in the case of this phrase there is a good deal more to find out) teaches us something we did not know about the way adjectives are positioned in front of a noun. But we all put these adjectives in the same order – no native speaker gets it wrong. And this is purely a question of usage, not of meaning: *a charming woman young decorator* is simply an incorrect way of saying *a charming young woman decorator*; it is not a way of saying something different. The linguist is not conducting his research in order to improve anyone's speech, but to find out how English speakers arrange their adjectives. He is not, that is, interested in prescription.

The arrival of descriptive linguistics, however, does not mean that prescription has disappeared, for many people want their language skills to be improved – and many others are willing, indeed eager, to do the improving for them. The clash between the describers and the prescribers shows no sign of disappearing, and it may be impossible for it ever to do so; for every denouncer of 'illiteracies' there is a denouncer of the denouncers. Daniel Defoe, writing fifteen years before Swift, put forward a similar proposal for an academy: he hoped that when it was established 'twould be as criminal to coin words as to coin money'. A modern descriptive linguist looks forward to the time when 'a claim to dispensing "correct" speech will be treated as being equal in fraudulence to dispensing a cure-all in medicine.' Describers and prescribers, we notice, would each like to criminalise the others!

Steven Pinker, in his otherwise wonderful book *The Language Instinct*, dismisses those he calls 'the language mavens' (*maven* is a Yiddish word for 'expert'), with the remark that 'most of the prescriptive

19

rules of the language mavens make no sense on any level. They are bits of folklore that originated for screwball reasons several hundred years ago and have perpetuated themselves ever since.' He points out that even the most incoherent speaker of 'ungrammatical English' is performing an operation of enormous skill, applying the complex grammatical rules that he knows without being able to say what they are.

> A preschooler's tacit knowledge of grammar is more sophisticated than the thickest style manual or the most state-of-the-art computer language system, and the same applies to all healthy human beings, even the notorious syntax-fracturing professional athlete, and the, you know, like, inarticulate teenage skateboarder.

This is an entertaining defence of the inarticulate teenager with his groping utterances, and what it says is certainly true; but the fact that even these inarticulate syntax-fracturers are exercising great skill does not exempt them from needing a few improvements. Let us think further about the skills of playing football or skateboarding. It is certainly true that the clumsy lad who drops a pass or falls off the skateboard is still exercising enormous muscular skill even to pick up the football or step on the skateboard; but that would not stop the football coach from observing how badly he plays. Descriptive linguistics has not eliminated the desire of large numbers of speakers to 'improve their English', or the desire of teachers to improve that of their pupils. Indeed, the ranks of the prescribers have recently been swelled by a new set of allies, very different from the defenders of traditional grammar: the believers in political correctness, or verbal hygiene, which is discussed at length in Chapter 9. They don't prescribe in the same way, or for the same reasons, as the Fowlers did, but they do prescribe.

How should we sort out the apparent clash between the prescriptive and the descriptive? What is meant by 'improving one's English', and when, if ever, is it necessary? Most obviously, this is the case when one learns a foreign language. Nobody says to a German learning English *You say 'sree' but we say 'three'*, or *You say 'I have done it yesterday' and we say 'I did it yesterday'*, and then leaves it as a purely descriptive observation; we teach them how to pronounce *th*, or what the difference is between our two versions of the past tense – two skills that native speakers have mastered but foreigners learning English often find difficult. We do this because they want to learn English 'better'.

Young children also make mistakes: they say *goed* instead of *went* and *holded* instead of *held*, which they cease to do as they grow up. Their situation, however, is not quite the same as that of foreigners, since they do not learn through being corrected, but through modifying their habits. Children whose parents do not correct their mistakes learn just as quickly, and just as well, as children whose parents do.

Foreigners learning English, then, need some prescription, and children probably don't. But those most in search of prescription are neither children nor foreigners, but adults interested in 'improving their English'; perhaps you, reader, belong to that category. The reason so many language users feel they need guidance is that using language is a continual making of decisions. Even as I wrote that sentence, I had to make decisions: whether to use *continual* or *all the time*; whether to write *making* or *taking* of decisions; whether to write *using language is* or *using language involves*. All tricky decisions. All decisions of a kind that we usually make without thinking in a casual conversation, but are more likely to ponder in a formal situation, and perhaps even more likely when writing. The descriptive linguist might note how often you use one form rather than another, and how far your usage is representative of that of native English speakers. The scientific student of grammar sets out to understand which decisions are possible and which ones are not in a particular language. The sociolinguist asks what sort of person decides one way, or another. The speaker (and the writer) – you and I – actually make the decisions.

If you want to speak and, more especially, write your own language better, what are you asking for? It could mean that you want to write with the brilliance of Shakespeare or Dickens, or with the precision of a great scientist or legal draftsman. That would be a wonderful achievement: to come up with a brilliant way of saying something is deeply satisfying, both to writer and reader. But it would be asking too much of the language teacher to make us all write as well as Jane Austen or Steven Pinker – that needs years of practice and a good deal of native talent. In ordinary life, improving one's English has a more modest aim: learning to use Standard English.

So we need to think about Standard English: what it is, how it relates to other forms of English, and why there are such furious arguments about its use. But before this we need to look at the one inescapable fact about English that must influence all our discussions: the fact that, along with all other languages, it is always changing.

CHAPTER THREE

Change

English, like any language, is always changing. This is a truth it has not always been easy to accept. When Samuel Johnson started work on his famous dictionary, he hoped that it would be able to 'fix our language, and put a stop to those alterations which time and chance have hitherto been suffered to make in it without opposition'. He 'flattered himself for a while' that he would be able to achieve this, but ended up with the realisation that it was impossible. The very words in which he described his hope show its impossibility: how could it be possible to prevent the alterations caused by time?

Let's look at a passage that was once familiar to everyone, and must still be familiar to many: 'Our Father which art in Heaven, hallowed be thy name. Thy kingdom come. Thy will be done in earth, as it is in Heaven.' None of us has any difficulty in understanding the language of the Lord's Prayer, though the three sentences you have just read were written in 1611. How would they run in modern English? Here is a possible translation into the language of today: *Our Father who is in Heaven, may your name be made holy. May your kingdom come, and your wishes be carried out on earth as they are in Heaven.* You will notice that 'which art' was used where we now say *who is*; also that whereas we would probably say *may your kingdom come* to express a wish, the old form was simpler: 'your kingdom come'. These are changes that have occurred in English grammar. *Hallow*, meaning 'make holy', is a verb that has more or less disappeared, though we still refer to the night before All Saints Day as *Hallowe'en*. This is a change in English vocabulary. The English of four hundred years ago is clearly not the same as the English of today, but it is not difficult to understand.

One difference between this version of the Lord's Prayer and a modern English version is particularly interesting: that is the use of *thy*. We don't say it in everyday speech any more, though we are quite likely to use *thou* and *thy* when we are praying, instead of *you* and *your*. Why? The answer many people might give is that these forms are more holy, and therefore show our reverence for God, but that is not the reason they occur in the Lord's Prayer of 1611. If you have learned another language, or even begun to learn it, you will have discovered that English is unusual in having only one pronoun for addressing other people. We call everybody *you*, but in most European languages the word we use depends on who we are speaking to. There is one form for addressing friends and family members (*tu* in French and Italian, *Du* in German), and another for addressing strangers or social superiors (*vous* in French, *Sie* in German, *voi* or *Lei* in Italian). English had this distinction too until the seventeenth century, when we lost the intimate form (*thou*) and began addressing everyone with the more formal *you*. Nobody knows the reason for this: can it be that the English got more polite, or less friendly, to one another?

The distinction was still alive when the *Authorised Version* of the Bible appeared in 1611, and it addresses God with the intimate form. There is therefore nothing holy about calling God *thou*, and a Frenchman praying will still address God as *tu*. But because we have lost this form, we no longer realise it is a way of addressing God as our father or friend, and many modern Christians think of *thou* as expressing not intimacy but reverence.

There is a further twist to the story of this pronoun. Those languages which retain the two different forms changed their usage in the twentieth century. Social inferiors used to be addressed as *tu*, but in our democratic age servants and workmen are thought of not as inferiors but as fellow citizens, and so are addressed as *vous*. (I once heard a French housewife quarrelling violently with her domestic servant, but she continued to call her 'vous'.) On the other hand, the use of *tu* has spread: children call their parents *tu* (they would not have done that a century ago), and students call one another *tu*. In this respect, French in the twentieth century has gone the opposite way from English in the seventeenth: with them the formal pronoun is becoming less common, whereas with us it was the familiar pronoun that dropped out of use.

Comparing modern English with that which was used to translate the Lord's Prayer in 1611 gives us some idea of how English has changed in four hundred years; and if we go back further in time the change becomes much more striking. *Fader oure that is i heuen, blessid be thi name … Oure ilk day bred gif us to day.* You probably had no great difficulty in realising that this is still the Lord's Prayer (in the English of about 1300), so let's go back even further, and look at the English of about 1000 AD: *Fæder ure, thu the eart on heofonum, si thin nama gehalgod … .* That really looks like a foreign language. If we took a time machine back to 1000 AD we would not be able to read what our ancestors wrote or understand what they said; yet they were speaking English.

This book is about English today, so the huge changes that have taken place over a thousand years will not really concern us – though I have begun with them to show how great language change can be. The changes we shall look at are those that have taken place in our lifetime, and that are still taking place today. And this introduces a new factor into the discussion. We are not likely to think that the English of 1000 AD was somehow better than the English of today, since nostalgia does not operate on such a large timescale. But for many older people the changes that have taken place during their lifetime are seen as decline: the language is not just changing, it is getting worse. That is a question we'll return to again and again in our discussions, and to give ourselves perspective let's begin with a glance at yesterday. *The King's English* by the Fowler brothers, a guide to correct usage published in 1906, was enormously influential through much of the twentieth century, and it still has many admirers. Here is a sentence from it:

> *Everyone has been told at school how* telegram *ought to be* telegrapheme; *but by this time we have long ceased to mourn for the extra syllable, and begun seriously to consider whether the further shortening to* wire *has not been resisted as long as honour demands.*

'By this time' was 1906. To mark the centenary of this sentence, let us ask what has happened to give it its old-fashioned air. First, clearly, no one reading it today was told at school that *telegram* ought to be *telegrapheme*: the correction will only mean anything to you if you know Greek, and very few of today's pupils have learned

Greek, and almost as few have been taught about English words in this etymology-conscious way. But who is – or was – 'everyone'? Even in 1906 a very small proportion of pupils would have been told this: those who had a classical education, roughly the same proportion as those who went to public school – perhaps one in twenty, at most. The word which has most notably changed its meaning is in fact *everyone*, which in the highly (if only half-consciously) class-oriented English of the Fowlers meant something like 'everyone who belongs to the circles who are likely to be reading our book'.

The other change that has taken place is very different: we no longer send telegrams. Now that almost everyone in Britain has a telephone (and this time *everyone* does mean 'everyone', or at any rate 'every adult'), the telegram has become a piece of outmoded technology, and it is no longer necessary to suggest that such a thing needs a nice short word.

Here we have come upon the two factors governing language change, or at any rate lexical change – the change that happens to individual words. On the one hand, the world changes, and language responds (no more telegrams, but plenty of email); on the other hand, change occurs *within* language, often for reasons we do not understand. Both these changes are going on all the time, are of great interest to speakers of English, and often rouse intense passions. In this chapter we shall look at some of these hot potatoes.

New Words – New Things?

Why do some words fall out of use and others come in? The most obvious reason (though not, perhaps, the most important) is that we need new words for new things. Fifty years ago we did not have the words *internet, email, eco-warrior* or *modem*. A hundred years ago we did not have the words *jet engine, computer* or *penicillin*. Two hundred years ago we did not have *motor car, psychoanalysis* or *helium*. Five hundred years ago we did not have *tobacco, pineapple, chemistry*, or *calculus*. Today we have virtually lost the word *groat*, because we no longer have a coin worth fourpence, and we may lose the word *shilling* unless we find other meanings for it than the now obsolete coin. And so on and so on.

These changes do not usually arouse much controversy. The inventions and innovations themselves often do: every new invention seems to be greeted by some as a great blessing, and denounced by others as a disaster. So the fact that an invention or a new social habit gives a new word to the language may easily be swallowed up in the arguments about the invention itself. Plenty of people disapprove of *bungee jumping* or *body piercing*, but there can't be many who like the activity but don't like the name. There are fierce arguments about the validity and legal status of a *living will* (the term dates from the 1970s), but both sides agree on what to call it. The invention of credit cards has brought great convenience to most of us, and dangerous temptation to some; we can disagree about the advantages of having lots of *plastic* in our wallets, but we don't disagree about the term.

Those are all quite clearly new terms for new things, but sometimes it is not easy to know whether what is new is the word or the invention. What of *user-friendly*, for instance? There has always been a distinction between instructions and explanations that are unnecessarily hard to understand and those where trouble has been taken to make them easily understandable by ordinary people. We expressed this in the past with words like *easy, comprehensible, straightforward*, and *clear*, contrasted with *jargon, complicated, obscure*, and *unnecessarily difficult*. But none of these words explicitly drew our attention to the user as a person, and to the relation between that person's experience and the way the machine was designed or the instructions were written. So is *user-friendly* a new and useful word which could have been coined in the past, but wasn't? Perhaps, but it may be that the invention of computers has introduced new levels of difficulty for users, and a new kind of gap between inventors and ordinary people; there is more that we need to understand, and more jargon to bewilder us (see page 124 for a discussion of jargon). So there is now a new and greater need for terminology and explanations that do not bewilder us. Designing one's system to help the inexperienced user is a new or at least a more urgent requirement, and in that case *user-friendly* is a new word for a new thing.

But what we are also looking at is a new use of *friendly*. Friendship is a relationship between human beings; it was sometimes applied in the past to non-human entities, but I think this was usually felt to be a metaphorical extension. When Juliet complains that Romeo, in committing suicide, has drunk all the poison 'and left no friendly drop To help me after', she is for the moment thinking of the poison as a living being, a friend to help her follow her lover into death. If we pause to think about our response to this line, we probably think of her as somehow extending the meaning of *friendly*. Nowadays this extension has become normal, so that as well as *user-friendly programs* or *instructions*, we have *eco-friendly policies* or *products*, and we now think of this as a normal use of *friendly*, not as a figure of speech. Once again, it is not easy to say if this is an extension of the language, or if something new is happening in our society which requires a new usage of the word. Where does language end, and human activity begin?

If you are *eco-friendly* you might also be an *eco-warrior*: is that odd? Warriors after all are not friendly. This shows us how much variety there can be in forming such compounds: *eco-friendly* means 'friendly to the environment', and an *eco-warrior* fights on behalf of the environment, and we have no difficulty in grasping these contrasting meanings of the compounds (see the section 'Knowing That We Know' on page 79).

And you might also be described as a *green*. This political meaning was unknown fifty years ago, and it is now probably the primary meaning of *green* when it's used as a noun: such is the speed of change.

Does the meaning of colour-words, then, change over time? A difficult – and fascinating – question. The common-sense answer would seem to be that the literal meaning of colour-words cannot change, since the difference between blue and green is a question of wavelength, and so quite objective; but that the feelings associated with a colour might well change. Like so many common-sense answers, however, this turns out not to be completely true.

What depends on wavelength is hue: blue, green, yellow, red. But our experience of seeing colours is not just a matter of hue: it depends on whether what we are looking at is in the sun or the shade, is keeping still or moving, is living or inanimate. There are a few colour words in English that do not denote hue but rather the total experience of seeing – for example *dun, wan, sallow,* and the more or less obsolete *fallow*. These words definitely refer to the experience of seeing, not to the associated emotions, but they seem to indicate a different, and older, way of classifying colours, and such words have an old-fashioned feel about them.

As for the associated emotions, what is striking about them is how ambivalent they are. Most colours can call forth a range of emotions, as we clearly see in the case of *red*. It is the colour of fire, of roses, of blushing, of blood: we *see red* when angry, our *sins are scarlet*, our love is *like a red, red rose*. The ambivalent feelings *red* suggests are brilliantly exploited in John Donne's line urging his soul to be '*red with blushing as thou art with sin*'. And just because colours have such contradictory associations, these do not change much: whatever feeling we associate with them, the opposite may not be far away.

So if I am right in suggesting that the new, favourable association given to *green* by its association with the ecological movement has somehow given the colour-word itself a more positive feel, this would not be a very typical example of change.

The colour with the least contradictory associations is of course *black*. The reason seems obvious: that black is the colour of night. Before the invention of gas lighting and then of electricity, very little of our social life can have taken place after dark, though it must always have been a convenient time for robbery and murder and other *black deeds*. A villain has always had a *black heart*; people have always *blackened* the character of their enemies. The eldest son of King Edward III struck terror into the French, and was known as the *Black Prince* – if the French called him that it would show fear and dislike, if the English did so it was a way of boasting about his prowess, mockingly referring to it as villainy.

Recently the racial meaning of *black* has become more prominent in our consciousness. Africans and African-Americans have, of course, always been referred to as *black*, but political changes and migration have made people much more aware of racial questions; and it is interesting to ask whether the racial meaning of *black* has changed our perception of the traditional way of using the term. It would obviously be absurd to claim that *black heart* is a racist slur, but a black person today might hesitate to use the expression. This takes us to the question of politically correct language, which is discussed fully in Chapter 9.

The feelings and judgements attached to colours, then, must have something to do with the changes in our society: not so much new inventions as new social arrangements and new political issues, and our attitude to the old ones. And it's not difficult to think of other, similar issues. What, for instance, should we say about *spin*? The meaning 'clever verbal trickery in order to deceive' is quite recent and so far is applied almost exclusively to politicians. It may derive from the meaning *draw out* or *lengthen*, often applied to storytelling – as in the expression *spin a yarn*: sometimes meaning just to tell a story, but often to tell a long, or even an unnecessarily long story. Madame D'Arblay wrote in 1787 about someone who 'spun out into an hour's discourse what might have been said in three minutes'. What is recent is adding the idea of deception to that of long-windedness (this may owe something to *spin bowling* in cricket, which is clearly intended to deceive), and – perhaps even more recent – its use as a noun. Recent as it is, the term is now understood by everyone: one effect of mass media is to speed up language change.

Inventions are not the only, and possibly not the most important, changes in our lives – social customs, habits, and ways of behaving also change, and these probably have even more influence on our language than does new technology. Let us think, for example, about the effect of feminism: it has changed not only the way we behave but also the way we speak. Here are three examples that seem to me particularly interesting.

A *glass ceiling* is an unmentioned barrier to promotion – almost always used of a policy of not giving the top jobs to women. Of course a glass ceiling presupposes that a considerable amount of emancipation has already taken place. The colour bar in apartheid South Africa or the southern states of America, the banning of Jews from the professions during most of European history, did not use glass ceilings – they used very visible and rigid barriers. When discrimination has to be secret, it produces barriers that are perceived by the victims as made of glass. Arguably, this means that it is going to disappear before long.

Power dressing by women is a way of wearing expensive tailored clothes that are the very opposite to the flowered and clinging garments associated with femininity and sexual attraction. It is a statement that the wearer is ambitious, even ruthless, possessing the qualities traditionally thought of as masculine. And both men and women, if they are so busy they don't get enough sleep, might take a *power nap* during the day. It's just a nap, really, but the name is meant to remind us that the napper needs it because he or she is someone with power, who therefore needs lots of energy.

Another product of recent feminism is the *new man*. This expression is modelled on the *new woman* of late Victorian times, who invaded the territory traditionally reserved for men (as well as seeking employment in traditionally male occupations, the new woman was supposed to go in for smoking and riding bicycles). The new man, therefore, takes on traditionally feminine occupations: cooking, childminding and helping to run a household (if he runs it completely, he is a *house husband* – clearly modelled on the term *housewife*).

It is not always easy to distinguish language from social reality. Take, for instance, *teenager* – a fairly new word, imported from America just after the Second World War. Quite obviously there have always been young people between the ages of twelve and twenty. Does that mean there have always been teenagers? If a teenager is someone taking part in modern teenage culture, then we can certainly say that this new word denotes a new thing. A mother who says *I have two teenage daughters* may simply be referring to their age, but she may mean something more: that they listen to pop music, stay out late, wear clothes that expose their midriff – even that they are always quarrelling with her. If she simply wanted to refer to their age, she might say *I have two young daughters*. If we are thinking in purely biological terms, there is nothing new about being a teenager; if in social terms, there is.

Or let us take *safe sex*. There have always been dangers associated with sexual intercourse: dangers of venereal disease, plus the risk (if it is thought of as a risk) of pregnancy. But avoiding these dangers was not called *safe sex* until the advent of AIDS, so it would look here as if we are dealing with a new word for a new thing. Yet the actual methods used to keep sex safe – condoms, bodily position, avoiding promiscuity – have been with us for a long time, so it could be argued that the new term *safe sex* does not describe anything new. Once again, where does language end and human activity begin?

Here are a few more examples, some recent and some a good deal older, of the shady frontier between 'new thing' and 'new word for old thing'. *Eurosceptic* presupposes the existence of European political union, *Afro* presupposes the popularity of a new hairstyle, *black hole* presupposes a new astronomical theory; they could all (with some hesitations over what we mean by *thing*) be considered examples of

31

new words for new things. What of *brain drain*? Emigration to the United States goes back at least to the seventeenth century, and it is quite arguable that the Pilgrim Fathers who sailed in the Mayflower in 1620, and perhaps most of the early Puritan settlers, were more intelligent than the average of the English population. But that is not the reason they went, and they were not being 'drained off' in the sense of going because they were offered jobs in America. We think of the brain drain as a new thing not only because of the movement of people it designates, but also because a new social movement gets named when we are aware of it as a movement.

Then what of *aerobics, hijacking, rollover*, and (a surprising example) *write*? I am at this moment writing a book; if I write it with a pen and then put it on a typewriter, we can distinguish between *writing* it and *typing* it. If I compose it directly onto the typewriter, we would describe that as *writing* not as *typing* it; from which we can see that to *write* has both the meaning 'to compose' and also the meaning 'to put down on paper', whereas to *type* always refers to the physical action of recording it. But being a modern person, I no longer use a manual typewriter, but a computer: I am still *writing* the book, but suppose I had begun with a draft in handwriting? What am I then doing when I sit down at the computer? I have seen an editor refer to *keyboarding* material that had been sent to him; to many eyes and ears this will seem ugly, but it is difficult to suggest an alternative – the contributions may already have been typed, and clearly a different word was needed for putting them on a computer. This example is one in which language must follow technology. Today an editor is likely to receive material on a disk (that is, it has already been 'keyboarded'), so a whole new vocabulary is now needed to distinguish the various ways of recording one's text, and that vocabulary will change as technology changes. The result of all this is that *write* has become inescapably ambiguous, and if we want to draw distinctions between composing and recording, or between different kinds of recording, we'll need to make them explicit.

So back to the question of where language ends and human activity begins. It is a question for philosophers – which means, for most of us, a question we'll leave unanswered. But we can say one thing, which may point to an answer. When the new word names an invention or discovery that exists in the physical world – *aeroplane*, *dishwasher, condom, black hole* – then we have a new word that denotes a new thing – or, with *black hole*, a newly discovered thing. When it names the way people behave, then we are dealing with an area in which words and things interact so much that it is very difficult (some would say, impossible) to distinguish them. That takes us to the edge of serious philosophy, and we can pause there and go on living.

Change from within Language

A good deal of language change – perhaps most of it – has little to do with inventions or changes in human behaviour: it takes place entirely within language. This is true of pronunciation, and of grammatical changes. Students of the history of the language have long been aware of the great vowel shift of the fifteenth century, when all the English vowels changed their pronunciation. An English speaker who died in 1400, if he had come back to life in 1500, would have been astonished to find almost all words pronounced differently. No one knows why this happened, and no one has been able convincingly to suggest any outside events in society that caused it. This was the time when English pronunciation changed most, but that does not mean that it was completely stable at other times: changes in pronunciation are taking place all the time.

As well as pronunciation, English grammar has changed – the past tense of verbs provides a good example. English verbs have two ways of forming the past tense. They usually add *-ed*, as with *walk – walked, try – tried, stun – stunned*; but some verbs (not all that many, but they are usually the common ones) form the past by changing their vowel: *sing – sang, get – got, think – thought*. The first group used to be called *weak* verbs, the second group *strong* verbs – though the names are misleading, since over the centuries lots of verbs that used to change their vowel have taken to using *-ed* instead. *Swelled* used to be *swole*, *helped* used to be *holp* – about three quarters of the verbs that were strong in Old English are now weak. (So it could be claimed that the weak verbs are stronger than the strong ones!) An interesting exception seems to be *hang*. It has two past tenses in modern English, *hung* and *hanged*. No one can say why they have both survived, but, since they have, a distinction has arisen between them: things are *hung*, people are *hanged*. But the second of these forms seems to be dying out, and *hung* looks as if it will soon take over as the only past tense (an exception to the tendency of the weak verbs to drive out the strong). There may be an explanation for this, though I am not at all sure of it. In the days of capital punishment, judges in Britain pronounced the formula *hanged by the neck until dead*. The chilling effect of this expression seems somehow intensified by the grim sound of *hanged* – though of course we should really put this the other way round, and say that *hanged* sounds rather chilling because we associate it with this grim formula. Now that capital punishment has been abolished in Britain, the word *hanged* seems to belong to the past, and to a rather forbidding past. If that is true – and I do not know of any evidence for this theory, though it sounds likely to me – then the decline of *hanged* is not something internal to language, but is caused by a change in society.

Yet however hard we look for explanations outside language, we constantly find changes that just seem to happen. A generation ago, a speaker or a book that inspired you was *inspiring*; today the word is more likely to be *inspirational*. No change of meaning, no discoverable influence from outside the language. (Or can you think of one? I can't.) Just two extra syllables. Suppose we are dissatisfied with the performance of our cricket team: Smith is a good wicket-keeper but he never scores any runs. Not being able to bat is a serious downside in a wicket-keeper, so we decide to line up a new one. A generation ago we'd have done the same, but we'd have said that not being able to bat was a serious *drawback* or *disadvantage* in a wicket-keeper and we'd have *chosen* or perhaps *appointed* a new one. *Drawback* and *disadvantage* are perfectly normal English words, understood by everyone. Why are they being replaced by *downside*, a word that was unknown a generation ago? (Unknown with this meaning, that is – you could hang something *upside*, *downside* or *end up*, though the word was never common.) *Advantage* has not been replaced by *upside*, so I can think of no reason for the sudden arrival of *downside*, or for the equally sudden popularity of *line up* for *appoint*. The new word seems to appear as unpredictably as an electron changes its orbit.

Why should those just below the top in an organisation be known as the *marzipan layer*? Why should an ideological gap between political parties be called *clear blue water*? Why should battles between rival gangs be known as *turf wars*? All these expressions are recent, yet the activities they describe are not new – nor are the activities from which the metaphors are taken. Making cakes with a layer of marzipan below the sugar icing goes back a long way, boat racing even further, and contests for territory among animals is older than humanity. Yet within the lifetime of those fairly young, each of these activities has given us a metaphor for something that human beings have long done. These new usages may have come from someone using an inspired analogy that then caught on, but we do not know; and often words seem to wear out for no good reason, and get replaced (less frequently, fortunately, than fashions in clothes) by other words that have nothing very striking about them.

Or we can take the words we use for praise or blame – what we could loosely call the 'hurrah words' or the 'boo words'. These are among the commonest words in the language, since we human beings spend so much of our time approving or disapproving, without pausing to particularise just what qualities we are praising or blaming. When I was young the commonest term of enthusiastic approval was *wonderful* but it has now been almost completely replaced by *fantastic* – or, not quite so frequently, by *fabulous*, which has a similar literal meaning. A young person today is likely to say that a footballer gave a *fantastic performance*, that the book she's just read or the meal he's just eaten was *fantastic*; if you remark that fortunately it was not fantastic but a real book or a real meal, they will understand the joke, and may give a faint smile, but will probably think of you as pedantic (or, as they might put it, *nit-picking*).

Words without Meaning?

If we ask what is the meaning of *fantastic* (or *wonderful* or *fabulous* or *terrific* or *marvellous* or *great* or *super* or *smashing* or *groovy* or *awesome* – once we attend to it we can see what a large number of terms of praise there are, some of them of course more up to date – or should we now say *up to speed* – than others!), it would be tempting to say that these words have no meaning: they are simply expressions of general approval. Of course (to touch the edge of philosophy once again), we could argue about what exactly we mean by *meaning* – in one sense, such emotional expression is separate from meaning, in another sense it is part of it. An even more extreme example of terms without meaning, found in the spoken rather than the written language, is what we can call *fillers*: expressions dropped into a sentence that seem to have no effect on its meaning. The basic filler is, of course, *um* or *er*. These are signs of hesitation which we know are very common in speech, and which we might think should not be thought of as words. But what about *you know* or *I think* or *sort of*? We all know the meaning of *sort* or of its synonym *kind*: apricots are a sort of fruit, lizards are a sort of reptile, adjectives are a kind of word. We are placing something in a larger category when we use *sort*, saying that it is a subdivision of that category. But if someone says *A sort of even more extreme example of terms – you know – sort of without meaning …*, there is no trace in that sentence of placing terms in a larger category: *sort of* is simply replacing *um* or *er*. When speaking French, if I was not sure of the gender of a noun, I sometimes used to say *J'ai trouvé une sorte de grenouille dans le jardin* (I found a sort of frog in the garden). By putting in the quite unnecessary *sort of*, I could conceal the fact that I couldn't remember if frogs were masculine or feminine in French – a useful trick for uncertain speakers, which had nothing to do with classifying frogs into a larger category. (Of course its usefulness was limited – it would not enable you to say that you had seen a green frog or a big frog in the garden.) By the way, they're feminine.

Similarly *you know* used as a filler has virtually nothing to do with knowledge, or *I mean* with meaning, except in the very general sense that you obviously should mean it if you are saying it. Some fillers are very simple, such as *like*, as in *He said – like – he'll come soon*; or *I mean – like – I was there*. This is not really very different from *um* and *er*. But sometimes a filler can be quite elaborate – elaborate enough to make us believe, if only for a moment, that it really does mean what it says. An elaborate filler that has suddenly become very popular is *at the end of the day*. It is difficult to listen to a politician or a footballer or anyone making a complaint on radio or television without, sooner or later, hearing those words. They do have some meaning: they direct attention to what is eventually going to happen rather than to an immediate consequence – like *sooner or later* or *in the end*. Such expressions can be meaningful if we are being asked to take a long-term rather than a short-term view. But usually they are just fillers.

Fillers attract a good deal of disapproval. Those who fear that English is on a downward path are likely to mention *sort of* or *you know* as signs of growing inarticulateness, as yet more evidence of the decline of standards in the modern world. This is very difficult to discuss meaningfully. We hear our children saying *sort of*, and we feel our grandparents never spoke like that, but we cannot listen to our grandparents to make the comparison. If we have any record of how they used English, it will almost certainly be of how they wrote. When they spoke, they used quite different fillers from today, or perhaps they just um'd and er'd while they looked for the right words. There is no reason to believe they were more fluent than we are.

There are two reasons why fillers are needed. One applies to everyone – or almost everyone. Which of us can always think of the right word when speaking? We need a moment's pause while we search our memory, but if that pause consists of just remaining silent, someone else is likely to step in and swing the conversation their way. So the *um* and *er*, the *like* or *sort of* or *when all's said and done*, the *I think* and *after all* are like traffic cones we put down in our parking space to stop anyone else putting their car there during the moments we leave it unoccupied. Few of us can do without them.

The other function of fillers can be described as cultural: those who are not fluent speakers are often suspicious of those who are. I call this 'cultural' because it is most likely to occur among the less educated, who might regard too much fluency as belonging to those who are richer and more powerful, towards whom they may feel some resentment. But perhaps we all of us, however well educated, have some suspicion of a speaker whose words seem to flow too easily. A good sprinkling of fillers, then, could allay this suspicion, and be a sign of genuineness.

Fillers obviously belong in the spoken language, and this makes them very ephemeral. Some of today's fillers were virtually unknown twenty years ago, and anyone reading this book in twenty years' time may have a wholly new set to contribute. Let us now turn to more long-lasting changes: to those that occur in writing as well as speech.

On the Cusp of Change

You may want to browse through this section rather than read it continuously, or perhaps return to it later (with the help of the index at the back). Some of these usages are hardly ever discussed or even noticed, others attract violent arguments; all are borderline cases, that is, they are well advanced into use but not yet universally accepted. Each time we use either the new or the old term we are making a contribution to change or retention, casting a silent vote for or against the new usage. (No one of course believes that their individual vote will decide the election.)

affect, effect, impact
The first of these words is a verb, the second a noun. *The economic recession has affected our profits, His behaviour last night has affected my opinion of him* – these sentences can be rewritten as *has had an effect on (our profits/my opinion)*. But it has grown common to confuse *affect* and *effect*, and so we increasingly see, or hear, *has effected (our profits)*. The situation is complicated by the fact that a verb *effect* does exist, with the meaning 'to bring about', so the second sentence could be rewritten as *His behaviour last night has effected a change in my opinion of him.* More usually this verb refers to an intended and perhaps difficult result, so the sentence is likely to mean that he behaved with the intention of improving my opinion of him and succeeded in doing this. It may be partly because of this complication that the word *impact* has stepped in. Dictionaries of a generation ago told us that *impact* is a noun, but they recorded occasional uses as a verb, meaning 'press closely upon', mainly in the form *impacted* (as in *impacted wisdom tooth*). The usage in *The economic recession has impacted on our profits* (or simply *impacted* – without the *on*) is recent, but has now gone a long way to replacing the normal *has affected*. We obviously need a verb meaning 'to bring about changes in', and there is nothing wrong with having two; and since this use of *impact* avoids the confusion between *affect* and *effect*, there is clearly something to be said for it, on the grounds that a new word is better than a mistake.

a.m. and *p.m.*
Not much difficulty about this, surely. Not everyone knows that the

letters stand for *ante meridiem* (before midday) and *post meridiem* (after midday); but everyone does know that a.m. is the morning, and p.m. is the afternoon and evening. The only problem concerns noon itself. There is a growing tendency to speak about *12 a.m.* or *12 p.m.* Midday itself cannot, clearly, be either before or after midday, so both these forms are logical nonsense. Language is not always logical, so it would be possible to defend them on the grounds of usage, except that usage is uncertain: I have seen midday referred to sometimes as 12 a.m. and sometimes as 12 p.m., so it is clear that users are confused. There are several correct forms for us to choose from: *12 noon, 12 midday,* or simply *noon* or *midday,* and *12 midnight* or simply *midnight.* I could add that *from 12 to 3 p.m.* is correct (though there's nothing wrong with *from noon to 3 p.m.*); but *from 12 p.m. to 3 p.m.* is wrong – as well as being more long-winded. As so often, the correct forms are also the easiest. And the restaurant that advertised 'Brunch served from 10 to 12 p.m.' must expect customers who turn night into day!

at least

We all know the meaning of *That dress must have cost at least a hundred pounds*: it means that you go upwards from a hundred. But what if you go downwards? *That looks a rather cheap dress – it must have cost ten pounds at most.* Straightforward, and logical. But suppose the price is being lowered, in a sale for example. *You should be able to get it for at least half as much.* Does that mean 'half or more' or 'half or less'? Most people use it to mean 'half or less', because they are thinking of the actual process of lowering, that the price will go down at least until it reaches the halfway mark, perhaps further. But in a sentence like *I'm selling my car; it's only two years old so I'm hoping to get at least half of what I paid for it*, it is clear that it must mean 'half or more'. If someone says to us *If you go to Brown's you'll pay at least half the price*, we'd need the context to know if they're telling us that Brown's is much cheaper, or isn't as cheap as we thought. When we are the speaker we can easily get round this problem by saying *at least half* and *at most half* (which will always be understood); when we are the listener we might sometimes have to guess. The excellent bus company in my local town paints in large letters on every bus how frequent it is: 'every seven minutes at least'. Does this mean you will wait at least seven minutes or at most seven minutes? Common sense tells us that they must mean the second, but logically the sentence means the first, since *at least seven* means 'seven or more'. It isn't easy to suggest what they should have written. *At least eight buses an hour? Every seven minutes – or less? The most you will wait is seven minutes?* If you have any suggestions, they might be grateful.

author
The noun is familiar and uncontroversial; what is new is its use as a verb. It has a technical use in computing, where it denotes the compiling of multimedia documents or page layouts for electronic publishing. But it now tends to be used simply to mean 'write', as in *He has authored three books.* This usage is mainly American, but is now found in Britain as well, especially in academic life, and (most especially) in applications for jobs or grants. I can think of three reasons for its prevalence. The first may be a simple spillover from its use in computing. The second – quite bluntly – is that it sounds more important. Anyone can *write*; only a distinguished scholar can *author*. Indeed *I have written two books* does not tell us whether they were published or not – but nor, actually, does *I have authored two books*, though we would probably be safe in assuming that the applicant would not have used such a grand word if they hadn't been published. The third reason is more specific: joint authorship is so common in academic life that the word *co-author* has grown up as an obvious convenience, and someone who has just written *I have co-authored one book* finds it natural to continue *and single-authored* or just *authored* one other. *To author* has now become almost a technical term in job applications, but I hope the day is far distant when we start saying that Shakespeare authored thirty-six plays (even though he did co-author two or three others).

A brief historical postscript to this item: *author* as a verb did have a brief life at the beginning of the seventeenth century. You could then *author foul things* or *author statements*, but the *Oxford English Dictionary* gives no examples of authoring a book. It was probably one of the many *inkhorn terms*, Latin words brought into English as scholarly borrowings, some of which survived, many of which (including this one) soon disappeared. The modern verb has no connection with it.

basis

If you do something every day you do it daily; if no one pays you for doing it, you do it unpaid; if no one compels you, you do it voluntarily. But these adverbs have begun to feel rather naked, so they are now bolstered with the nicely vague noun *basis*. You work for your employer, you visit your aged aunt, *on a daily basis, on a voluntary basis, on an unpaid basis*. This makes it sound grander, and somehow more official, so it will probably not be possible to halt this practice; and there is perhaps one thing to be said in favour, or at least in explanation of it. Two of these adjectives – and probably the two that are most often used with *basis* – end in *-y*. *Voluntarily* sounds rather awkward, and we probably feel we'd rather avoid it. And *daily* is an adjective that, because of its ending, looks like (indeed, can also be) an adverb, and we perhaps feel uneasy about its status if we use it adverbially: ought we not to be saying *dailily*? But there's no such word. We can avoid these slight awkwardnesses if we use *basis* on a regular basis.

British

The United Kingdom consists of England, Scotland, Wales (these three make up Great Britain), and Northern Ireland. If we ask a Londoner what country he's from, he can say *Britain, Great Britain, the United Kingdom* or *England*; someone from Glasgow can say *Britain, Great Britain, the United Kingdom* or *Scotland*. If we ask what their nationality is, they will probably use an adjective: *English* or *British* in the one case, *Scottish* or *British* in the other. Someone from Belfast has the choice of *Ireland, Northern Ireland, Ulster* or *the United Kingdom; Irish, Northern Irish* or *British*. Which terms are they likely to use, and why?

The person from Belfast will almost certainly be guided by politics. If he is an Irish nationalist, he will probably not say he's from *Northern Ireland* or *Ulster*, and will certainly not say he's *British*; if a Unionist, he will not say *Ireland*, and is quite likely to say he's *British*. The Glaswegian will either say *Scottish* or *British*, and will obviously not say *English*.

Britain (with *British*) is a convenient term for the Scots, the Welsh and (some) Northern Irish; and it is the term normally used by Americans, for whom *English* is primarily the name of the language,

41

so that Americans study *British Literature* and *British History*, and will usually refer to an Englishman as a *Britisher* – or more colloquially as a *Brit*. These terms often sound odd to British ears. Fowler, writing in 1926 in *A Dictionary of Modern English Usage*, went so far as to find them ludicrous: 'How should an Englishman utter the words *Great Britain* with the glow of emotion that for him goes with *England*?' We do, however, speak of the *British army* and the *British navy*, since in some contexts *British*, along with the rather old-fashioned noun *Briton*, has a glow of rather jingoistic patriotism about it (*Britons never, never, never shall be slaves*). So perhaps the glow of emotion that Fowler referred to belongs with English country lanes and English literature rather than battles and the British Empire!

And to complicate matters even more (or perhaps in an attempt to simplify them!), the term *United Kingdom* – in speech almost always shortened to *UK* – has in recent years come to be used more and more frequently. In certain official contexts it is of course the correct term (*Residents of the UK are not required to answer question 3b*), but it has crept into semi-official and even quite informal contexts (*How long have you lived in the UK?*). I confess that to my ears it still has the ring of officialese, and in practice I can usually manage by saying *England*. A tricky situation might arise if one were speaking to a Pole or a Jamaican who had come to live in London and then moved to Glasgow, and one wanted to ask *How long have you lived in …? In this country* would be a way of evading the problem, but it is not accurate, since Scotland is not the same country as England. And suppose one were actually asking the question when abroad. I would probably, in this case, say *Britain* and accept that there is no glow of emotion. And if he had moved not to Glasgow but to Belfast? Well, I have heard it suggested that *Britain* (without the Great) is used informally to refer to the whole of the United Kingdom …

Faced with all these complications, it is tempting to envy the French or the Swedes, for whom no such minefield of terminology exists.

decimate

A military practice in ancient Rome (and occasionally in later times) was to punish a regiment – usually, no doubt, for mutiny – by killing every tenth soldier; the term derives from the Latin word for ten.

This barbarous practice has now died out, and the term, if kept to its original meaning, would die out too, except in writing military history about past ages. (It had other, non-military meanings, always connected with tenths, which are now quite obsolete.) The word has now taken on a less precise meaning, of killing off a large fraction of a group: typhus fever *decimates* a school (that example comes from the mid-nineteenth century), a hurricane *decimates* a population. Is this extension of meaning useful? The answer, surely, is Yes, since there is no other verb which means 'kill off a substantial number of'; but those who feel that the sense of 'a tenth part' is inescapably part of the word (which may in practice mean those who know Latin!) will dislike this looser use.

exception that proves the rule
Your friend makes a bold statement that you know is wrong: he might say *Women are no good at science,* or *Old people are always conservative.* You reply *What about Marie Curie, or Dorothy Hodgkin, who won Nobel Prizes?* or *What about Karl Marx, or Tony Benn?* He replies, with the air of making a shrewd point, *Ah, that's the exception that proves the rule.* This is so obviously nonsense that we might wonder how such an expression ever came about, except as a useful saying to help the obstinate. There are two theories. One says that exceptions prove the existence of a rule; the second – which seems to me the more likely – is that exceptions *test* the rule. This is an old meaning of *prove*, which still survives in the expression *put to the proof*, which means 'put to the test'. You can explain all this to your friend, but you may not have much success: he may smile, and say *Well, that's your theory.* After all, to the really obstinate, *theory* has two meanings: other peoples' theories are not likely to be true, while their own are not called theories but simply asserted.

female, feminine, feminist
It is not difficult to describe the difference between these three terms, and most people use them correctly. *Female* and *feminine* both refer to the sex of whoever is spoken about, *female* being usually a straightforward biological term that can be applied to both animals and humans, whereas *feminine* is almost always applied to humans and refers to those qualities that are usually associated with women:

feminine wiles, or *feminine charms*. The difference between the two terms is very similar to that between *sex* and *gender* (see page 183). No doubt there is often a lot of prejudice involved when certain qualities are designated as *feminine*, and some uses of the word are therefore likely to be objected to by *feminists*.

Feminism is a political movement, aiming to promote the rights of women, and has nothing to do with the sex of the person professing it: men can be feminists, and women can be anti-feminist. Indeed, Mrs Thatcher when prime minister used sometimes to declare that she was no feminist. Of course when she said this she was referring to feminist programmes of the 1980s which she felt were making unreasonable demands; traditional feminism, in the late nineteenth and early twentieth century, had as one of its main demands the right of women to vote and enter politics, and she was clearly not against that.

There is a long literary tradition which makes fun of women, regarding them as fickle, sexually insatiable, bad-tempered and unreasonable: Chaucer's *Wife of Bath* and Kate in Shakespeare's *The Taming of the Shrew* are famous examples. It has become quite common to refer to this as the *anti-feminist* tradition. It is not confined to the distant past – a respected book on T. S. Eliot's early years cites some of his derogatory remarks about women and calls them *anti-feminist*, though they are about bitchiness and vanity, and have nothing to do with feminism. That tradition should be called *anti-feminine* or *contemptuous of women*.

Most linguistic mistakes are committed by the less educated – what, one might feel, is education for, if not to enable you to avoid mistakes when using your language? So I am pleased to be able to include a mistake that is more likely to be made by the educated.

flaunt, flout and similar muddles

What is the meaning of *flaunt*, and what is the meaning of *flout*, and have they anything to do with each other? Can you answer this without looking in the dictionary – or before reading on?

To *flaunt* is to move ostentatiously, to show off; it can be used transitively or intransitively, so you can *flaunt your new clothes*, or you can simply *flaunt*, meaning 'swagger'. To *flout* something is to mock or defy it: if you went to a formal party dressed in dirty jeans, you would be *flouting* the dress code. The two words have no connection with each other, so why do they now get confused, so that people say *flout* when they mean *flaunt*? The reason must be that they are rather similar in sound and neither is very common. And this is by no means the only pair that gets confused for no better reason than a similarity in sound.

We have a similar pair in *mitigate* and *militate*. *Mitigate* comes from the Latin word for 'mild', and means to make something milder: you *mitigate a punishment*, or a drug can *mitigate the effects of an illness*. *Militate* comes from the Latin word for a soldier (so is related to *military*); it used to mean 'to serve as a soldier', but now it is a rather unusual word, and means 'to be a piece of evidence' or 'to be a reason why something is not likely to happen'. It is usually followed by *against*: this piece of evidence *militates against his guilt*, this item in a party's programme *militates against their chance of success in the election*. Once again, it is hard to see any reason why these two words should be confused, except the resemblance in sound and the fact that they're both rather unusual. It is the slightly more common word, *mitigate*, which tends to be used instead of *militate*.

Another pair of this kind is *discreet* and *discrete*, which are actually pronounced the same, and which do, this time, both descend from the same Latin word; indeed, they have more or less changed meanings with each other over the centuries. *Discreet* is the commoner word, and means 'tactful and careful about what you say', as in *She is very discreet, and you may be confident that any secret you tell her will go no further*. *Discrete* means 'separate', as in *These are two discrete ideas, and should not be confused* (this is more or less what the original Latin word meant). We can manage perfectly well without ever using *discrete*: its meaning is quite adequately covered by *separate* and *distinct*. *Discreet*, on the other hand, is a useful word, since no other single term describes a person's character in exactly the same way. It not only means you can trust the person to keep a secret, but suggests that she is a person of few words, tactful and rather reserved, and is normally a term of praise.

A further pair is *turgid* and *turbid*, though in this case the two words are fairly similar in meaning. *Turgid* means 'swollen', and applies normally to something solid, like the stem of a plant, whereas *turbid*, which means much the same as *turbulent*, applies normally to liquids.

45

And finally there is *fortuitous* and *fortunate*. This time the two words come from the same source: the Latin word *fors*, meaning 'chance'. Anything which is *fortuitous* happens by chance, as in *It was quite fortuitous that she turned up at the same time as I did* – we did not plan it. Things that happen by chance can be good or bad, and though we speak about *good or bad fortune*, the adjective *fortunate* now has only the meaning 'by good fortune'. So her *fortuitous* presence just when I was there could have been either *fortunate* or *unfortunate*, depending on whether I wanted her to be there or not.

imply and *infer*

This is yet another example of confusion, though in this case I doubt whether the words are similar enough for the confusion to come from their sound. It is more like the case of *refute* and *reject*, where two different mental processes, which have something in common, have been confused. We all know that words and sentences can suggest (or *imply*) an underlying meaning. You arrive late for an appointment, and I say *Oh, it doesn't matter, I had a book to read*, but in a rather stiff tone which *implies* that it does matter; and you *infer* from my remark that I am offended. The speaker (or the writer) *implies*, the hearer (or the reader) *infers*. But it is growing common to use *infer* in both senses: *Are you inferring that it's my fault?* instead of *Are you implying ...* . This mistake is now so widespread that it may before long become standard usage. In the meantime, if you wish to cast your vote for preserving the distinction, you will not be misunderstood if you continue to use *imply*. As I have more than once remarked, your hearers will recognise, even if they do not use, the correct form.

lay and *lie*

These are two separate verbs in English, one transitive and one intransitive. The transitive verb (that is, the one which takes an object) is *lay* (past tense *laid*): You *lay* the table, a hen *lays* an egg, you *laid* the table yesterday. The intransitive verb is *lie*, past tense *lay*: *She's gone to lie down, Your coat is lying on the floor, I lay down for half an hour this morning*. Clear enough, surely? But not always clear, it seems. The fact that the past tense of *lie* is the same as the present tense of *lay* is confusing enough; then if we look at *The dog is lying on the floor* and *The boss is laying down the law*, they seem so similar that we might not notice that the first is using the intransitive verb, and the second the transitive. It's impossible to know what will eventually happen to these two verbs, and my best advice for the time being is just to use them correctly and do your charitable best to understand those who use them wrongly.

literally
I was literally knocked out cold by his impudence. I was literally dead with exhaustion. She's literally a slave to that husband of hers. We are all familiar with utterances like these (more often, in the case of *literally*, in speech than in writing). The one thing we can usually be sure of is that the first speaker did not lose consciousness, the second is still alive, and the third statement is not about a society where slavery is legalised. In other words, whatever *literally* means when used as an intensifier, it doesn't literally mean 'literally'. Does this matter? There is no intensifier in English which is so readily and thoughtlessly available as *literally*, though there are of course alternatives. *Absolutely, truly* and *really* release us only partly from the illogicality, since they all make a claim rather similar to *literally*. If we want to avoid the (literal) untruth of *literally*, the best alternative, surprisingly, is *almost (I was almost dead with exhaustion)*, which, although strictly speaking it modifies (or mitigates) the claim of what follows, often has the effect of seeming to intensify it.

This may seem odd, but intensifiers sometimes behave oddly. If we hear something described as an *absolute* or *total* disaster, we can be fairly sure that it was actually quite trivial – the loss of a cricket match, wearing the wrong clothes, or the dinner spoiling. A serious disaster (an air crash or trapped miners) is never referred to with these apparently extreme intensifiers.

may and *might*
When referring to future events, these two forms do not differ much. *I may come tomorrow* and *I might come tomorrow* both indicate the possibility that I shan't come – although *might* makes my coming rather less probable. But when referring to the past they have a different meaning. *He may have done it* means that the speaker does not know whether he did it or not; *he might have done it* normally means

that he didn't, but would perhaps have done it if … . Thus we can say *He might have done it if you hadn't warned him against it.*

To complicate matters, it is possible to use *might* instead of *may*: *he might have done it* can be used instead of *he may have done it*, to mean that we do not know. But we ought not to use *may* instead of *might*: *He may have done it if you hadn't warned him against it* is not grammatically correct.

Or rather it was not grammatically correct; but it has now become quite common in speech. You will hear sentences like this nowadays: *He took a risk parking there: he may have got a parking ticket.* In the (quite recent) past this would have meant that I do not know whether he got a ticket or not; nowadays it is often used when I know quite well that he got away with it. Of course if you use the correct form and say that he *might have got a ticket* when you know that he didn't, you will certainly be understood. Once again, we have here an example of passive knowledge outliving active knowledge. Older speakers may well lament the loss of a distinction when they hear the newfangled *He may have got a parking ticket* in cases where it is known that he didn't; but since we already use *may* and *might* interchangeably for the cases when we don't know the facts, it could be argued that no great loss is involved in using them interchangeably when we do.

modern

This, surely, once we have learnt to think historically, and to contrast the past with the present, is the one unavoidable word; yet it dates only from the sixteenth century. Its early uses were rather limited – dividing history into *ancient* and *modern* (later, into *ancient, medieval* and *modern*), or contrasting *ancient* and *modern languages*. But as historical ways of thinking become more and more established, anything can be modern: so we get *modern literature, art* and *music, modern politics, thought, machinery* and *communications*, always with a contrast, explicit or implied, with what came earlier. The next step, once we have decided that each of these has a distinctive new style or method, is to describe this newness by calling it *modernist*. This does not happen in those fields where progress is assumed: *modern machinery, modern communications, modern transport* will obviously use the most up-to-date methods, so there is no need to call them *modernist.* We speak of *modernist fiction, modernist music* or *modernist architecture* to contrast them with novels or symphonies or buildings that may be modern in time, but do not use the revolutionary new techniques that we associate with *modernism.* This terminology has been with us for almost a century by now, so the earlier *modernist* composers and artists are quite far back in the past: what about those who then tried to go further in being modern? So the term *post-modernist* came into being, though there is very little agreement about what *post-modernist thought, architecture* or *literature* are actually like. The term most nearly agreed on is *post-modernist thought,* often equated with *post-structuralism* (also known as *deconstruction*), a philosophy based on the belief that language itself is essential but unstable, so that there is no escape from its limitations. To venture further into these muddy waters would be beyond the scope of a book on usage. Not surprisingly, there have been attempts to speak about *post-post-modernism*, but at this point common sense has exercised its veto.

present a lecture

This is another Americanism now spreading in Britain. Professor X lectures on, say, American foreign policy. The normal verb has for a long time been *give a lecture*, and just as it is somehow more prestigious to author a book than just to write one, so it seems grander to *present* than just to *give* a lecture. The trouble is that *present a lecture* already has a meaning: the lecture is given by Professor X but is presented by the Foundation or University that invited her, pays her, and invites us to come and hear her. For this reason, and in defence of our lovely English monosyllabic verbs, I refuse to use the term.

quantum leap

Is this a big leap, or a small one? The term comes from physics. Not many of us know enough about modern physics to understand exactly what it means, but you do not need to understand nuclear theory is order to use it correctly – or do you? Electrons sometimes leap from one orbit to another for no apparent reason, and quantum theory is concerned with the mathematics of such events. The important thing about such a *quantum leap* is that it is uncaused, and that it can have drastic consequences; but since everything at the subatomic level is so tiny by our ordinary standards, we cannot, surely, say that a quantum leap is large. If we say that the economic growth of a country took a quantum leap, meaning that its cause is unclear and it had striking consequences (for example by reducing unemployment), that seems a correct application of the analogy with physics. If we simply mean that there was a sudden large increase, it doesn't. But since so few of us really understand the physics, is it pedantic to insist on this? Has the expression left the analogy with physics behind and simply come to mean 'a very great leap'? Perhaps we need to ask the physicists.

regrettably and regretfully

To be *regretful*, as the word clearly indicates, is to be filled with regret; it is always a person who is *regretful*. But to be *regrettable* is to be the object of regret, so it is an action or a decision which is *regrettable*, because we regret it. This is a parallel to the example that began this book, *hopefully*. I explained there that *hopefully* can be an adverb that qualifies the whole sentence (*Hopefully, he'll be here soon*). *Regrettably*, too, is usually used to modify the whole statement: *Regrettably, he can't come after all.* But when *hopefully* is used to mean 'full of hope', it corresponds grammatically to *regretfully*. So we might say *They began the game hopefully* – thinking they were going to win – and after they had lost they *regretfully contemplated all their missed chances.*

retiree

This is now quite common in America and beginning to be used in Britain. It means 'retired person', but its form is odd, since the -*ee* suffix is normally passive: a *payee* is someone who is paid (in contrast to the *payer*), a *trainee* is being trained (perhaps by a *trainer*), a *nominee* has been nominated. So we would expect a *retiree* to be someone who is being retired; *retire* is usually an intransitive verb, but it can be used transitively, often with the meaning 'to make someone retire against their will'. But the many companies and universities in America who keep in touch with, or make generous payments to, their *retirees* have not forced them to retire (or if they had, that is not why they call them *retirees*). The normal English usage would be *We bid farewell to all those retiring* (when they are in the process of leaving) and *We like to keep in touch with our retired colleagues* (afterwards). Perhaps the use of *retiree* arose to avoid these circumlocutions and replace them with a single noun. But I confess I find it difficult not to think of *retirees* as the unfortunate victims of (to use another fashionable term) company downsizing, and I would not use the term.

The use of the *-ee* suffix is found in other verbs too. A notice in a bus that might once have read *No more than five standing passengers allowed* might today say *No more than five standees allowed*. I find this odd, almost comic: *stand*, like *retire*, is usually intransitive, and the *-ee* suffix, as I've pointed out, is normally passive, so it should really only be attached to a transitive verb. Looking for a transitive use of *stand*, I wonder if a *standee* is someone whom I am standing a drink – or even someone whose foot I am standing on!

societal

The adjective from *society* is *social*, and it has a range of uses. You may enjoy *social intercourse, social occasions* and *social gatherings*, such as parties; but you may also be a serious student of society – a *social scientist*, no less, studying *social change, social development* or *social factors* that influence the individual. It really would not do to allow anyone to think that such serious study had any connection with parties and other frivolous social activities, so by adding an extra syllable to the adjective we can make it clear that we are scientists, studying *societal change, societal development and societal factors* that demand careful, perhaps statistical, analysis. There is no way of stopping the social scientists from adding their extra syllable, but the rest of us can at least continue to do without it. There is no occasion on which it is necessary: confusion with the frivolity of *social gatherings* is adequately avoided by the noun we attach to it. As can be clearly seen by the fact that there has been no effort – yet – to add the extra syllable to the expression *social science* itself.

sorts of

Sort in the singular is a collective noun. *I like this sort of tie, of soup, of car* refers to a number of different ties, soups and cars, all resembling one another in one respect (plain ties, perhaps, or peppery soups, or small cars). We are referring to several ties but one sort. Yet speakers now feel much more conscious of the ties as plural than of the sort as singular, and so the idea of plurality has got dragged back to *sort*, so that you will usually hear *these sorts of ties*. Strictly, this should mean two sorts (not only plain ties but also woollen ties, say), but everyone understands it as meaning the same as *this sort*. This has now become more or less accepted usage. It does make it awkward to say that there are two different sorts of tie that you like, but this is not something we often do want to say; so this usage, now very common, does no great harm.

substitute

There was a white tablecloth on the table, but we decided that a green one would look better; we therefore *replaced the white one with the green*, or we *substituted the green for the white*. If we want to put this in the passive, *the white one was replaced by the green*, or *the green one was substituted for the white*. Straightforward, surely? But not any longer: it is growing common to use *substitute* in both senses. The explanation for this may lie with football. A manager is permitted a limited number of substitutions in the course of a football match. If he decides that Smith is not playing as well as Jones, he may replace Smith with Jones when he picks the team; but if Smith is hurt and has to come off during the game (or if the manager decides to take him off for tactical reasons), and Jones is sent on in his place, then the manager has performed an official substitution, and so we are usually told that Smith has been *substituted*. Obviously this can cause confusion, since it is really Jones who has been substituted for Smith. Is the verb *replace* beginning to drop out of use? Even if it is, it will still, of course, be understood.

the 1800s, the 1900s

The years from 1801 to 1900 are the nineteenth century, the years from 1901 to 2000 are the twentieth century, and so on. The years from 1830 to 1839 are the eighteen-thirties, those from 1820 to 1829 are the eighteen-twenties – and before that? We can speak about *the eighteen-tens*, though to some the term might seem a little odd. But what of the years 1800 to 1809: what are they? Clearly they ought to be *the eighteen hundreds*, so if *the mid-eighteen-fifties* means, more or less, 1854 to 1856, then *the mid-eighteen hundreds* ought to be, more or less, 1804 to 1806. But it is now increasingly common to re-fer to the twentieth century as *the nineteen hundreds*. As a result, *the mid-nineteen hundreds* has become ambiguous: it can mean 1904 to 1906, or (perhaps more frequently) 1940 to 1960. It is probably too late to halt this now, so we have lost a convenient expression: we can speak about *the McCarthyite tyranny of the early and mid-1950s*, but *the events of the mid-1900s* is ambiguous, so it is probably prudent to avoid it.

And now, to conclude, here is an example to show how evanescent change can be.

permanent quad
Are you puzzled by this expression? If so you are probably under 40. During the 1970s there was a sales campaign by which shopkeepers gave out Greenshield stamps with purchases, and when you had ac-cumulated enough you could redeem them for free gifts. It was not a scheme which made much economic sense, and soon died out. Some shops (and especially petrol stations) would offer double, treble or quadruple stamps on certain days (presumably the days when busi-ness was quiet). So there would be notices saying 'quadruple stamps on Tuesdays' – then, as competition became more desperate, 'quad-ruple stamps every day', which turned into 'permanent quad'. It has taken me over a hundred words to explain a now incomprehensible but once ubiquitous expression: such are the drawbacks of change.

CHAPTER FOUR

Standard English

We have looked at the differences that occur over time; now we must add that there are also differences that occur over space. To distinguish them from change, these differences are usually called *variation*. Imagine a conversation between a New Zealand shepherd, a professor from India, a housewife from Belfast, a factory worker from Manchester, a clergyman from London and a New York taxi driver. They all speak English, and four or five of them probably speak no other language, but they might have great difficulty in understanding one another. Clearly they don't all speak the same kind of English.

We use two different words to describe the differences between their English. Those from London, Manchester and Belfast speak different dialects of British English; the New Zealander, the American and possibly the Indian, are said to speak different varieties of English. That difference in terminology is not really important, and almost everything I'll now say about dialects applies to varieties as well.

If you have spent some time in Manchester or Belfast you'll be familiar with many of the features of their dialects. The person from Belfast will offer you not 'a little drink' but *a wee drink* (and even a large drink might be called *a wee drink*); if you ask her if she can do something for you she is likely to reply not 'Yes' but *I can*, and she will pronounce *can* to rhyme with *barn*. Here we have three different kinds of variation: in vocabulary (using different words), in grammar (using different constructions), and in pronunciation. The last is the one we are most likely to notice, and is what we usually mean when we speak of a Belfast accent or a Lancashire accent.

What is a dialect, and who speaks in dialect? The answer to that last question is: everybody – including you and me, and yes, including the London clergyman. A dialect is a way of speaking that belongs to a particular group and differs from the way other groups speak. Some languages have more dialects than others. The language of a small tribe in Papua that has little contact with the outside world is not likely to show much variation, but not many of the world's population now live in such tribes. If a language is spoken over a large area by a status-conscious society it will develop dialects, and there is probably no language today which has more dialects and varieties than English – but they are all forms of English. More about this in the final chapter.

How do we tell a dialect from a foreign language? Do the people in Barcelona speak a Catalonian dialect of Spanish, or a separate language, called Catalan? Do the Scots speak an English dialect, or a separate language, called Scots (or Lallans)? Why are there four Scandinavian languages (Danish, Swedish, Norwegian and Icelandic) when their speakers can understand one another perfectly well – probably better than a Cockney can understand a Glaswegian?

To decide when two dialects should be considered separate languages is partly a linguistic question, and partly political. The linguistic criterion is mutual intelligibility: when speakers can no longer understand one another, they are speaking different languages. The political criterion is, to put it bluntly, that a dialect which has an army and a national flag is called a language. Catalan is often called a language now because of the intensely independent spirit of the Catalonians; in the Spain of Franco, strongly opposed to separatism, it was not officially regarded as a different language. If Scotland were an independent country, the pressure to regard Scots as a separate language would be stronger, even though the difficulty of it being understood in England would not be any greater.

Neither of these criteria will always apply. Mutual intelligibility is a matter of degree, and there are always borderline cases – often quite literally borderline cases when we come to the border between two linguistic zones, and there are some interesting exceptions to the political criterion. The German spoken in Germany, Austria and Switzerland is called German throughout, even though Swiss German is about as different from High German as Dutch is. And the exception that we are all familiar with is of course American English, which nobody considers a separate language, even though the United States has been a separate country for over two hundred years.

At this point we must add that there are two kinds of dialect: it is not only those who live in a different place who speak differently, but also those who belong to a different social class. The English spoken by those who are poor and powerless is a class dialect; the English spoken by those who live far from the centre is a regional dialect. (For this purpose, the 'centre' is roughly the Oxford–Cambridge–London triangle, though in these days of commuting, London could be said to extend linguistically down to the south coast.) Clearly there is some overlap between the two; a working-class person in Manchester will speak a dialect further away from Standard English than a teacher or lawyer in the same town, who has received a similar education to teachers and lawyers in London, perhaps even in the same institutions. Cockney English (the term is getting old-fashioned) is purely a class dialect, since Cockneys live in the same region as Standard English speakers. Now it is very clear that class dialects carry more social stigma than regional dialects. Indeed, it could be regarded as part of the definition of a class dialect that it carries an element of social stigma; that is inherent in the very concept of social class. And stigma is the underside of prestige: if one person speaks a worse (that is, socially inferior) form of English than another, then the other speaks better – and may be proud of the fact. Though in our democratic age, such superiority can only be indulged in if it's also laughed off.

Here is a nice short example of class dialect. Coming to school on the first day of term, a teacher was surprised to see a boy there, since she thought his family was moving to another town. When she asked him about this, he answered 'We was but we never.' She was so taken with the conciseness of this that she wrote to a linguist about it, citing it as an example of pithy working-class speech.

Now suppose the positions were reversed, and the pupil was surprised because he thought the teacher was moving, and said so. She might well reply *We were but we didn't*. The boy's working-class speech says *we was* and the teacher's Standard English says *we were*; the boy uses *never* where she uses *not*, and he leaves out the verb where she combines verb and negative into *didn't*. Both are concise, both are clear, and any native speaker who was listening would immediately recognise the class difference.

Feelings run high about class dialects. This was vividly shown by the U and non-U discussion of the 1950s and 1960s. In 1954 a Professor of Linguistics, A. S. C. Ross, published an article in a Finnish journal of linguistics on what he called U and non-U English (the U standing for 'upper-class'), in which he classified usages into the two categories. *Writing paper* was declared to be U, *notepaper* non-U; *drawing room* U, *lounge* non-U; *lavatory* U, *toilet* non-U; and so on through dozens of words and phrases. The article claimed to be purely factual, a scientific study of class dialect; but the astonishing success it had when republished in the magazine *Encounter* in a less technical form showed that there was a widespread, even obsessive interest in the matter which was by no means merely factual. It sparked off a popular book, *Noblesse Oblige*, edited by Nancy Mitford, which contained a satirical poem by John Betjeman that revels in non-U expressions:

> *Are the requisites all in the toilet?*
> *The frills round the cutlets can wait*
> *Till the girl has replenished the cruets*
> *And switched on the logs in the grate.*

Sometimes it is non-linguistic practices that are being ridiculed here, such as artificial log fires and paper frills round chops, but for the most part this is a list of non-U expressions; the U equivalents would be *requirements, lavatory, chops, maid, filled, salt cellars* – though *requirements* may be questionable, since to use an abstract noun instead of naming the objects is itself considered non-U. I can still remember the innumerable discussions that broke out everywhere, and the self-examination by ordinary speakers of English, eager to discover that the English they spoke was genuinely U.

The episode showed, of course, how far English society was (and still is?) obsessed with social class, and how language practices can be a class marker of almost obsessive power; but it also showed the lopsided form which this obsession takes. Any serious sociological analysis of modern English society will start from occupation, wealth and power, and will offer a broad division into bourgeoisie and working class (though it may not use those terms), followed probably by subdivisions that will be based largely on occupation. The distinction between aristocracy and commoners, once so important, has now become little more than a quaint relic; if there is an aristocracy in Britain today, it consists of business leaders, politicians, civil servants, scientists and academics who have received titles (nowadays non-hereditary) for their achievements. Our hereditary aristocracy has become a quaint survival, whose wealth depends on their investments and business interests; in other words, they are now members of the bourgeoisie. The distinction that Ross was exploring was essentially that between a tiny hereditary aristocracy and the rest of society – or rather the rest of bourgeois society, since he observed that 'habits of speech peculiar to the lower classes find no place here'.

The enormous interest which the U/non-U discussions aroused, therefore, though it tells us that class dialects are of obsessive interest to the English, also tells us that this interest is in the frills of class distinction, not in the reality of where power and wealth lie (as the speaker of Betjeman's poem was perhaps more interested in the paper frills round the chops than in the quality of the meat itself!) Language practices obsess the popular imagination for what they tell us of power and privilege in a previous age rather than today, and the U/non-U episode, though it tells us a lot about what people are interested in, does not tell us much about class dialects.

The best-known attempt to study class dialects in English in a socially more responsible way is probably that of Basil Bernstein. In the 1960s Bernstein set out to investigate why intelligent working-class children, and especially children from the bottom end of the class spectrum, do badly in school, and to discover whether the reason is a linguistic one. He drew a distinction between what he called *elaborated code* and *restricted code*. (*Code* in this usage has nothing to do with secret writing, but is a term that linguists use to denote one of several varieties of a language.) If you are describing an event, you may assume that your hearer knows nothing about it, and so explain everything to him; or you may plunge into the story, assuming that he is taking part along with you. If you do the first you are likely to use longer and more complex sentences, with plenty of subordinate clauses; if the second, your sentences will be shorter and simpler. *I was getting off the train yesterday when a young man I'd never seen before came up to me; for no reason I could make out he started swearing at me, just as if I was someone he knew who'd offended him.* That is an example of elaborated code. The same story in restricted code might begin: *So this bloke comes up to me – I'd never seen him before. Tells me to bugger off. I ask you – what does he think? Like I'd been swearing at him, or what?* Both codes have their usefulness, but in written English we are more likely to use the elaborated code, and for some purposes (for scientific explanations or historical narrative, for instance), it is necessary. Bernstein maintains that middle-class children use both codes, but many working-class children use only the restricted, and this holds them back in their school work.

This theory is very controversial. Some critics see it as a way of demeaning working-class children; others see it as a very useful analysis, without any element of prejudice. The argument is complicated, and sometimes heated (though not as heated as the very similar American arguments about 'black English'); too complicated to enter into here. What we can say is that Bernstein did try to study class dialects in a socially responsible way, investigating real and present divisions in English society rather than the colourful fringe at the top of the social ladder, as the U/non-U controversy did.

Variation is always growing and always shrinking. Regional variation was kept alive in earlier centuries by the simple fact of geographical isolation; those who never travelled might hear nothing except the local dialect. Those days are gone, but there is still local pride. If you call a cat a *moggy* or trousers *kecks* or a bad mood a *cob*, you might not care whether a Londoner understands you or not; *if he wants to talk to people from Liverpool, let him learn Scouse.* We could feel that this independence is something admirable; but it obviously has practical drawbacks. So if we want more uniformity, if we think it would be better if we all used more or less the same English, how do we achieve this? Obviously, by replacing dialects with a standard form of the language; that is, by using Standard English.

Putting a brake on something that is widespread among ordinary people will not always be popular, and the imposition of Standard English on everyone has its opponents. The political objection is that it is authoritarian. Since Standard English is on the whole the speech of the more powerful sections of society, to insist on it is to demean the speech of social groups which are less powerful. This too has produced some violent argument. John Honey, for instance, in his books *Does Accent Matter?* and *Language is Power*, claimed that, although dialects (class or regional) serve the function of communication within a particular social group perfectly well, if children were not also taught to speak Standard English then the education system was doing them a disservice – not preparing them for the situations when they needed or wanted to use Standard English instead of their dialect. He was of course dealing mainly with speech in claiming that.

Speakers of regional dialects are probably more likely than speakers of class dialects to feel proud of their speech and to insist on sticking to it. This becomes clearer still when we look at those regions of Britain which enjoy a degree of political independence: moderate Welsh, Scottish and Northern Irish accents carry virtually no social stigma, and their speakers show little wish to speak like Londoners. Both regional pride and democratic sentiment, then, operate against the imposition of Standard English as the only acceptable form of the language; and in recent years this case has had some success. You have only to compare a sports commentator of fifty years ago with one today, who is now allowed to have a regional or class accent. A newsreader is less likely to have a class accent, but one who speaks with a Welsh accent, for example, might actually be welcomed.

There are not many people today who want to see regional dialects abolished so that everyone speaks Standard English (or if there are, they tend to keep quiet about it). Standard English can be seen not as a weapon to kill off dialects, but as an alternative. So individual speakers in Manchester or Belfast could become bilingual, switching in and out of their local or class dialect according to the situation – as many do already, and as Honey would like to see them doing more easily. Much of the political case against the imposition of Standard English is an objection to getting people to change their speech, an objection to encouraging children in Liverpool to speak Standard English and so make their parents feel inferior. One can see why this makes people angry, and why they write books and articles to express their anger. The books and articles, however, are in Standard English.

So far, as you may have noticed, I have used the term *Standard English* as if it applied equally to the written and the spoken language. It is now time to separate these.

A Few Taps of the Keyboard

Anthony Burgess described writing as 'the mutation of a mouthful of air into a penful of ink'. We can bring this up to date (since we use ink less and less these days) by calling it 'the mutation of a mouthful of air into a few taps of the keyboard'. It's a definition worth pondering. First, it reminds us that speech is much older than writing – probably many hundreds of times older, since humanity has used some form of speech for as long as it has been on earth, whereas writing as we know it may not be much more than three thousand years old. And, of course, we all learn to speak before we learn to write.

But speech is primary not only in a historical sense: it is primary because only in speaking does the language really exist. Ferdinand de Saussure, the founder of modern linguistics, went so far as to say that language is what we say, that the only reason for the existence of writing is to record spoken language, and he warned against believing that writing is in some way more important than speech. 'It is rather', he writes, 'as if people believed that in order to find out what a person looks like it is better to study his photograph than his face.' Saussure is certainly right; but humanity has been writing for so long that written language has begun to develop habits of its own, and to lead a separate existence. I am writing this book as you, reader, write letters, as scientists write learned papers and journalists write copy: without having spoken it beforehand. And if any of us had spoken it beforehand (in a conversation, for instance), it would have been very different, for we do not speak in the complete, well-formed sentences that are normal in writing. The six imaginary characters who began this chapter, from London, New Zealand, India and wherever, would pronounce this sentence very differently, but would all write it more or less the same.

So when does writing become primary? The answer is obvious: when we write something which we have not previously spoken. A good example of this is provided by medieval Latin. For hundreds of years Latin was the common language among the European nations, sometimes spoken but more often written. When it was spoken, the situation was rather artificial, since it was no one's mother tongue; it was like a Russian and a Spaniard conducting a conversation in English. They may understand each other perfectly, and even if they make mistakes these might go unnoticed and will probably not interfere with communication; if their English is so good that they don't make any mistakes, they may still use constructions that a native speaker would not use. If a native speaker happened to be present, he might be impressed by their fluency, but might also be tempted to intervene and correct them. But in the case of medieval Latin there were no native speakers.

Indeed, genuine spoken English does not often find its way into writing; we switch more or less automatically into the more formal mode of the written language once we pick up a pen or sit down in front of our keyboard. And not only then, for nowadays the frontier between written and spoken English is not clear cut. Just think of all the occasions when (this is one way of putting it) we speak as we write. Politicians delivering speeches, professors giving lectures, candidates being interviewed for jobs, scientists explaining their theories in television documentaries; all use rather formal English, closer to the written than to the spoken language. Of course there is a gradation between the two: the newsreader on the radio or television uses a much more formal English than the competitors in a television quiz or footballers being interviewed after a game, though even these last do not speak to the interviewer in quite the same way as they do to their mates. A good way to hear the gradation is to listen to the recorded message on someone's answerphone. At the one extreme is the elderly gentleman whose message runs *You have reached 0123456. I'm afraid no one can take your call at the moment. Please leave a message after the beep.* At the other extreme is the teen-ager whose voice (barely audible above the background music) says *Hi. This is Fred. How ya doing? What is it?* And there are plenty of levels in between. There is no one point at which the careful syntax of the first turns into the casual fragments of the second, but we can say that somewhere along the gradient the speaking of written (and therefore Standard) English begins to give place to casual speech. So the best way to describe the situation is to say that in writing, and when speaking more or less as we write, we try to use Standard English.

There is however another way of crossing the frontier between the spoken and the written language. As well as speaking more or less as we write, it is possible to write more or less as we speak. It is not only possible, it is actually quite common; that is the way our tabloid press is written – or at least that is the impression it wishes to give. *The Sun*, which is the most widely read newspaper in Britain, likes to write English in a way that its readers will feel at home with, and will perhaps recognise as – more or less – the way they themselves speak (or would like to think they speak). To study this, I took a single issue of *The Sun* (25 February 2005) and examined its language.

Sun English

Perhaps the feature of its language which this newspaper would most like us to notice is the wordplay. Like its great rival *The Daily Mirror*, it loves to use puns; I counted eighteen in the issue I studied, and no doubt missed a few. It's not easy to think up eighteen good puns every day, and there were probably others so feeble that I didn't notice them. The shocking record of accidents when young people are taught to drive by their parents was headed 'It's L driving with parents'. Under the picture of an almost naked young woman on page 3 was 'News in Briefs'. Those were probably the two best.

But that is not the most prominent feature of Sun English. Much more frequent, and much more striking, is what I shall call elegant variation: replacing an ordinary word by a less frequent one – sometimes a familiar colloquialism, sometimes a less familiar one, sometimes a variation that seems to have been thought up by whoever wrote the column. Instead of reaching cinemas by a certain date, a new film is going to *hit* screens; instead of a mistake, a goalkeeper commits a *clanger*; instead of increasing, a quantity *climbs*, or *peaks* or *ups*; instead of hiding information, culprits *bury* it; instead of questioning someone, you *quiz* them; instead of being ready, a footballer is *primed* to change clubs; instead of intending, you are *set* to do something, or it's *on the radar*; a boxer does not withdraw from a contest, he *dumps* it. It's not easy to know if there is a general principle behind the choice of variants; sometimes it's difficult to see any motive except the desire for variation. But quite often it seems an attempt to make things sound more violent: a football team is not eliminated from a competition, it *crashes out*; to begin something, one *kicks off* or *kick-starts* it; there is not an increase but an *explosion* of MRSA deaths; and (this is my favourite) instead of losing her temper, a pop star *throws her rattle out of the pram*.

Where does this elegant variation mainly occur? My investigation suggests that there are three areas: praise, success, and sex. Let us save the last until the wider discussion of the language of sex (page 158), and since the other two suggest very similar conclusions I shall concentrate on praise. I have already pointed out that general praise (what can informally be called the 'hurrah words') is an area of meaning where change is very fast, and popular newspapers race to keep up with the speed of the spoken language. In the one issue of *The Sun* I found *cool*, *hot* (yes, these two have the same meaning!), *coming good, the real deal, simply now* (a furniture store offers an *inspiring new simply now* collection), *groovy, up there with, fab, hotty* (used as a noun for someone who is *hot*), *awesome, sparky, stupidly* (that's not a mistake – a footballer is described as *stupidly talented*, meant as high praise), *spicy, prime* (the astrologer tells us it's *prime time* to look for a new home) and *fast forward* (the same astrologer tells us that our life will be *sent into fast forward*). Compared with this rich collection of 'hurrah words', there are astonishingly few 'boo words' – terms of criticism and dispraise. Should we draw the reassuring conclusion that our popular press is full of positive attitudes, praise and encouragement?

Three articles in the issue I studied were not written in Sun English. Two were in Standard English: one about a woman who killed her nine-year-old son and was convicted of manslaughter, the other a comparison of various makes of car seat for infants, the facts taken from the pages of *Which?* magazine. This latter did begin with a touch of wordplay in the headline (*Hot Seats*), but thereafter its language was quite straightforward. Anything that involves the killing – or the safety – of children is clearly considered too serious to be described in anything but Standard English. The third article that avoided Sun English was about an Anglican clergyman who performs exorcisms, describing how he drives evil spirits out of those who are possessed; this one was almost entirely in Standard English, but spiced with one or two old-fashioned solemnities. 'Be gone,' the clergyman cried to the possessing spirit, 'leave this child.' *Be gone* is archaic, even obsolete; no one says it today. It was an adult, not a child, who was being exorcised, and calling a grown woman a *child* is traditional for priests (especially if they are called *Father*, so that they reply *My child*): not exactly obsolete, but suggesting what some might consider an old-fashioned world where clergy are kept distinct and the laity treat them with deference. He exhorts the evil spirit to 'disperse in peace', and later claims that he has 'banished entities from bars, hotels and hospitals'. I would have expected him to say *depart in peace* (another rather old-fashioned clerical solemnity); perhaps by *disperse* – if it isn't just a misprint – he was suggesting that the evil spirit would melt into thin air. *Entities*, I presume, was the clergyman's own word for what we would normally call *beings*; it suggests to me the language of philosophy rather than of religion, but perhaps our clergyman fancied himself as something of a philosopher. These few small departures from Standard English are all in the direction of the formal and the archaic, as clearly was felt appropriate for writing about exorcism.

So far I have discussed the language of the newspaper descriptively, without objecting to its departures from Standard English; but there must be those among my readers (though not, presumably, among the readers of *The Sun*) who regard it as slovenly, and a sign of declining standards in the language. So let us ask as the next question how many of the departures from Standard English could be considered mistakes (remembering of course that today's mistakes may eventually come to be considered correct; not <u>will</u> be considered correct, but may possibly be). I found seven instances that I would describe as mistakes. Read them through and see if you agree.

1   A singer's new record proves that an earlier phase of his career is over *with this hard-hitting debut.*
2   If returning a bottle of wine in a restaurant, you are told to explain what's wrong with it. *This focuses [the waiter's] mind on your complaint, and are likely to agree with you.*
3   Three companies in the business section are said to have *gained from their latest figures.*
4   (also from the business section) *The potential impact of war, terrorism and natural disasters remain, but appear to have lessened.*
5   *Horse A is tricky to predict, so Horse B rates the danger ahead of dodgy jumper C.*
6   *The alarm bells will really start clanging if Team A are beaten by Team B at the impregnable JIB Stadium.*
7   *To put up with the crowd abuse he did in South Africa suggests …*

First of all, what is wrong with these sentences? Here are my answers:

1   If a record is a singer's debut, that means it is his first (*debut* means 'beginning'), which this record clearly isn't.

2   What is the subject of *are*? As it stands, it must be *this*, which doesn't make sense. We need to insert a subject before *are*, which will obviously be *the waiter* or *he* – or, since the verb *are* is plural, no doubt it was meant to be *they*. This makes me think that the word *they* may have been deleted, so that we have a misprint rather than an actual mistake.

3   The companies did not gain from the figures; we need *judging from their latest figures.*

4   A common mistake, this. The subject is *impact*, which is singular, so the verbs should be *remains* and *appears*, but the writer forgot that he'd begun with *impact*, and treated the three following nouns as the subject.

5   This sentence is written in 'racing speak', the jargon of punters and tipsters (see page 124 for a discussion of jargon). *Predict* here means 'predict its chances of winning'; *rates* means 'is rated as', or – in Standard English – 'is considered to be'; *danger* must mean 'danger to its chances of winning.' To the reader unfamiliar with racing speak the sentence will seem incorrect and even puzzling, but could be considered an example of jargon rather than of actual mistakes.

6   The stadium is not impregnable (it's not a fortress being attacked), but presumably Team A are considered impregnable when they play there.

7   Should it be *the crowd abuse he received in South Africa,* or, more probably, *to put up with the crowd abuse as he did in South Africa?* Here again I suspect that it may be a misprint, not a mistake.

Now this can teach us something about mistakes, or rather can confirm something we have already observed: most mistakes do not actually prevent us from receiving the meaning. At most one out of these seven did that. If the readers of the newspaper do not notice the mistakes, or if they do not mind reading a paper that uses the language incorrectly, then in six (or even all) of these cases the mistake has done no harm. (Whether those who write the paper are content to be thought of as using the language in what educated readers will think of as a slovenly manner is a question only they can answer.)

Now I must add that there were two other sentences in that paper which I had difficulty in understanding:

1 *The overall number of convictions* (for rape) *fell from six per cent the previous year.*
2 In an article about whether there have been more MRSA deaths than has been admitted, a doctor states *most people would accept this is an under-representation. The number of deaths linked to MRSA is going to be much higher.*

The first sentence could mean that there were six per cent in the previous year and the number fell the following year; or that in the previous year the number fell from six per cent (so six per cent is the figure for the year before that). There is no way of knowing.

In the other example, the second sentence is certainly saying that the number of deaths is going to increase; but when we combine it with the previous sentence, and indeed with the whole article, it is clear that the speaker is not talking about how many people are going to die, but about the cause of death being misrepresented. So he actually means that in the future it will be realised that more of the deaths were due to MRSA than has yet been admitted. Now neither of these sentences is grammatically incorrect, from which we must conclude that not getting your meaning across and writing incorrect English are by no means the same thing. Bad grammar is not the main cause of bad communication.

– and the Quality?

A short postscript to this discussion. English newspapers are usually divided into two categories, *popular* and *quality*. The quality newspapers have longer and more scholarly articles and much fuller treatment of politics; the popular ones have more pictures and more personal gossip about pop singers, sports personalities and the Royal Family. They are sometimes described as the *broadsheets* and the *tabloids*, terms that refer to their size and shape. Now that the more serious papers have discovered that the tabloid format is very convenient for readers, several have started using it, so these terms may fall into disuse. Terms often outlive their accuracy, however, so they may survive.

We have seen that a popular newspaper like *The Sun* departs frequently and deliberately from Standard English – not of course by using a dialect, but by using some non-standard devices such as spoken forms in writing; would we be correct in assuming that the quality papers don't?

Well, almost correct. To test this, I looked at an article from *The Times* about Angela Merkel becoming Germany's first female Chancellor. Its departures from Standard English were, by comparison, minor, but they were interesting. Here are a few examples.

We are told that Merkel 'has been billed as the German equivalent of Margaret Thatcher, and so political observers have been watching carefully how she deals with privatisation of the country's national treasures'. A later paragraph tells us that disagreement over where savings should be made will 'make the next four weeks of horse trading very complex'. Information about who is to be in the cabinet is introduced with 'The Cabinet line-up unveiled yesterday …'.

These departures from Standard English are now so familiar in newspapers that we probably do not notice them as we read; but the normal terms, surely, would be not *billed* but 'described', not national *treasures* but 'assets', not *unveiled* but 'announced'. Each of the journalistic variants used is more colourful and rather more dramatic than the more abstract term it replaces; this is very much the case when discussions and bargaining about policies are described as *horse trading*. The normal term for a colourful variant in language which is now so familiar that we no longer notice it is *cliché*, and the Standard English of *The Times*, we now notice, is peppered with journalistic clichés. (*Peppered*, of course, is also a cliché.) And since these clichés belong particularly to journalism, they could be described as journalists' jargon.

Writing the Spoken

There is of course another very different situation in which spoken English does find its way into print – or seems to. This is in novels, where the dialogue is an attempt to write down the spoken form of the language. This practice is actually quite recent. In Mary Wollstonecraft's novel *The Wrongs of Women*, published in 1798, a wronged wife informs her husband that she is leaving him in these words:

*I have borne with your tyrannies and infidelities. I disdain to ut-
ter what I have borne with. I thought you unprincipled, but not
so decidedly vicious. I formed a tie, in the sight of heaven – I have
held it sacred; even when men, more conformable to my taste, have
made me feel – I despise all subterfuge! – that I was not dead to love.*

No wife, surely, ever spoke like that. On a solemn occasion like this
an angry wife might choose her phrasing carefully, and thus come
closer to the written language than speakers usually do (though we
might equally imagine that she would get carried away by emotion
and become more incoherent). But those grammatically well-formed
sentences, with their balanced subordinate clauses and the carefully
placed parenthesis, belong to the written language, not the spoken.

Mary Wollstonecraft would probably not have been disturbed by
this criticism; eighteenth-century novels did not usually try to show
us how dialogue is actually spoken. For that we need to wait for the
nineteenth century, and especially for Dickens, who was perhaps the
first novelist to try to write down the spoken language as it really is
spoken:

*It's time for me to go to that there berrying ground, sir, … Where
they laid him as wos wery good to me, wery good to me indeed,
he wos.*

Jo, the illiterate crossing sweeper in *Bleak House*, does not speak
English as it is written, and Dickens has tried to write down what he
actually said. He has tried, but I am not at all sure he has succeeded.
I can easily believe that Jo pronounced *very* as if it were 'wery', and
that he repeated phrases, as he does here. But I am not at all sure
that he would have said *indeed*; its use as an intensifier of *good* belongs in a rather formal way of speaking, and does not seem likely
in the speech of the illiterate Jo. But the real giveaway is 'wos'. Why
has Dickens misspelt *was* in this way? It cannot be to show us how Jo
pronounced it, since we all pronounce *was* as 'wos'. It is Dickens' way
of reminding us – of what? Not, surely, that Jo cannot spell, since he
almost certainly cannot write at all. Rather it is a signal between author and reader that says *We know English better than Jo, don't we?* – a
kind of reassuring nudge. The same can be said for *berrying*, which
once again represents not just Jo's pronunciation, but also yours and
mine.

The conventions Dickens uses to represent Jo's dialect are very like those used to represent the speech of foreigners in boys' adventure stories in the twentieth century. The English hero in such stories often meets a helpful foreigner who says things like *Me likee you*, or perhaps a bloodthirsty foreigner who says *Me not likee you*. Some of these conventions probably go back to *Robinson Crusoe*, the adventure story which Daniel Defoe wrote in 1719, and which became a children's classic (though it was not written for children). Crusoe's servant Friday, whom he finds on his deserted island and teaches to speak English, is the original of all those *Me likee you* foreigners. Here are some specimens of Friday's English: 'Me die, when you bid die, Master. … He be much O glad to be at his own nation. … No, they no kill me, they be willing love learn.'

How has Defoe chosen to represent Friday's English? In the first place, Friday's vocabulary is much better than his grammar; he can usually find the right word, but he can't arrange words correctly in sentences. This is quite plausible, and often happens when people are struggling to speak a foreign language. If we now ask why Friday makes the particular mistakes he does, we can't answer, because we don't know (and Defoe doesn't know) what his own language is like. When we make grammatical mistakes in a foreign language we are likely to use the grammar of our own language; this makes Friday's mistakes quite different from Jo's, since Jo is speaking his own language. There is however one mistake of Friday's that strikes me as implausible – and, perhaps surprisingly, this is the one that became the commonest way for boys' stories to mark the speech of foreigners: his use of *me* instead of *I*. The word *I* is so common that Friday must have heard Crusoe use it thousands of times, and it is unlikely that his own language fails to distinguish between *I*, the subject, and *me*, the object. So *Me die* and *Me not likee you* became conventions meaning 'this speaker is from a primitive tribe', rather than attempts to be plausible.

Spoken and written forms of English, as of any language, are very different. It is in writing more than in speaking English that most people want guidance, and it is easy to see why. The rules are stricter, much less variation is permitted, mistakes are permanently recorded to be noticed, and we usually reflect far more on what we write than on what we say. In writing, almost everyone (except the journalists on popular newspapers) aspires to use Standard English.

A Guide for the Perplexed

This is the title of a book by the medieval Jewish philosopher Maimonides. It sounds like a book we all need. In this welter of change and controversy, how are we to decide what to say and what to write? The truest answer is the one which sounds most unhelpful: that no one else can take your decisions for you. But what can help is to bear one or two principles in mind.

What governs our choice when we are hesitating between alternatives in language? The obvious answer is that we wish to be understood. We do not say *I'll meet you at six o'clock* when we mean 'seven o'clock' or *on Wednesday* when we mean 'Wednesday week', because of the endless trouble it would cause. So, surely, we would cause trouble by saying *the late 1800s* when we mean 1880, if our hearer takes it as meaning 1808–9; or by telling someone that she has not refuted the argument if she is going to reply indignantly *But I do refute it*, meaning 'deny it'. Clearly what we need to be aware of is the situation we are in. In most cases, this means to know what words mean and (in the occasional controversial cases we have been discussing) what our listeners think they mean. If they think wrongly, then we either correct them, or ignore their error (at the cost of misunderstanding), or decide to swim with the tide and adopt their mistake. That is not a linguistic decision, it is a social one.

But there is a linguistic point which can be very useful here. I have mentioned it more than once, but it bears repetition. It is the fact that our passive vocabulary is often more conservative than our active; that is, listeners recognise and understand earlier usages even when they themselves don't use them. These usages may originally have been the only correct ones, and to more conservative speakers will still be that. If, out of natural conservatism or for any of the particular reasons discussed in 'On the Cusp of Change' in Chapter 3, you go on using them, you will be understood. Given reasonable goodwill in your listener, you can say that you have been reading a diarist who wrote in the mid-1900s, and because he was not sufficiently disinterested he offered a view of Lloyd George (full of anti-Welsh sentiment, say) which needs refuting. You will not be misunderstood to be claiming that Lloyd George was alive in the 1950s, or that the diarist was not very interested in the subject, or that it would be enough to deny what the diarist said.

What happens when we misunderstand? There was a story circulating shortly after the Second World War concerning the export of grain from America to France. French bread in the late 1940s was often a curious yellow, and the reason believed by many people was that the French trade negotiator had told the American supplier that they wanted *corn* – and because he had learned British English only, he did not know that *corn* in American English always means maize, whereas the purchaser wanted wheat. The story may well be false, but it gives us a good example of misunderstanding because of a mistake in vocabulary. Another example is *contemporary*. This means 'at the same time': Thackeray is a *contemporary* of Dickens, because they lived at the same time. Our *contemporaries* are those alive at the same time as us. There is not much likelihood of misunderstanding when *contemporary* is used as a noun, but the adjective can be trickier. Because we live in the present, the commonest usage of *contemporary* is likely to be 'at the same time as us': *contemporary styles* and *contemporary furniture* refer to the styles in use now. This usage is now so widespread that it might seem to some people to be the only meaning of *contemporary* – but of course it isn't. I once saw an examination paper in which candidates were asked to compare the philosophy of Hobbes (or Plato, or Marx, or whoever) with that of 'contemporary thinkers'. It emerged that the examiner, who should certainly have known better, meant 'present-day thinkers', but of course the more accurate reading was 'contemporary with Hobbes (or whoever)'. Misunderstanding of that kind, however, is not very common. Much more frequent is puzzlement; when communication fails, it is more likely to be because the hearer is not sure what we mean rather than believing we meant something different.

But conveying our meaning accurately is not the only aim of language. Because speech (and, in a less immediate way, writing) is a social activity, it has another purpose, which we can call self-presentation. What sort of person do you wish to come across as? Without our giving conscious thought to it, this aim governs a good deal of language use. Are you more afraid of appearing ignorant, or pedantic? Of appearing trendy or stick-in-the-mud? That is a choice only you can make.

Illiteracy?

Is there a case to be made against writing correctly similar to the case against 'speaking proper'? Should we even want to correct our (or other people's) mistakes? Let us look at a really drastic example:

> ### Smocking in the houes
>
> *One night in bed I had a puff,*
> *Wil reading literature and,*
> *lsning to hear if the sairs would creek*
> *so I was not cort indiscrest*
> *not a sound I could hear*
> *utill the door was open*
> *as quick a flass the fag was in bed*
> *But my mums got a bludy good Nos*

This is a poem written by a schoolboy of about fourteen, in one of the lower streams of his school. There are so many spelling mistakes that it is almost easier to count the words he has got right; and if we do that we might be surprised to see that he has spelled *night*, *literature* and *quick* correctly – all more difficult, one would think, than *house* or *flash*. Let us divide his spelling mistakes into two kinds: those where he has inadvertently spelled a different word (*smocking*, *Nos* – and perhaps we should add *wil*, which looks as if he was trying to spell *will* rather than *while*), and those which are just mistakes. In these latter cases, is it always clear what word he intends? We might hesitate before realising that *cort* is meant to be *caught*; but the only real puzzle, I think, is *indiscrest* – *indiscreet? in distress? in disgrace?* It's not at all certain that he knows himself.

One's heart sinks at the prospect of teaching this boy how to spell. According to David Holbrook (from whose book *English for the Rejected* I have taken the poem), the best method would be to praise him for what he has done, and wait for his command of the language to improve. But suppose we ask a slightly different question: would we *want* to teach him to spell? My favourite spelling mistake in this poem is *lsning*, which seems to slither into hearing, sounding like the half-caught sounds he is listening for. It leads one to wonder if there is something creative about this boy's mistakes. Is he smiling at himself (or at us) when he describes what he was reading as *literature* – spelling that word right, as if to suggest *You see, I could if I wanted*

73

to? That might make us wonder whether the baffling *indiscrest* was a deliberate portmanteau word. And perhaps also whether the way the poem ends so suddenly and leaves us to imagine the outcome is also a sign of narrative skill.

It is not easy to say whether the very mistakes in this piece of writing are a sign of a certain vitality, even of narrative skill; and harder still to say if that would be lost if the boy managed to learn to spell and punctuate correctly. But what we can say, of course, is that if he wants to get a job for which literacy is required, that is what he needs to learn. In other words, his bad spelling has not led to any serious misunderstanding by the reader; it has led to his being identified as someone who is uneducated. Its bad effect on his job prospects might not be very different from turning up for an interview in ragged and dirty clothes. His mistakes are not doing much damage to the ability of the writing to communicate what he has to say; the damage is to the picture of himself that he is putting across. So if he does not want a job that requires literacy or even cleanliness – if he does not want a job at all – why should he learn to spell?

We are out of language now and into politics. If we think it important that the boy should improve his English, it is because of our view on what sort of people we want our society to consist of, not because we want his writing to get its message across.

Let's turn now to a very different – and less extreme – example of someone whose command of English is not as good as it might be. This passage is from a letter written by a woman in her sixties, who is looking after her deaf 85-year-old aunt.

> *Your letter went astray and did not reach here till the 13/2/67. I see by your letter you wrote it on the 31/1/67. It seems you did not have the right number, but the letter has been to different places that its difficult to see the number now ... Am sorry I have not written before but have been almost immobile with Lumbago and still cannot go out. Dora washes up for me and if I give her the utensils will do the vegetables but am afraid she gets so confused she does not remember things. I have to write things down. Perhaps she will make no comment on my written notes so I have to write again to ask her if she understood the last note. She is very well in herself and eats even more than myself. Of course you know all of her idiosyncrasy but she is*

not unhappy. Dora says she waited on me hand and foot when I was young and now I must do the same for her. I may be the same when I get her age, one never knows what is before us does one. What a lovely morning, the Sun is shining but oh how cold, but then you are young and have plenty warm young blood in you.

My love to you all, Edith.

The first and most important thing to say about this letter is that the mistakes really do not matter. It is a private and personal document, and to point out what is wrong with the English would be inappropriate and even cruel. But since the writer is dead and not known to us, we can treat it impersonally and ask what would need to be corrected if for any reason the writer wanted it to be in correct English – if she were writing, say, to her doctor and did not want him to think she was uneducated. We could even imagine that she brought the letter to us and asked us to correct it for her.

We might begin by saying that there are not many actual mistakes (spelling and grammar mistakes, that is), but quite a lot that is clumsily or inappropriately worded. Let's begin with the actual mistakes: *reach* in the first sentence is a transitive verb, so she should really write *did not reach me* (or else, *did not arrive*); the second sentence should say that the letter has been to *so many different places that*, or (slightly less idiomatic) has been to different places *so that*; and *its* should be *it's*. *Lumbago* should not have a capital letter, since it is not a proper noun (it's not a person or a place) – though perhaps Edith has such strong feelings about her lumbago that she sometimes thinks of it as a person. *All of her idiosyncrasy* sounds odd, since if you know *all of* them, they should really be in the plural (*all of her idiosyncrasies*, or perhaps *her eccentricities*). It's arguable that by *idiosyncrasy* the writer means Dora's idiosyncratic nature taken as a whole, but in that case she should not have written *all of*, which introduces a list of separate items, but simply *all her idiosyncrasy*. *Get her age* should be *get to* (or *reach*) *her age*. The switching between *one* and *we* in that sentence is awkward: she should have written either *We never know what is before us, do we?* or *One never knows what is before one, does one? Plenty warm blood* should be *plenty of*.

A detail that is odd without being an actual mistake (though the boundary between oddities and mistakes is sometimes uncertain) is her way of writing the date. We don't normally write dates out in figures (*13/2/67*) when we're writing continuous prose, just as we don't normally use that form in the spoken language. Perhaps Edith, having written the date like this at the top of her letter, felt vaguely that you write all dates that way in letters. Another detail that could be considered technically a mistake is surely quite all right: the structure of the last sentence, which breaks into spoken English (*but oh how cold*). This breaking of the syntax corresponds exactly to the way an exclamation can break into what we are saying, and brings the writing to life at that moment; I would not even want to turn it into *oh how cold it is*, though technically that might be more correct.

Once we start looking closely at the language of the letter, all sorts of speculations become possible. Was Dora teasing or defending herself when she said she had waited on Edith hand and foot and now Edith must do the same for her? If we'd heard the sentence spoken we might know – especially perhaps from the emphasis she gave to *must* – but from the letter we can only guess. Similarly we can't be sure whether the account of Dora's confusion about reading the notes is a complaint or an expression of sympathy or just a factual account. If the letter occurred in a novel, the novelist would probably have taken the trouble to make these implications clear to us; if we knew Edith and Dora, we'd probably know how to read between the lines in this way. As it is, a lot of these implications remain open.

What's at Stake?

Why do we want to improve our English? One thing is surely clear from both these texts: getting our meaning across without misunderstanding is not usually a problem. We are not often misunderstood in the way that French official (if he ever existed) may have been misunderstood when he said *corn*. The main reason for writing correctly is that we care what kind of person we come across as.

It is spoken English that generates the bitterest arguments. Should schoolchildren in Glasgow or rural Yorkshire be told to speak Standard English, abandoning their local pronunciation along with dialect words and constructions? Should they be in effect bilingual, speaking their dialect in the playground and at home, but Standard English in the classroom and at job interviews? And how standard should their Standard English be?

There are furious controversies about this, but when we turn to writing, most of these arguments melt away. I have already remarked that polemical defences of the value and dignity of regional and class dialects are themselves written in Standard English; no one would expect this book, for example, to be written in anything else. The term Standard English is best used for the written language; for pronunciation the most convenient term is probably Received Pronunciation (often shortened to RP). Since I am not discussing pronunciation, I can therefore avoid most of the bitter controversies.

One final question to end the chapter: why did Standard English arise? It is so convenient to have a standardised language, that our first answer is likely to be that it arose for purely practical reasons – to enable us to communicate better, and to prevent misunderstanding. Radical historians, however, looking for social and political conflict behind most movements, would be likely to claim that the standardisation of English was not a response of the whole community to the need to communicate better, but was the authoritarian creation of a small and powerful elite. Standardisation, like so much else, can always be interpreted either as politically neutral and useful to the whole community, or as an exercise of power. There will always be disagreement between different historical schools about how far change comes about in the interests of all, and how far to serve the interests of the powerful. Standardised weights and measures are very convenient for customers – but can also be seen as serving the interests of manufacturers. And so Standard English can be attacked as the dialect of the privileged, imposing itself on less powerful regions and classes of society, or defended for its great practical advantages. Language can be seen as serving us all because it joins us together, or as dividing us because of its variations.

That argument will never be settled; but because of it, I think it necessary to end this chapter with what I believe to be a fundamental truth about language, which is that unity is more important than variety. Let us ask ourselves a very fundamental question: what is language for? Here is an answer, from Noam Chomsky, the most famous of living linguists. He lists its purposes as follows: to transmit information, to establish relations among people, to express or clarify our thoughts, for play, for creative mental activity, to gain understanding. For every one of these purposes, except perhaps for play and for some kinds of creation, like poetry, language needs to be clear; making it clear therefore serves the interests of all. And so I think the radical political interpretation of what lies behind Standard English, though it can be illuminating on many details, is less important than the interpretation which places clarity and communication at the centre. Different speakers can fit the same words into very different political interpretations. When a foreigner learns that 'money' is the English for *argent* or that 'politeness' is the English for *Hoeflichkeit*, it does not matter if she believes money to be the root of all evil or to be an invaluable means of distributing goods and services, or whether she believes politeness is a very valuable moral attainment or a way of being hypocritical that we would be better without. She is now able to express any of these opinions in English as well as in her own language. Languages change over time and vary across society, but what makes them languages is comprehensibility, the fact that they enable us to understand one another. That language can be used for oppression and discrimination is an incidental consequence of its main function: to rescue our thoughts and our social practices from incomprehensibility and oblivion. It is our most precious gift.

CHAPTER FIVE

A Spot of Grammar

This is not a grammar book; it does not set out to describe systematically the rules by which English sentences are constructed. There are plenty of such books, some very detailed and elaborate. *A Comprehensive Grammar of the English Language*, by Randolph Quirk and others, has over a thousand pages, and will answer all your grammatical queries. My aim is more modest: to explain what grammar is, and to indicate when we need worry about it.

The one thing we can all do, if we are native speakers, is speak English more or less correctly. We know that it is correct to say *John left his book at home*, but not *John his book at home left*; correct to say *John left his book at home and so did I* but not *and so I did*. If we were asked why, could we answer? We might suggest that after *so* we reverse the order of pronoun and verb; but we can say *He told me to leave my book at home, and so I did*. (In that case *so* has a different meaning: 'therefore', instead of 'the same'.) We might suggest that we want to emphasise *I*, and so we put it last; but emphasising is a very complicated procedure in English. In spoken English it depends a good deal on intonation; that is certainly not the reason why we say *John left his book at home and so did I*. We could go on suggesting explanations for the word order, and they would all turn out to be wrong. A grammarian would know the rules, or would know where to look them up. The rest of us do not need to; we still get it right when speaking.

Knowing That We Know

Clearly there is a difference between knowing English, and knowing what its grammatical rules are; we are not usually aware of these, even though we are quite capable of following them. I will call this the difference between what we know (English grammar in practice) and what we know that we know (English grammar in theory). There are of course other – and more scientific – ways of describing this difference. For Chomsky, the very influential linguist we have already encountered, the first goal of grammar is to discover 'the nature of the intuitive, unconscious knowledge which permits the speaker to use his language'. This knowledge is sometimes astonishingly complex; and it is this complexity which has led a large number of experts in linguistics, including Chomsky himself, to speak of a 'language instinct'. They claim that we do not learn our native language because we are taught it, or because we imitate our parents, but because small children already have grammatical structures hard-wired into the brain, and can fit what they hear into these.

Let's look at another example of the English grammar that we all know, but do not know that we know. We say *I've been reading a novel of Trollope's*, or *I believe you know an uncle of mine*. Pause and think about those sentences, and you will notice the double genitive. That the novel is by Trollope or that the uncle is mine is indicated twice: in the first sentence by *of*, plus *-'s* at the end of *Trollope*; in the second by *of* plus *mine*. Other European languages do not do this – French, for example, can't, since it has only one way of indicating the genitive, whereas we have two. When do we use both of them together? The answer is, when Trollope wrote more than one novel, or when we have more than one uncle. It would sound awkward to say *I have been reading a novel of Trollope* – we'd say *by Trollope*. And if we said *I've been reading Trollope's novel* that would change the meaning: it would mean that Trollope wrote only one novel. On the other hand, if I say *I believe you know my uncle*, that could mean either that I have only one uncle or that I have several; but *an uncle of mine* always means that we have more than one. The double genitive indicates that we are choosing one out of several possibilities.

The genitive in English is very tricky, and native speakers are very unlikely to know the rules, but they get it right. I haven't given this as an example of something we need to learn; it is something we all know, and use automatically. I have used it to show that you do not need to know English grammar in order to speak and write English correctly. This undoubted truth is by no means always accepted. When Kenneth Baker, Minister of Education in the 1980s, campaigned for the teaching of formal grammar in schools, he declared 'Pupils need to know about the English language if they are to use it effectively.' There may be many good reasons for knowing about the English language (and some of them, I hope, have led you to read this book), but that is not one of them. For every thousand people who use the double genitive correctly, I doubt if there is one who can explain what it is.

But once we start discussing grammar, once we start trying to explain why something is wrong, we naturally look for an explanation. The true explanation, almost invariably, is simply that that's the way it's done in English; attempts to say why are often colourful but hardly ever correct. Take, for instance, the sentence 'The American force battles the insurgents.' It is quoted by John Humphrys (in his book *Lost for Words*), who quite correctly considers it incorrect, and remarks 'No they don't, they battle against them. Better still, they fight them. Battle is a noun.' We'll return later to the question of using nouns as verbs, but first, let us look at Humphrys' explanation of why we need that preposition: 'The abandonment of certain prepositions is regrettable. Properly used they act almost as a lubricant, easing friction in a sentence. Remove them, and the sentence jars.' Well, there's plenty of friction involved in the American forces fighting the insurgents, but it isn't grammatical friction. English is full of pairs of verbs with similar meanings, where one is followed by a preposition, and the other isn't. A car can *hit* a wall, or it can *crash against* the wall; we can *hear* someone, or we can *listen to* him; we *curse* those who annoy us, or we *swear at* them. *Battle*, when used as a verb, is normally followed by the preposition *against*; but *fight*, the more usual verb, isn't. It would be absurd to claim that *hearing*, *hitting* and *cursing* are somehow self-lubricating, whereas *listening*, *crashing* and *swearing* need a preposition because they have to be lubricated. They need a preposition because that is the way those English verbs behave; knowing English means knowing which verbs are followed by a preposition and which ones aren't. And it means knowing that there are even verbs with which the preposition is optional: we can say *Arsenal played Chelsea* or *Arsenal played against Chelsea*.

This doesn't seem very satisfying. Aren't there any rules, then? There must be, and surely it is the job of grammarians to tell us what they are. This sounds a reasonable expectation, but it bedevilled the study of our language for centuries. Grammarians were quite willing to give us rules, but they weren't the rules of English grammar. They were, or tried to be, the rules of Latin grammar, and they were taught in the fond belief that any self-respecting language must be like Latin.

English Grammar for English

Latin grammar is largely a question of word-endings: a noun in Latin has six or eight possible endings (known as the different cases of the word), according to their function in the sentence. The nouns for *boy* and *girl* are *puer* and *puella*; that is how they appear when they form the subject of a sentence, but when they are the object they become *puerum* and *puellam*. So *the boy loves the girl*, where *boy* is subject and *girl* is object, is *puer puellam amat* in Latin, and *the girl loves the boy* is *puerum puella amat*. The reversal of meaning is brought about in Latin by changing the endings of the nouns, in English by changing the order of the words. The word order has no grammatical importance in Latin; you can say *puella puerum amat, puella amat puerum*, or any other order you like, and all mean *the girl loves the boy*. As well as the case used for the subject (known to grammarians as the nominative) and that used for the object (known as the accusative), there is also the genitive or possessive case (*pueri, puellae*). In English this is indicated by using an apostrophe (*the boy's book, the girl's face*), or sometimes by using the preposition *of* (*a picture of the boy, the left hand of the girl*). There are still two more cases, but the terms for them (dative and ablative) are not needed at all in English, since we usually convey them by using prepositions. We give a book *to a girl*, we get the book back *from the girl*, and we go for a walk *with a boy*. In this last example, Latin would also use a preposition, but would still have to worry about getting the case right: *cum puero*. Then in Latin we need to know another set of case-endings for the plural of the nouns. English nouns, however, have no case-endings: prepositions and word order have freed us from one bit of grammar that Latin (and German) still have.

To see how important word order is in English grammar, consider the following sentences:

1   *Only Henry Martin slept in the House of Commons last week.*
2   *Henry Martin only slept in the House of Commons last week.*
3   *Henry Martin slept only in the House of Commons last week.*
4   *Henry Martin slept in the House of Commons only last week.*
5   *Henry Martin slept in the House of Commons last week only.*

The difference between them is not just a question of elegance but actually of meaning. Try indicating the differences, to see if you agree with my suggestions, which are:

1   No one else slept there, only Henry Martin.
2   This can have two meanings: (i) he only slept there, he did nothing else; and (ii) as a matter of emphasis we (perhaps ironically) point out how shocking this was. In speech, our intonation would indicate this difference.
3   He didn't sleep anywhere else.
4   Again, there are two possibilities, distinguished in speech: (i) if we pause after *only* we attach it to *the House of Commons*, which gives us the same meaning as sentence number 3; and (ii) if we pause <u>before</u> *only* we then attach it to *last week* in order to emphasise how recently it happened.
5   There was no other occasion when he slept there.

Can you add any other possibilities? You will notice that although *only* can move around freely, it cannot go anywhere; it cannot, for instance, be placed between *last* and *week*. In fact the only other position it could have is between *the* and *House of Commons*, where it would mean that there is only one House of Commons.

Since word order is so important in English, mistakes in word order are likely to strike us forcibly – not that this always prevents people from committing them! On the packaging of a sponge pudding I saw the serving suggestion 'Pour over custard for a delicious dessert.' To *pour A over B* and to *pour B over A* have different meanings in English: the noun that comes before *over* is what you pour and the noun after *over* is where you pour it. So you pour cream over your baked apple. The instruction was therefore clearly nonsense, since you can't pour a sponge pudding. Common sense tells us that it should read *pour custard over it* – or (more casually expressed) *pour custard over*. Common sense in the reader, as so often, comes to the rescue of carelessness in the writer. And what do we mean here by common sense? In this case, we mean guessing what the writer meant, even though it was not said correctly; we do that all the time in our native language.

What is this knowledge which native speakers have but which they do not know they have? The answer should by now be clear: it is knowledge of the rules for joining words together. Linguists therefore distinguish between studying lexis (individual words) and grammar (the rules for joining them together). Simple. But, alas, not always simple, for it is not always easy – and sometimes not possible – to distinguish questions of meaning from questions of grammar. Suppose you wanted to explain (to a foreigner) the meaning of *make up*. Knowing the meaning of *make* and of *up* will get you nowhere. You can *make up a story*, *make up your face*, or *make up a deficit*, and it is very difficult to see what these have in common. The difference between *make a face* and *make up a face*, too, is not something you could possibly arrive at by knowing the meaning of *make* or of *up*; what you need to know about is sulky children and cosmetics. Now is this a question of what the words mean, or of how they are used; of semantics, or of grammar?

That is a further reason why Latin grammar cannot be used for English. The rules governing the use of *make* with various prepositions (*make out, make for, make off*) depend on what *make* can and can't mean, and this range of meanings is quite different from that of *facere* in Latin. English grammar needs to describe English. It needs to indicate how English differs from other languages; and sometimes, in ways we have not noticed, how it resembles them.

Let me take the example of English and German nouns. There is no need to know any German to appreciate this point, though some of the long words you will meet may look unpronounceable to you. German has a habit of (some would even say a fondness for) making compound nouns: joining two nouns together to make a single word. This habit enables German to build very long nouns, and other nations have often made fun of this. The mass media are *Massenmedien* (not really different from English); research into the mass media would be *Massenmedienforschung*; you might get a scholarship for research into the mass media – *Massenmedienforschungsstipendium*. In theory, you could go on and on building the word, though this is as far as any German is likely to go. The longest word in their language is sometimes said to be *Donaudampfschifffahrtsgesellschaftskapitän*, which literally means 'the captain of the company for journeying on the Danube in a steamer'. I have no idea whether this title has ever been used, and nor, probably, have the Germans, but they like to think so, and there is even a comic song about him.

To check how fond German is of compound nouns, I opened an essay by Heine at random and found five compounds in the space of four lines: *Welthistorie* (world history), *Räubergeschichte* (story about robbers), *Geistergeschichte* (ghost story), *Haupthebel* (main lever), and *Privatzwecke* (private purposes), along with two compound adjectives, *ehrgeizig* (ambitious, literally 'covetous of honour') and *habsüchtig* (greedy, literally 'seeking for possessions'). We seem to have noticed a difference between the two languages, and it has often been remarked that the culture which produced Kant, Hegel and Schopenhauer, philosophers with a strong taste for abstract ideas, has a fondness for abstract thinking that leads Germans to regard elaborate nouns with a kind of awe. (And after all, they do spell all their nouns with a capital letter!) We, in contrast, would not dream of constructing these very elaborate nouns in English. Or would we?

Next time you are looking at newspaper headlines, pause and think about their grammar. The police who operate in Leeds are the *Leeds police*. If they have a scandal it's a *Leeds police scandal*; if it's being investigated there's a *Leeds police scandal investigation*, which might have a breakthrough, leading to the headline *Leeds police scandal investigation breakthrough*. That's probably as far as we'd be likely to go, though I can just imagine *Leeds police scandal investigation breakthrough confirmation*. When it comes to headlines, we are quite as addicted to stringing nouns together as the Germans are; the only difference is that we leave a space between them.

How would we translate these German compound nouns into English? The most famous example is probably *Schadenfreude* (literally 'damage-joy'), which means 'taking pleasure in someone else's misfortunes'. This we have decided not to translate, and we use the German word. Why? Like so many linguistic questions, this is not easy to answer. Perhaps we admire the neatness of the single word – but then why choose this one in particular? Perhaps – rather unkindly – we like to think of the Germans as taking pleasure in other people's troubles. Or perhaps, like so many linguistic oddities, it just happened. Your theory on this may be as good as mine.

But if we do want to translate? We say research *into* the mass media, a scholarship *for* such research, the holder *of* such a scholarship. Our fondness for prepositions pushes its way forward here, as it did with my version of the captain *of* the company *for* journeying *on* the Danube *in* a steamer. Turning to the examples from Heine, we see that the first of them is two nouns in English, but we prefer to leave a space between them (*world history*), that in three cases we inserted a preposition, and that in two we would probably prefer – as I did – to use a simple adjective, *ambitious* or *greedy*. German, we might even suspect, prefers to remind itself of how the meaning of such words comes about. Are the English less inquisitive linguistically?

Another striking feature of English nouns is their habit of turning into verbs. This is only possible because we have lost so many of our word-endings. We can *man* a stall, we can *house* the homeless, we can *butter* a slice of bread, and we can wonder whether a plant has *flowered* yet. *Man, house, butter* and *flower* are nouns, yet it is perfectly normal to use them as verbs. French cannot use *homme, maison, beurre* or *fleur* as verbs; even with the last two, where a French word can replace the English verb, it is necessary to turn them into a verb form, *beurrer* or *fleurir*.

There is nothing controversial about this, but it is precisely the extension of this very English practice to new words that arouses indignation. When we come to discuss jargon in Chapter 7, I shall suggest that using nouns as verbs is a favourite device in jargon. It can on occasion be a way of sounding important; but it is also a widespread practice in Standard English. We *catalogue* the items we are selling, we *garage* our car, we *group* items together. Each of these examples can arouse protest – and, as we saw earlier, we *battle* instead of fighting a battle. If you dislike these examples of the modern carelessness about the difference between a noun and a verb, you might like to speculate which of them is a modern example. The answer (to save you looking it up in the *Oxford English Dictionary*) is that in every case the verb is almost as old as the noun. In the case of *garage*, of course (brought in from French at the very beginning of the twentieth century), the word itself is recent; it arrived first as a noun, and within four years it had been used as a verb.

The way in which nouns can – and can't – become verbs shows us how far apart grammar and logic can be. Let us, as an example, look at travelling. We can travel (among other methods) on foot, by bicycle, by car, by bus, by ship or by plane. Which of these nouns can become a verb?

The answer turns out to be unsystematic and very complicated. *Bicycle, car* and *plane* are hardly ever used as verbs. *Chambers Dictionary* gives *plane* as a verb, but I don't think I have ever heard it used this way. *Car* is never a verb, but the earlier form of the noun was *motor car* (still sometimes heard), or *motor*. This can be used as a verb (*We motored down to Brighton*), though it is definitely old-fashioned, both as noun and as verb. *Bicycle* also sounds old-fashioned as a verb, but to *cycle* is quite normal, and you can sometimes hear *bike* as a verb, mainly in America. To travel on foot is normally to *walk*, but we do use *foot* as a verb – usually when the walking is strenuous, and usually in the form *foot it* (*We had to foot it up a long steep hill*). *Ship* is only used as a transitive verb; goods are *shipped* to their destination (even if they are travelling by land), and the person who despatches them is often a *shipping clerk*. As for *bus*, the disputes about racial and educational integration in America in the sixties gave the word a new lease of life as a transitive verb, meaning 'to move groups of children to a school outside their area'.

A short digression here on spelling. The practice described above became known as *busing*, a spelling which one would expect to be pronounced to rhyme with *fusing*, and which still looks very odd to me. Since the word rhymes with *fussing*, why is it not spelt *bussing*? Monosyllables with a short vowel normally double their consonant when -*ing* is added (*fitting, batting, stepping*). If you look in a dictionary, you will find that the spelling *bussing* does exist, but I have never seen it used in the sense of 'shifting schoolchildren' – certainly not in America (where the practice began). There are, then, two reasons for spelling the word with only one -*s*. The first is to distinguish the meaning 'shifting schoolchildren' from the earlier, broader sense of 'transporting by bus'. That may well be the correct explanation, but there is another possibility which is quite interesting linguistically. It may derive from the feeling that *bus* itself is an unusual spelling: verbs with a short vowel ending in -*s* usually double the -*s* in their simple form (*kiss, pass, mess*). And the reason for the spelling of *bus* is that it is an abbreviation of *omnibus*, which you can still sometimes hear, and which is Latin for 'for everyone'. So whoever produced the spelling *busing* may have had a feeling (whether or not they knew the origin of the word) that *bus* isn't an ordinary English word, so shouldn't form its participle in the ordinary English way.

But to return to our main point, the quite irregular way in which English turns these nouns into verbs (or sometimes doesn't) makes it quite clear that usage has little to do with logic. Yet there are some nouns whose use as a verb does jar even on quite unprejudiced readers, and it is often difficult to decide why. One of my aversions is *showcase*, which when used as a verb means 'display' – or even, sometimes, the same as *show* or *show off*. A publicist showcases the achievements of her client, a cricketer showcases his ability to score runs, performers showcase their talents. There would be a certain logic in saying that a museum showcases its exhibits, but I have never seen it used in this more or less literal sense. Am I just prejudiced in objecting to this usage, or is it really an indication of our publicity-mad, exhibitionist culture? I can't decide – can you?

The Apostrophe – and Other Awkwardnesses

Almost every English noun can have an *-s* added to it. When? If you think about it, you will realise that there are three occasions: to turn it into a plural, to turn it into a possessive (or genitive), or to abbreviate the word *is* after it. So we can say to a cousin *Our fathers were brothers* (plural), or we can say *My father's age is 55* (possessive, with an apostrophe before the *-s*), or we can say *My father's somewhere in the house* (an abbreviation of *My father is*). English doesn't put an apostrophe before *-s* when it indicates a plural, but does in the other two instances. However, for lots of people nowadays this is a pitfall, since they either do not understand or do not bother to use this distinction. Now one might expect that if a grammatical feature, such as the apostrophe, is not clear to users, it would drop out of use. And it might be an improvement if English just lost the apostrophe; German manages perfectly well without it. But the opposite has happened. If your local greengrocer puts up a notice saying *Nectarine's 30p each* instead of *Nectarines 30p each* (as my local greengrocer did), he clearly does not understand the use of the apostrophe. But instead of simply leaving it out when it should be used, he has used it when it should be left out. This has become a common error, which I cannot explain; except to suggest that, feeling anxious because he does not understand when to use it, he has decided to play safe by putting it in whenever he is in doubt.

You will see superfluous apostrophes wherever you look nowadays. Here is a sentence that appeared in my favourite newspaper: 'The nation's from a Western Christian tradition and the Islamic world are still learning how to co-exist.' After reading the first seven words, we can only understand the apostrophe to mark the shortening of *The nation is.* So we assume that the nation in question is probably Britain, and that the sentence, continuing with *and the Islamic world,* is presumably going on to say that the Islamic world is from a different tradition. A second reading is necessary to realise that *the nation's* is meant to be a plural and should therefore be *the nations* – without the apostrophe. The confusion between *-s* and *-'s* does not, I have to admit, cause any lasting damage; it just requires us to give a second reading. And leaves a (more lasting) awareness that even a leading national newspaper does not always use the apostrophe correctly.

Since it is the short simple words that are the most complex in their grammar (we'll come back to this in the next chapter), you will not be surprised to learn that the word which presents the trickiest problem with the apostrophe is the word *it. It* has no plural form (the plural, of course, would be *they*) but it could logically take an *-s* in both the other instances: as a possessive, and as an abbreviation for *it is.* But as both might be expected to require an apostrophe, to distinguish them it is helpful to use the apostrophe in only one instance. Since we write other possessive pronouns (such as *hers, ours* and *yours*) without an apostrophe, it is only consistent to do the same for the possessive *its.* This separates it from the abbreviation for *it is,* which we write as *it's.* And so it's important to distinguish the right use of this pronoun from its wrong use.

Pronouns are in fact the one area in which English grammar <u>can</u> be likened to Latin, for our pronouns have retained the case-endings that our nouns have lost. *I, we, he, she,* and *they* still behave like the pronouns in Latin – and indeed in most languages – by changing their form when they are the object and when they are in the genitive case. So *I* changes to *me* or *my, he* to *him* or *his,* and so on. We all know this, and don't need to be told; and therefore pronouns cause us no difficulty.

Or hardly any. Take the sentence *I can run faster than Billy*. Its meaning is clear, and we do not need to worry what case *Billy* is, because English nouns are the same whether they are the subject or the object. Now replace *Billy* with a pronoun, and we have to decide whether it's the subject or the object: *I can run faster than he* or *I can run faster than him?* We all say *him*, though if we stop to think we'll realise that it ought, logically, to be *he*, since the sentence is a shorter way of saying *I can run faster than he can run*. That too is not really a problem; we can shrug our shoulders and smile at one of the many ways English idiom allows us to say something illogical. But suppose we say *I gave Mary more money than Billy*. Now that there are three people involved, the sentence is ambiguous: does it mean 'I gave Mary more money than I gave Billy' or 'I gave Mary more money than Billy did'? There is no way of knowing, so we need to repeat the verb, as I have just done, to make it clear whether Billy is its subject or its object. This means that if we now replace Billy with a pronoun, we need to get it right. *I gave Mary more money than him* ('than I gave Billy'), or *I gave Mary more money than he* ('than Billy gave Mary')? This last sounds odd, even pedantic, to most people, so the best solution in this case is to say *than he did*.

Why have our pronouns kept their case-endings when our nouns have lost them? Probably because they are so often used. It is usually the frequent and familiar forms that cling to their bits of grammar when other words have lost them. We see this very clearly if we think about the verb *be*, easily the most common verb in English and in most other languages, which has more (and more varied) forms than any other: *am, is, are, was, were, being, been*.

The grammar of pronouns causes us hardly any trouble, because the forms are so familiar. We probably don't even notice (until we stop to think about it) that the one pronoun which does not change its case is *you*. In earlier centuries, English used *ye* as the subject (corresponding to *he*) and *you* as the object (corresponding to *him*), but *ye* has disappeared – or at least disappeared from use. We still recognise it, and at Christmas we sing *O come all ye faithful*. But no one, except students of grammar, realises that it would actually have been wrong, in Middle English, to say *O come all you faithful*, since *you* was used only for the object of a sentence.

I have no explanation for why *you* has behaved in this way in English; the same thing has not happened in other European languages. Perhaps there is something slightly eccentric about *you* in English. We don't, for instance, spell it with a capital letter; although we do for *I*, in contrast to German, which spells *ich* (meaning 'I') with a small letter, and *Sie* (the polite form for 'you') with a capital. This difference between English and German could make us look very self-centred to the Germans!

Even odder is the way *you* seems to prefer *I* to *me*. Consider the sentences *She likes you* and *She likes me*. Now suppose she likes both of us; the natural way to say this would surely be *She likes you and me*. Certainly we can still say this, but there is a growing tendency to say *She likes you and I*. It's hard to see the reason for this, since it is still probably normal to say *She likes him and me*. Have we got an odd feeling about *you* that makes us feel *you and me* is somehow improper? Is it modesty or arrogance about ourselves that makes us do this? The habit, though now quite widespread, is not universal, and we can certainly get away with being logical and still using *you and me* as the object of the verb: *It concerns you and me*. If you join me in doing this, reader, then both you and I are being logical, and a new habit has been rejected by both you and me.

English nouns do not change their form much. They usually have a singular and a plural form, and that's all. This is very different from Latin, where, as we saw, a noun has a number of different endings (or inflections as they are technically called), according to its function in the sentence. The contrast between inflected languages and those (like English) that have lost most of their inflections is even more striking if we turn to verbs. Let us take any English verb – *love*, for instance. You may love your mother, and she loves you; each of you loves and will continue to love the other; few sons or daughters love their mother as you love yours. If you had not loved her, would she have loved you? Will you ever love anyone else as much, and will anyone ever love you as she does? If she loved your father more, would such love make you jealous; do all men love their mothers? Have mothers always loved their daughters? … We can go on making up ever more complicated sentences with the verb *love*, and we shall use only three or at most four forms: *love, loves, loved,* and *loving*. If you learn Latin, you usually begin with what used to be called the conjugations: *amo, amas, amat, amamus, amatis, amant,* meaning *I love,*

91

you (singular) *love, he or she loves, we love, you* (plural) *love, they love.* If you learn French or German, or indeed many other languages, you will find a similar set of changing forms; the word *love*, which has only four forms in English, will have dozens in French, scores in Latin, and perhaps even more in some languages.

One final comment on grammatical rules. You may have noticed that almost all the examples we have looked at were cases where people sometimes make mistakes, or argue about which form is right. The previous sentence could have begun *You might have noticed*, which would also have been correct, though with a very slight difference in meaning: if I write *You might have noticed*, I suggest a higher probability that you did not in fact notice it. A grammar book will certainly discuss this difference, because it is one on which speakers might feel they need guidance – or might want to give guidance to others! But it will not bother to tell us not to write *You have may noticed*, because that is not a construction anyone would use. It is the cases we might argue about that get formulated as rules.

Grammar and Meaning

To say that we need grammar in order to convey our meaning is to state something obvious. Yet we saw in the last chapter that a sentence can be grammatically wrong while its meaning is quite clear; and that it can be grammatically correct, but ambiguous. Does grammar lead a life that is partly independent of meaning, so that we can find a sentence grammatically correct but meaningless? Since the work of Chomsky we have become aware of this possibility, and the sentence he made up to illustrate the point has become famous: 'Colourless green ideas sleep furiously.' Chomsky claimed, quite rightly, that we all recognise this as a perfectly acceptable English sentence, as far as the grammar is concerned; but that it means nothing. One might create other, similar sentences: *A woolly hedgehog threw an artful dream* or *My purple patience fell without Milan* – it can be quite fun making them up.

Although grammar is necessary if we are to say anything meaningful, it should not surprise us that it's possible to construct English sentences which have more than one meaning, because more than one grammatical pathway can be found through them. *Time flies* is a familiar saying in English, meaning, of course, that time passes too quickly; but *time* can be a verb, and there are *flies* in our house every summer, so those two words might occur in the sentence *It's hard to time flies, because they move so quickly.*

Even more striking are those sentences which can have two directly opposite meanings. *That'll teach you to arrive early*, for instance, could be spoken to someone who came late and missed something important, or to someone who came early and had to sit round doing nothing until the others arrived. This is because two rather different meanings of *teach* are being used: we can be taught because we did something with an unfortunate result (arrived early and were bored), or because we failed to do it and missed something valuable.

Or consider the sentence *You can't be too careful.* This almost always means that you ought to be careful; it is such a familiar saying that this meaning has become firmly attached to it. But suppose you said *You can't be too fierce.* This could be advice on how to handle a sensitive and nervous pupil, telling you not to be fierce. Or it could be telling you to stand no nonsense from a persistent heckler, and that the fiercer you are the better. Both meanings are perfectly idiomatic, and we would have to know the exact situation to decide which one is intended – and sometimes not even that would tell us. The ambiguity in this sentence does not actually belong to *fierce* (the meaning of which is quite clear) but to *can't*, which in the first case means 'you ought not to', and in the second case means 'it's impossible to'. My feeling (though you may not agree) is that these possibilities of totally opposite meanings are an enrichment rather than a fault in our language.

A Language without Grammar?

The points I have been making in this chapter are often summed up by saying that modern English has hardly any grammar, but I hope it is now clear that this is a misleading way of putting it. It is just as possible to make grammatical mistakes in English as in a highly inflected language. Recently I received a letter from someone I did not know, which began by saying that our common friend X *has been so kind to suggest your name.* The meaning is clear, and I naturally did not feel it necessary to inform the writer (who was Dutch) that he should have written that X *has been so kind as to suggest your name,* or else *has been kind enough to suggest your name.* If we think of how often foreigners say *I have done it yesterday* instead of *I did it yesterday*, or how difficult they sometimes find it to distinguish between *I walk* and *I am walking*, we can soon realise that English has plenty of grammar. It is just that we have shed one particular piece of grammar – we do not indicate grammatical differences by word-endings. Instead we do it mainly by word order, and partly by the use of the little all-purpose extra verbs such as *do, be, would* and *get,* that grammarians call auxiliaries.

It is not possible for a language to have no grammar – if by grammar we mean the rules for joining words together to make complex statements. No language can exist without such rules. The alarm calls of animals consist of something like words (*danger,* for instance), but they have no way of distinguishing between *Look out! Danger approaching* and, say, *That's dangerous, That might be dangerous, I was in danger yesterday, Johnny is always courting danger, She avoids danger more than I do,* and so on. Unless we have a grammar that enables us to draw such distinctions, we have not really got language.

CHAPTER SIX

What Does That Mean?

What *does that mean?* someone asks. A simple enough question, surely. Or is it? Like so much in language, it gets less simple when we think about it. We could ask *What does that mean?* because we haven't understood a word or a sentence. The sentence might be in a foreign language which we are still learning. A Russian or German listener, hearing you say *That was a terrific performance*, might not know the word *terrific*. She knows *terrible*, and wonders if the performance was very bad; she knows *terrifying*, and wonders if the performance frightened the audience; she suspects – rightly – that the word doesn't mean either of these, and so she has to ask what the word means, or look it up in the dictionary. Then she will find that it's an emphatic way of saying 'very good', and knows what it means.

Or we might have found the sentence pretentious or obscure. It might have been written by a philosopher whom we find difficult to understand, and we're not sure whether it's very profound or just a way of bewildering us:

The concept determines itself, posits determinations in itself, and then sublates them, and through this sublation wins for itself an affirmative and truly richer, more concrete determination.

Reading (or hearing) this sentence by Hegel, many a person who is not a professional philosopher could be forgiven for wondering whether it is a valuable though difficult insight into the history of ideas, or whether it is just playing about with abstract nouns in order to impress us. And might therefore ask impatiently *What does that mean?* Or perhaps, in this case, *What on earth does that mean?*

There are other possibilities; the question could be a way of indicating that we dislike what we have heard. Someone says to us *Of course that's probably too difficult for you to understand*, or *I know you don't like me to get too technical*, or just *Here we go again*. We suspect that the speaker was putting us down, showing off his superior knowledge, commenting on our idiosyncrasies; and we respond, perhaps indignantly, by saying *What does that mean?* This example clearly belongs in the spoken language, and our intonation will show our displeasure.

All these possibilities – and perhaps others – are covered by the simple question *What does that mean?* Indeed, it's not a simple question at all, because the idea of meaning is not a simple one. As I shall now try to explain.

Dictionaries

If they don't know what a word means, most people go to the dictionary. So let's start there. Look up a word – any word – in a good dictionary. What will you find? First of all, that the dictionary tells you a good deal more than the meaning of the word. Obviously you will find how to spell the word; since the dictionary is written, it could hardly avoid that. You will find what part of speech it is (noun or verb or adjective or whatever), and you will soon notice that a lot of English words are both noun and verb: you go for a *walk* and you *walk*. Most dictionaries will tell you the origin (or, to use the technical term, the etymology): either the Old English from which the word derives, or the foreign language from which it came into English. But by far the largest part of the entry will be about the meaning – or meanings – of the word. You will find that the entries vary greatly in length, and also that the commoner the word the longer the entry. Let's take a moderately common verb like *tear*. Most of us would probably think its basic meaning is 'to pull apart', as in *to tear your shirt* or *to tear a letter*, but there are plenty of others: we can *tear out of the house, tear down the road*, or *tear a letter out of someone's hand*. We might not have noticed, till the dictionary tells us, that when I *tear a letter* the letter is damaged, but when I *tear the letter out of your hand* it may be undamaged. This is something we all know, but until we read it in a dictionary (or in this book!) we may not have noticed that we know it.

Some dictionaries will then explain the meaning of the verb when it is paired with a preposition, and this may well be the most complicated part – think of *tear up, tear into, tear off, tear away, tear apart.* Perhaps the verb which has the richest collection of meanings when followed by different prepositions is *get*; just think of *get at, get by, get in, get out, get on, get off,* and so on. Then think of *get on a bus* and *get on with your mother-in-law* and you will see that even with the same preposition it can have two very different meanings. Indeed, even with two prepositions this is possible; as well as *getting on with your mother-in-law* you could be *getting on with the job*. This is one of the hardest things in English for foreigners to master, and even those who speak English well are likely to use *manage* instead of *get by, enter* instead of *get in, rise* instead of *get up*, and so on. To the English this sounds a little stiff, but to the foreigner who learned English not at her mother's knee but in a more formal situation, these common verbs plus prepositions do not come very naturally. And even without prepositions, the really common English verbs (*come, go, get, put, have, do, run*) have huge variations of meaning. Just think, for instance, of the number of things that can *run*: a person who's in a hurry or a person running through something in her mind, a film, a tap, a stocking, an engine, a train. These very short and familiar verbs are among our most complex words. They are not complex in the sense that *nuclear fission* or *psychoanalysis* are complex: those words refer to activities that are complex, but they have only the one meaning, so we could say that as words they are quite simple. These familiar verbs are complex because they have so many different meanings. More about this in a moment.

But first let's return to *tear*. You may have noticed that there is also the word *tear*, referring to what we weep, spelt the same as the *tear* we've looked at, though pronounced differently; and you may have wondered if it's the same word. The fact that it's pronounced differently is irrelevant, since words change their pronunciation so much. Similarly you may have wondered if *fry* in *They're only small fry, not the leaders,* and *fry* in *Let's have a good fry of bacon and sausages* are the same word. Or whether *facility* in *The job looked difficult, and I admired the speed and facility with which he carried it out,* is the same word as *facilities* in *Are there facilities for changing one's clothes here?* How does the linguist decide that to *tear down the street* and *a tear in your shirt* are two different uses of the same word, but that the *tear* you shed is a different word? How do we distinguish different meanings of the same word from different words? What do we mean by 'the same word'? You might like to think of your own answer to these questions before reading on.

The answer is historical: by looking at the history of a word we can see how it has branched out into different meanings. *Facilis* means 'easy' in Latin, so to say that someone's answer is *facile* means that it was easily arrived at (perhaps too easily, since the adjective has acquired a touch of disapproval in English). *Facilities* for changing therefore suggests a place where it would be easy to change, but the idea of 'easy' has more or less disappeared from this meaning, and *changing facilities* has come to mean simply a room where you can change. But the linguist does not hesitate to consider them to be the same word, because these uses have branched out from the same origin. The *tear* we weep, however, because it derives from a different word in Old English, is historically quite separate from the *tear* in your shirt. And the *fry* we might enjoy for breakfast is a word that came into English, first as a verb, from French, whereas the *fry* of *small fry* came into English from Scandinavian; it originally meant 'seed' or 'offspring', and then 'the young of fish'. Quite unconnected with frying.

So if two meanings go back to a common origin, then they belong to the same word. Clearly dictionary-makers need some knowledge of the history of the language; even if their dictionary does not give etymologies, they still need to know how to tell one word from another. And not all dictionaries use this historical principle in arranging their entries. A dictionary might, for instance, list *facile* and *facilities* as separate items if it was simply considering the convenience of the user, who might not realise that they are, historically, the same word. This does not alter the fact that the only consistent way to distinguish between two different words, and two different meanings of the same word, is to treat the matter historically.

The greatest and most famous dictionary of all, the *Oxford English Dictionary (OED)*, is historical in a much more central way. It was originally called *A New English Dictionary on Historical Principles*, and its aim was to give us the complete history of every word in the language. The entry for *tear* (or rather the two entries, since the

OED separates the entry for the noun from that for the verb) is very much longer than any of those we've so far looked at; that for the verb occupies a large page of very close print. It gives us all the spellings the word has ever had and devotes a dozen lines to discussing its etymology. It arranges the word's meanings very carefully, starting with the oldest, and tries to show how this developed into the other meanings the word has (or had). It gives the date of the first recorded use, and the date of the first use of each meaning (plus, if any of the meanings are now obsolete, the date of the last). And everything it says is illustrated; examples of every meaning are quoted (roughly, one for each century) and dated, so that we can share in the research that went into the entry. If we want to find out what the word could and couldn't mean in, say, the year of Shakespeare's birth, the information is there – though it will need some patience on our part to work it out.

Everyone has heard of the *Oxford English Dictionary*, and everyone is vaguely aware that it is the authority that somehow lies behind all the others. But obviously it is a work for scholars, and most of us are likely to feel that it offers more information about the word than we need – and perhaps that such a bulky volume is more than we have space for (although nowadays we can buy the compact edition, complete with magnifying glass, or the electronic version, for use with our computer). Even the *Shorter Oxford English Dictionary*, which omits many of the quotations and some of the detail, but is still organised on historical principles, might seem more than most readers want. Once one has started on the happy hours of exploration of the language which it offers, however, it is very easy to get hooked!

Completeness?

We would of course like a dictionary that is complete, so that if we are looking up a word we can be sure that it will be there. But what does that mean? Does it, for instance, mean that the dictionary will include all the words in the language? How many words are there in English, anyway?

That's an easy question, and the answer is – nobody knows. It is, in the first place, impossible to decide what counts as a word. *Tear, tears, tearing, tore, torn*: one word or five? And what about *untorn, tearable, untearable?* My computer programme does not recognise these as words – but I could easily instruct it to do so. If I did, it would be absurd to claim that I have added new words to the language. Clearly, we cannot know how many words there are in English unless we first sort out our definition of a word, but that is not a practical problem; whether we call *tear, torn, untearable* and the rest different words, or variants of the same word, we can ask that an exhaustive dictionary should include them all. It is not such variations that provide the real problem, but the fact that a language has no firm boundary. If you look at the Introduction to the great *OED*, you will find a famous diagram, which shows the *Common Language* in the middle, surrounded by two areas labelled *Literary* and *Colloquial*. Beyond *Literary* we find *Scientific* and *Foreign*, beyond *Colloquial* we find *Slang* and *Dialectal*. No one knows how many words there are in each of these categories. If we included every scientific term there is, we would probably have to include more words than in all the other categories put together, most of them known to only a handful of specialists. As for slang, it is changing all the time; if we tried to include all the slang terms, our dictionary would go out of date while it was being printed. So the *OED* comes to the conclusion that 'The circle of the English language has a well-defined centre, but no discernible circumference.' Every dictionary-maker has to decide how far out from that centre to travel.

When Samuel Johnson set out in 1747 to compile what was the first serious dictionary of the language, he began with high hopes, resolving 'to leave neither words nor things unexamined'. After enquiring into the words, he intended 'to show likewise my attention to things, to pierce deep into every science'. But as the years went by he found 'that one enquiry only gave occasion to another', and that he was chasing the sun, which when you reach one hill has disappeared behind the next. What he here discovered was the difference between a dictionary and an encyclopedia: put at its simplest, the one deals with words, the other with things. The dictionary can tell us what a *teal* or a *partridge* is, but to find out about their habits we need a bird book. So Johnson's abandoned hope of piercing 'deep into every science' was one which he need not have entertained in the first place.

But that was not the only limitation he felt it necessary to apologise for. 'I could not visit caverns to learn the miners' language,' he wrote rather defensively, 'nor take a voyage to perfect my skill in the dialect of navigation, nor visit the warehouses of merchants, and shops of artificers, to gain the names of wares, tools and operations, of which no mention is found in books.' Although Johnson's great dictionary is now hopelessly out of date, and no one would dream of using it today, things have not changed all that much; modern lexicographers, who spend most of their time looking through books and sitting in front of computers, do not visit these places either. Most dictionaries set out to record the written language – though, as we saw earlier, the boundary between written and spoken is not easy to draw.

So a dictionary aims for as much completeness as possible, limited by space and by its decisions on what really belongs to the language. And also, we must now add, by what it is allowed to print. Until recently, dictionaries did not print the 'four-letter words' that were considered indecent. The *OED* left them out of its final version in 1928, but printed them in the *Supplement* which appeared in 1972, either because the taboo had relaxed, or because scholarly insistence on completeness triumphed over it. But one difficulty was overcome only for another to appear – as Robert Burchfield, editor of the *Supplement*, discovered to his chagrin. The new prudery concerned not obscenities but political incorrectness. This is discussed more fully in a later chapter, but here we need to anticipate that discussion briefly. If you are told to avoid abusive language, you clearly need to be told which words are considered abusive: do not call Pakistanis *pakis*, or Jews *yids*, or African-Americans *niggers*, and so on. In writing that sentence, have I not just used the abusive words? Well, not really; we could claim I have not used them, but only mentioned them. The distinction between use and mention is very important for dictionary-makers, who see their task not as using the language but as recording, or mentioning, the way it is used. Burchfield found to his alarm that the mention of racist or sexist terms could arouse as much indignation as their use, and he even invented the term *Guralnikism* to denote the attempt to keep such words out of the dictionary. David Guralnik was the editor of *Webster's New World Dictionary*, published in 1970, who explained in his Foreword that it had been decided not to mention 'those true obscenities, the terms of racial or ethnic opprobrium, that are, in any case, encountered with diminishing frequency these days'. This rather optimistic statement must have saved Dr Guralnik a good deal of hassle – hassle that Dr Burchfield had to endure. Much of the controversy that he was embarrassed by concerned politics (how to define *Pakistani* or *Palestinian*, for instance), where the issue concerned definition, not mention; but there were also objections to the very inclusion of terms such as *nigger*. The term which got the *OED Supplement* into most trouble, however, was *Jew*. A Jewish businessman went so far as to bring an action against the publishers, Oxford University Press, in a blaze of publicity, complaining that the *OED Supplement's* explanations of the abusive meanings of Jew were 'derogatory, defamatory and deplorable'. He lost the case, but not on the grounds that mention is not the same as use; the judge simply ruled that the words in the definition did not refer to him personally. This leaves open the possibility that mention could be considered as bad as use, so not even the lexicographer is safe from politics.

Ambiguity

The purpose of language is (surely) to enable us to say what we mean; if the hearer, or reader, is puzzled because we could mean one of two things, we have (surely) failed to communicate. If we say *The lecture lasted an hour; I wasn't paying attention the whole time*, it is not clear whether we were paying attention most of the time but not the whole time, or if we failed to pay attention for the whole time. If we ask *Where were you wounded?* the answer could be *in the right leg* or *in France*. If we say *He likes me more than you*, it could mean *more than you like me*, or *more than he likes you*. The context or – if we are speaking – the intonation might make each of these sentences clear, but if it does not then they need changing, since they are all examples where we presumably intend the meaning to be clear.

Of course there are always cases where we don't intend this. We might be making a joke, as in *If the baby doesn't like cold milk, boil it*. We might wish to be ambiguous, as in the story of the wife who wished to buy an expensive dress and sent her husband a telegram asking if they could afford it, and received the reply *No price too dear*. Now that we no longer send telegrams this joke is clearly dated (and anyway the husband could surely have afforded to pay for a comma!), but we do still make New Year resolutions. I once heard someone introduce a remark which he thought his listeners might think inappropriate by saying *I intend despite my New Year resolution to continue my bad habit* – and he then paused, leaving us to guess whether the resolution was to continue the bad habit or to give it up. When we are deliberately ambiguous we clearly want the listener, or the reader, to think of both meanings. This is often the case in poetry.

Thomas Gray's *Elegy in a Country Churchyard* – once among the most famous poems in the language – describes the simple lives of those who are now buried in humble graves, and tells us that they are none the worse for not having flattering epitaphs: 'Can flattery soothe the dull cold ear of death?' This line could be personifying death, telling us that it's no use flattering the grim reaper, who will cut us all down regardless; or it could be telling us that it's no use whispering flattery into the dull cold ear of someone who is dying. Which is the right reading? Both of them fit the sentiment so well that both are possible, and there is no need to choose between them. The poem is richer if we keep both in mind.

Ambiguity can even be central to the meaning of a poem:

> *I fear a man of frugal speech,*
> *I fear a silent man;*
> *Haranguer I can overtake*
> *Or babbler entertain*
>
> *But he who weigheth, while the rest*
> *Expend their furthest pound –*
> *Of this man I am wary:*
> *I fear that he is grand.*

This haunting poem is by Emily Dickinson – in my view the finest of all American poets, but her poems are often strange. This poem takes a bit of getting used to, but once we make out the rather odd use of some of the words it is not very difficult – I have made it more accessible by modernising its very odd punctuation. *Haranguer* and *babbler*, who bombard us with long, wordy speeches or chatter away non-stop, are obviously contrasted with the *silent man*; she can cope with them – even though she uses rather odd terms (*overtake, entertain*) for the way she deals with them.

We can explain most of the oddities in the poem, but we can never explain away its central ambiguity. Is it telling us that the man of frugal speech is to be feared and disliked, that by weighing his words while the rest babble he is somehow alienating us? Or is it saying that the silent man, though unattractive at first, is more impressive and more deeply to be admired? This ambiguity at the heart of the poem is summed up in the last word, since by calling him *grand* she could be paying a high compliment or dismissing him as pompous and self-important; both are possible meanings to give to the word. And the more I ponder the poem, the more I feel that I do not need to resolve that ambiguity; it lies at the heart of how we feel about strong, silent, imposing men, and makes the poem more powerful.

Comedians and poets, then, for quite different reasons, often seek out ambiguity; but the rest of us usually need to avoid it, and make our meaning clear.

There are two causes of ambiguity: grammar and individual words. *He likes me more than you*, which we discussed on page 102, is ambiguous because it can be taken in two different ways – it is a case of grammatical ambiguity. *Did you hear the lecture?* could be a way of asking whether you were present at the lecture, or, if the lecturer spoke very softly, whether he was audible; and this can be regarded as an ambiguity depending on two different meanings of *hear*. But these two kinds of ambiguity cannot always be firmly distinguished. *Professor X lectures on the moon*, which is clearly a kind of linguistic joke, depends for its effect on the ambiguity of *on*; but since prepositions are not so much words with meanings of their own, as words with the job of arranging the meaningful words into sentences, this example of ambiguity could equally be seen as depending on grammar.

Now our brief study of dictionaries has surely taught us that most of the commoner words in English are richly ambiguous; the longer their entries in the dictionary, the more ambiguous they are. That is why the question *What does that mean?* is so often necessary and important; and we should never feel too embarrassed to ask it. It is impossible, in a book of modest length like this, to discuss all the possible ambiguities; to do this we'd need a book considerably longer than a dictionary. All we can offer is examples, and I have chosen three verbs which we all know, though we may not always have sorted out their possible ambiguity; they are *recognise, antici-pate* and *appreciate*. Can you think up sentences in which these words would be ambiguous?

Firstly, let's look at *recognise*. We are all familiar with the usual meaning: we *recognise a face, recognise a quotation, recognise an idea.* It involves remembering, and identifying. We might not have seen a distant relative for twenty years, but we *recognised her immediately.* We might not be very familiar with Shakespeare's plays, but everyone *recognises that 'To be or not to be' comes from Hamlet.* No difficulty about these. But *recognise* also has the meaning of granting a sort of approval, as when the government of one country refuses to recog-nise that of another. A number of Western countries *did not recognise East Germany*, a new revolutionary government somewhere *is now recognised by most other countries*, and so on. It is possible for these two meanings to be confused. I once read the minutes of a meeting which had discussed one of the practices of those applying for funds. 'It was agreed', ran the minutes, 'that this practice must be recognised as a way in which such bodies can obtain revenue.' Because I had been at the meeting, I knew that the practice was being disapproved of, so we had the common meaning of *recognise*. But it could easily (and probably would usually) be understood in the other meaning of *recognise*, that the committee was granting approval to this practice.

That was a minor example, a quibble of concern mainly to lawyers and committee members. *Anticipate* has a wider interest. The first part of the word derives from the Latin word *ante*, meaning 'before', so that it refers to something in the future; and it has therefore come to be used to mean 'expect'. But the second part of the word is from the Latin *capere*, meaning 'to take', and *anticipate* originally always meant to take some action, to do something, in advance. A chess player who *anticipates* his opponent's moves does not merely expect him to move, but arranges his own pieces in order to guard against the move. When Macbeth declared 'Time, thou anticipat'st my dread exploits', he meant that his exploits were being frustrated, since Time (which he is here treating as a kind of God or Fate) was not just ex-pecting the exploits, but guarding against them – that is, was *doing* something. (You may have noticed that I used the word with this meaning on page 101.) Whether we intend the word simply to mean 'expect', or use it in this older and more precise sense, will often be clear from the context – but not always. To *anticipate your holiday* usually means, in modern colloquial English, to look forward to it. But if your employer told you sternly that *you should not anticipate your holiday*, you might find his language a bit old-fashioned but you would (I hope) realise that he was telling you not to stop work until the holiday began. To *anticipate marriage* is a particularly interesting example. When sex before marriage was generally considered sinful, the distinction between the two meanings of *anticipate* ('to look forward to' and 'to do something before') had great moral importance. If you like to preserve traditional – and useful – distinctions of meaning, you will refuse to replace the perfectly good word *expect* with *anticipate*, and will refuse to anticipate yet another blurring of meaning.

And thirdly, *appreciate*. Once again, it will be useful to look at the origin; it comes from the Latin word for 'price', and its meaning was originally connected with the idea of value. *Appreciate* can be used transitively (that is, with an object) or intransitively (without one). The intransitive use – which is much less common today – is always used in this older sense; if your house or your shares *appreciate*, that means that their value goes up. In its more common, and transitive use, the idea of price or value can still be present. If you *appreciate* a fine wine, or someone's cooking, or the paintings of Rembrandt, that clearly implies that the wine, the cooking, and the paintings are of good quality. If you *appreciate someone's kindness* that too makes it clear that the kind deed was valuable. But there are looser uses of the word. The man who sends you a bill and would *appreciate prompt payment* is just saying he would 'be grateful' for it; and the employer who *appreciates the hard work you have put in on the project* may not mean anything different from 'realise'. If he continues by informing you that he is *letting you go* (see page 149), you can be sure he was just using an empty formula.

The Meaning of Meaning

Our discussion mentioned complex words earlier, and pointed out that words denoting complex activities – *psychoanalysis, nuclear fission, metaphysics, radiocarbon dating* – are really quite simple as words (and therefore require only a short dictionary entry). *Tear*, on the other hand, is quite a complex word, and, as I mentioned, such verbs as *put, get* or *go* – short, familiar and known to us all – are very much more complex. So what are the most complex words of all? My suggestion may seem surprising, but I am quite serious in advancing it: the prepositions.

What is the meaning of *on*? The first answer that would occur to most of us probably concerns relations in space; *on* means something like 'above and touching', as in *The book is on the table*. Thinking a bit further, we might add that it is the opposite to *off*, as in *This light is on, that light is off,* where it means something like 'functioning'. Well, not quite 'functioning': a light may function perfectly well, but not be on at present. *The light is on, so you'll be able to see* – that, surely, is the same usage as *The show is on, go in very quietly please*, where the meaning is 'functioning now', or 'taking place now'. But we can also say *I hear the actor is ill; is the show still on?* where *on* can mean 'taking place as scheduled', not 'now'.

We can also contrast *on* and *off* when referring to physical movement; *get on the bus* and *get off the bus* form a clear enough contrast. What of *he tore off up the road*? That means he ran away from me – but then so does *he tore on up the road*! So can *on* and *off*, those basic opposites, actually have the same meaning? Well, there is a slight difference between these sentences; *he tore off* suggests that he began running, whereas *he tore on up the road* suggests that he was already running, and kept on. This does correspond to one element in the contrast between the two prepositions, that you go *on* doing something you were already doing, and you start *off* doing something new. And then there are some *on/off* contrasts that have nothing to do with movement. Someone tells us a far-fetched story and we say *Come on!* – which means much the same as *Come off it*. But *come on* is usually an encouragement, not a sign of dissent or scepticism. Sometimes we don't even need the *on/off* contrast: *go on* with one intonation is an encouragement, with another a sign of disbelief. We *take on* a job, which means much the same as to *take up* work, and when we have done so we *get on with* it. We *take off* our clothes, which is the opposite to *put on* rather than to *take on*. We can even use *on* and *off* as nouns – cricketers do, striking a ball *to the on* or *to the off*.

We could *go on* making this list for a long time, but it might *get on* your nerves. And then we could turn to all the other prepositions – *in, out, up, down, to, from, at, by, with* – each of which has just as long a story to tell. I shan't try to tell any of them, but there are one or two conclusions we can draw.

We have been exploring the meaning of *on*; but we have also, surely, been discovering something about what we mean by *meaning*. We usually feel that there is a clear distinction between language and the world it refers to. There is the sun, here is the earth, and the earth goes round the sun. It does so whether we talk about it or not, whether we say *The earth is going round the sun* or *The sun has the earth going round it*, or *La terre tourne autour du soleil*, or the same thing in Japanese. *Meaning* here refers to a relationship between language and a world which is quite independent of it. But that is not the only way meaning works – and that is not how dictionaries tell us what words mean. There are a few dictionaries that in an attempt to be helpful include pictures, showing us what a *crocodile* or a *tall-boy* looks like. This can be useful for showing the different kinds of grass or fungi, or for explaining *eclipse* by means of a diagram; but in that case the dictionary is taking on the function of an encyclopedia. Most words (verbs, prepositions, abstract nouns) can be explained only by means of other words. The physical universe may be quite independent of the language we use to talk about it, but we cannot say the same of human actions and thoughts; for much of the time, language is used to refer to something that is already partly linguistic. If we say *He has a guilty conscience*, we mean, among other things, that he reproaches himself, wonders if he should confess, and wishes he had not done what he did; and the reproach, the wondering, the wish are at least partly expressed in language.

Much the same can be said about abstract nouns; *love* and *hate*, *virtue* and *wickedness* are words that denote not only the actions of our bodies, but the attitudes, intentions and wishes that these actions express, and those attitudes are closely involved with language. So to *mean* is not always to apply language to a world independent of language; it is also to operate within language. And the prepositions, we now see, operate almost entirely within language. That is why we cannot separate the meaning of *on* from the way it is used; the study of the meanings of words and the study of grammar are inextricably bound together. If dictionary-makers had to deal only with words like *teal* and *bird*, *earth* and *sun* and *crocodile*, their task would be comparatively easy. It is above all the prepositions that show us just how difficult their task is.

So difficult, in fact, that it is tempting to maintain that compiling a dictionary which is wholly correct is an impossible task. If I were feeling mischievous, I could probably show how impossible it is. While I was about it, I could probably show, too, that learning a language is so impossibly difficult that no one can ever learn to speak or write. Why would this conclusion be wrong, as it so obviously would be? The answer takes us back to a point which I made in the chapter on grammar; we need to distinguish between what we know and what we know that we know. If we had to go through that elaborate exploration of the meaning of *on* in order to use the word, we would slow down so much that we could not speak at all. It is clear that what we call 'knowing English' is more like possessing a skill than having any conscious knowledge, and that it is an amazingly complex skill, far more complex than we realise. Children have the ability to master this skill, and some lucky ones find themselves in a situation where they master more than one language in childhood. But, for reasons no one understands, this skill fades, and it becomes extremely difficult for an adult to learn a foreign language well enough to speak it like a native; learning to play chess looks easy in comparison. Kasparov displayed more skill when he spoke Russian than when he won the World Championship.

CHAPTER SEVEN

The Company We Keep

T hink of the number of ways in which you can ask people not to smoke. You could put up a notice saying *No Smoking* or *Strictly No Smoking* or *Please Do Not Smoke* or *This is a No Smoking Zone*. If someone lights up you could say *Do you mind not smoking?* or *Didn't you see the notice?* or *Excuse me*, and point to the notice; or *Hey, watch it!* (or just *Hey!*), or even *Put that bloody fag out!* And there are dozens, perhaps hundreds, of other possibilities.

All these messages have the same simple purpose, yet they sound very different from one another; so clearly there are two different language functions at work here. Let's look at another example before we try and sort this out.

Good evening. Welcome to the show. Would you please take a moment to make sure that all mobile phones and pagers are switched off. That's one way of getting people to turn off their mobile phones, and anyone who goes to a theatre nowadays is pretty sure to hear that or something very similar before the performance. Here are some other ways of making the same request: *This is a quiet carriage: please do not use mobile phones*; or *Oh God, there goes another of those dreadful mobiles*; or *For God's sake, shut up!* All these sentences have the same content, but they are very different from one another.

What this shows is that our choice of language is determined not only by what we are saying (that is, by the content), but also by the situation: who we are talking to and under what circumstances, and – especially – what our relationship is to them (family member, close friend, casual acquaintance, boss, employee, stranger, etc); also by whether we are speaking or writing, and whether we are broaching a new topic or continuing an old one. The usual term for this aspect of language is *register*. Register is the imprint that the situation leaves on what we say. If we speak in, say, a Yorkshire accent, that is because of who we are and where we grew up, and we are likely to use it all the time. If we speak in a particular register, that is because of what we are doing at the moment and who we're speaking to, and we are almost certain to use different registers on other occasions.

Let's look a little more closely at these examples. You'll have had no difficulty in realising that the first four no-smoking injunctions were written, and the rest spoken. Which of the anti-mobile messages was written? That should be easy: it's the second, which is a notice put up in a train. There is actually, you may have noticed, a small difference in content between the written and the spoken injunctions: the written are addressed to everyone, the spoken are addressed to one person who is smoking (or telephoning) or who looks as if he is going to.

Or rather, that is almost but not quite true. One of the spoken messages (the one beginning *Good evening. Welcome …*) was also addressed not to an individual but to everyone present, and was in complete, well-formed sentences – two of the main characteristics of written language. This is a case of spoken language behaving as if it was written.

And while we're on the question of who is being addressed, what about *Oh God, there goes another of those dreadful mobiles*? I included this as one of the 'requests' to turn off a mobile phone, but it has not got the grammatical form of a request. Much will depend on how – and especially how loudly – it is spoken. It could be addressed as a remark to one's companion, but it could also, if spoken loudly, be intended for the ears of the person using the mobile. In that case, we can notice that, though it is not grammatically addressed to that person, he is the recipient. And it could be spoken in such a way that it is not clear (perhaps not clear even to the speaker!) whether the culprit is meant to hear it or not.

Of the four written no-smoking injunctions, the first, *No Smoking*, is the most usual – and the most neutral. *Strictly No Smoking* is clearly a stronger prohibition, likely to appear in a hospital ward or a scientific laboratory. *Please Do Not Smoke* is obviously trying to be more polite. And *This is a No Smoking Zone* perhaps has something of the flavour of the counter-culture of the nineteen sixties and seventies, suggesting that an enlightened group are uniting to keep the establishment out.

What do we learn from these examples? They remind us that everything we say is part of a human situation: even when talking to ourselves, we are usually imagining a situation. And that means that register is always present when we use language. Whatever we are saying, it is always possible to say it differently: that makes it possible to vary the register almost indefinitely. Compare *Do you think I could have an advance of fifty pounds until the end of the month?* with *Can you lend me fifty quid till payday?* They are both making the same request, but the situations are different: the first sounds as if addressed to the boss, the second to a friend. So the first says *fifty pounds* and the second, more informally, *fifty quid*; the first says *until the end of the month*, which is more formal than *till payday*. *Payday* is a word the boss probably doesn't use, whereas the friend is perhaps being nudged by this reminder that he'll be paid back. The use of *advance* when speaking to the boss is a matter of content, since the boss would technically be making us an advance and the friend wouldn't; but it is a matter of register as well, since it serves as a reminder of the boss's power and so conveys a touch of deference.

One more example. *I asked you a question, and I expect an answer; Please answer me; Oh come on, don't keep evading the question.* Once again, three different ways of saying the same thing. They are all probably spoken, though it's just possible that the first could be written in a private letter. The first clearly comes from someone in authority (the boss, a teacher, an angry father), and is likely to come after previous unsatisfactory attempts to get an answer. The second might also presuppose previous unsuccessful attempts to get an answer, but instead of sounding angry it sounds pleading; it is, however, very flexible, and we'd have to hear the tone in which *please* was uttered, and perhaps know something of the situation, to be sure of the register. The third is probably addressed to someone the speaker knows well, and the use of *come on* could suggest either impatience or pleading. In all three cases, and especially the second, we'd have to know more about the previous utterances to be quite sure of the register, though in the case of spoken language the tone of voice will tell us a good deal.

The range of different registers is much greater in the spoken than in the written language, both because of the way we can use intonation to vary the impact of what we say, and because there are usually so many colloquial ways of saying it that are available to us as alternatives. In writing, the choice of register is likely to be more global – that is, it will be determined once and for all by the nature of what we are writing. Thus there are differences between the register of a textbook (*In the space at our disposal it will not be possible to discuss all the cases*) and that of its blurb (*This encyclopaedic work is based on a masterly command of all the important thinkers*). There is a register of legal English, which likes to use several terms for the same idea, in order to cover all possibilities (*I give and bequeath*, or *shall apply and be incorporated herein*); and there is a register of scientific English (*three grams of sodium chloride were then added to the solution*), which instructs us not to use the first person, to use the passive a great deal, and to use technical terms for the sake of accuracy.

Let us take a slightly fuller look at the register of scientific English. We can begin with a sentence like this: *The warping of space in effect lengthens the path of light approaching and leaving the sun.* If asked what sort of book that comes from we would probably say it is from a book about astronomy, and it is in fact part of an explanation of Einstein's theory of relativity. Yet it is clearly not written for astronomers, but for you and me: if it was real astronomy it would be full of mathematical formulae and only a trained mathematician would understand it. But even a real scientific paper has some sentences in English in between the mathematics – could it not be one of those? Look at the sentence again, and you will see that one phrase makes this very unlikely: *in effect.* What that means here is something like 'This is more or less what happens, but I cannot explain it fully without getting too technical.' Those two words have shifted us from the register of scientific research to the register of popular science. Now let's shift the register still further:

> *When I heard the learn'd astronomer,*
> *When the proofs, the figures, were ranged in columns before me,*
> *When I was shown the charts and diagrams, to add, divide and measure them …*

The speaker of those lines is certainly not an astronomer. His response to the learned astronomer who, as he goes on to tell us, *lectured with much applause in the lecture room*, is hostile, or at least impatient. We might not notice it on a first reading, but *the charts and diagrams*, the way he was being asked *to add, divide, and measure them*, tells us how wearisome he found the scientific approach. So it is not surprising to read on and find this:

Till rising and gliding out I wandered off by myself,
In the mystical moist night air, and from time to time,
Look'd up in perfect silence at the stars.

You may have noticed that the word *stars* was never used in the lines about the astronomer and his explanations: trotting it out like that as the last word of all enables it to convey a sense of wonder that was destroyed by the *charts and diagrams*. I am sure that many astronomers would feel that this short poem by Walt Whitman was highly unjust, that they too can feel a sense of wonder looking at (or thinking about) the stars; but we are not concerned here with justice but with the use of register. Writing about astronomy can move from the highly technical language of scientific research, through the register of popular science, to the register of wonder.

So far we have looked mainly at sentences; though usually, to make them manageable, at fairly simple sentences. If we turn now to look at a single word – or rather at four words which are all variants on one another – we shall be looking at the smallest units out of which register can be built. There are four main words for 'woman' in everyday English: *woman, lady, female* and *girl*. It is quite easy to indicate the register of the noun *female*: its usual context is scientific, and it can denote animals as well as humans. An archaeologist might describe either a human or an elephant's skeleton as belonging to a *mature female*. But it also has a common ironic use in which the writer amuses himself by pretending to take a scientific position. Kipling's poem 'The Female of the Species' offers parallels between female bears and cobras on the one hand, and women on the other, to suggest that a mother's intense commitment to protecting her offspring should be seen in biological, not social, terms; and its refrain ('For the female of the species is more deadly than the male') has become a kind of proverb. It is difficult to be sure how seriously Kipling took the biological parallel; and certainly when that line is quoted nowadays it is almost always jokingly.

The primary difference between *woman* and *lady* is one of social class, though usages that refer to class will often take on a flavour of more general approval. *His wife is a lady* is therefore ambiguous: it can mean that she has a title, and is entitled to be called *Lady Dorothy*, or it can be a compliment, usually poised somewhere between complimenting her character and complimenting her manners. His wife can be a *lady* because she is gracious to people (especially, perhaps, her social inferiors), or because she would never say anything to give offence. But in our era of social change and democracy this distinction is often blurred, and even reversed, as in the cartoon which shows a female caller saying to a housewife 'Are you the woman who advertised for a cleaning lady?'

As for *girl*, its primary meaning is of course 'young female', and its colloquial application to adult women is often objected to as patronising. It can certainly be patronising, though there is a considerable difference between addressing a group of 17-year-olds and a group of 30-year-olds as *girls* – and a group of 70-year-olds might rather like it. But what do we say of the young wife who announces that she is *going out with the girls tonight*? Is she defiant or self-deprecating? Is she mocking her husband who *goes out with the boys*, or saying in a perfectly friendly way that it's her turn now? Much will depend on her tone of voice – and perhaps also on knowing the exact state of her marriage.

To conclude this item, here are two details about female members of the royal family. Queen Victoria's groom and personal servant John Brown addressed her as 'woman'. That was clearly intended as a direct defiance of etiquette, and members of the court found it shocking – so shocking, perhaps, that there was little danger of its serving as an example to others. Though shocking, it was not at all hostile: everyone knew that he had a great respect for her. (If someone were to address Queen Elizabeth II as *woman* today, would that be more or less shocking?) Apparently similar, though perhaps very different, is the habit of the media of referring to Queen Elizabeth, the Queen Mother, in her last years, as the 'Queen Mum'. *Mother* and *mum* have the same meaning: all that has changed is the register. This is a very different case from that of John Brown, who would probably have been deeply shocked if he could have seen into the future and discovered that perfect strangers were speaking about her in that casual way. *Queen Mum* was no doubt partly a sign of affection (though a rather impersonal affection, felt by those who did not know her); and partly, no doubt, a sign of the general move away from formality in public life.

The John Brown story also shows us something else – that to address someone as *woman* is very different from referring to her as *a woman*. That form of address is found in some English translations of the Bible – Jesus addresses his mother as *woman* – but today its use is always humorous or disapproving. As for *lady* as a form of address, there is a (perhaps surprising) difference between the singular and the plural. It is quite normal to address a group of women as *ladies* (just as it is normal to address a group of men as *gentlemen*), but when used in the singular it is usually disrespectful, as in *Look, lady, I'm a busy man* – which I feel to be still American, though it can certainly be heard in Britain.

Gender

Should we include, among the factors governing register, the sex of the speaker – or of the listeners? Is there, that is to say, a feminine and a masculine register?

Certainly such gender differences are much less marked in English than they are in some other languages, especially 'primitive' ones. I call them *primitive*, since that is the commonest word for illiterate cultures, but terminology here is controversial and shifting: not only is the term felt by some to be 'politically incorrect' (see Chapter 9 for much more about this), but we also need to remind ourselves that though we think of 'primitive' societies as less complex than ours, so-called 'primitive' languages have grammar that is far more complex than ours. The most famous example is that of the Caribs of the West Indies, who were reported in the seventeenth century to have something very close to two different languages for the two sexes; but since the language has died out it is no longer possible for us to check this. Modern Japanese (which no one could describe as a primitive language!) has considerably greater differences between masculine and feminine usage than any European language: men and women use different words for 'stomach', for 'eat', and for the first person pronoun 'I'.

If there are such gender differences in English, they are most likely to show up in single-sex conversations, and by definition none of us has experience of both of these. The one thing we all know – or claim to know – about single-sex conversations is that men are far more likely than women to swear, and to use the 'four-letter words' when speaking of sex or other bodily functions. This was much more true a generation ago than it is now, just as a group of women getting drunk was very unusual in British culture until recently; but although much has changed, swearing and coarse speaking are probably still commoner among men than among women. There are other differences, too, between masculine and feminine registers: *fib* for 'lie', *awfully* and *terribly* as adverbs (*That's terribly kind of you*), *common* in the sense of 'vulgar', are all more feminine than masculine in register. Women until recently tended to avoid saying *naked*, preferring *without a stitch*, and (even more old-fashioned and rather quaint) *in one's birthday suit*. There are claims that women make finer colour discriminations than men, and are more likely to use words like *beige, crimson* and *ultramarine*. There are also claims about women's syntax and how it differs from men's: that they are more likely to use tag questions (instead of saying *Yes, that's true* they are more likely to say *Yes, that's true, isn't it?*) Then there are claims about women's conversational habits, that they speak co-operatively whereas men speak competitively, sympathising with one another instead of trying to score points: strictly speaking, that is perhaps an observation about social behaviour, not just about language – though it also shows us how fluid is the distinction between the two.

But I must immediately add two points. First, that all this is changing, perhaps more rapidly than anything else in contemporary English: as the position of women in society changes, so does their language, and gender differences in language are nowadays more marked among older than younger women. (Does that mean they are about to disappear? Or that the younger women's linguistic habits will change as they grow older?) And second, that all this is controversial because it is not merely descriptive, but easily turns into prescription (I discussed this distinction in Chapter 2). That lands us firmly in the area of political correctness – the subject of Chapter 9.

The Real Language of Men

Poets can do fascinating things with register. Should poems be written in ordinary language, or in a special 'poetic' register? For many centuries the second was considered normal (though good poets often broke the rule). The most famous rejection of a special poetic register is that of Wordsworth, who in the Preface to *Lyrical Ballads* in 1800 declared that poetry should be written in the language 'really spoken by men', and should avoid what was called 'poetic diction'. He was rejecting the view that to mark its dignity a poem should replace everyday terms with a more elegant expression: that instead of *birds* a poem should refer to the *feathered choir*, instead of *fish* should speak of the *finny drove*. *Diction* in this case means much the same as 'register': the meaning of *finny drove* is the same as that of 'fish', but the more elegant phrasing is a sign of the dignity of poetry. In rejecting this, Wordsworth made the famous democratic statement that a poet was 'a man speaking to men', rejecting the view that the poet should be a gentleman speaking to gentlemen.

And by a sad irony, this radical statement has now become something for radicals to attack. For Wordsworth was so anxious to attack discrimination by social class that he overlooked discrimination by gender: indeed, I feel sure that though he was quite willing to read the work of women poets, it did not enter his head to write that a poet is a human being speaking to other humans, rather than a man speaking to men. This seems a perfect illustration of the fate of radicals: that they will in turn come to be seen as a conservative.

Here now is an example of a modern poet using the real language of – well, in this case he does seem to be using the language of men rather than of men and women. There is really no difference in principle between the way a poet can use register and the way it can be used in prose; but we'd be lucky to find in prose such a brilliant exercise in transgressing register as Philip Larkin's *Vers de Société*:

> *My wife and I have asked a crowd of craps*
> *To come and waste their time and ours: perhaps*
> *You'd care to join us?* In a pig's arse, friend.
> Day comes to an end.
> The gas fire breathes, the trees are darkly swayed.
> And so *Dear Warlock-Williams: I'm afraid –*

Vers de société is a technical term in literary criticism, denoting a light poem dealing elegantly with the superficial concerns of upper-class life. Larkin's poem is not at all light, since it deals with loneliness and even despair, and how social gatherings are a way of coping with this, and it starts off by deliberately shocking us through its use of register. The invitation from the luridly named Warlock-Williams is translated by the author into a very different register, as he cynically turns it into the hollow social ritual he sees it as, until its last sentence (*perhaps You'd care to join us?*) reverts to what looks like the actual wording of the invitation. The poet's first response (*In a pig's arse, friend*) is in a register he would never use to Warlock-Williams, though he might use it about him, and the use of this register makes the word *friend* heavily sarcastic. Then come two lines of description of the evening in a register quite normal for poetry, hinting at a deeper melancholy than can be contained in the polite refusal, which was in a register of politeness. (The fact that Warlock-Williams is addressed by his surname, without 'Mr', shows that he is a social equal, and an acquaintance rather than a close friend.) The rest of the poem, consisting of the poet's own reflections on loneliness and social intercourse, does not need any play upon register.

Register is central to all discussions of political correctness, or verbal hygiene, the subjects of Chapter 9. We shall see that campaigns for political correctness urge us to avoid particular undesirable words and expressions; and since it is virtually impossible actually to ban the use of a word, what this means is that its register changes, so that it becomes less acceptable in normal conversation. And how is register controlled? To understand that fully would be to understand what holds society together. When social control – including control of language – is functioning successfully we hardly notice it; when we start demanding that control be exercised, that is a sign of some sort of breakdown.

We are all familiar, nonetheless, with the commonest way of controlling register, which is by expressions of approval or disapproval. *Mind your language, please* (or, sometimes, just *Language!*); *Gentlemen do not speak in that way*; *Talking posh, are you?*; *Now Johnny, you shouldn't use such words in front of your mother* – or *That was very nicely said, Johnny, I like to hear you talk like that*; *If I hear you say that again I'll tell the Headteacher/my Dad/your Dad/the boss* (or, sometimes, just *If I hear you say that again!*) These are examples of how we try to get people to use the right register, or stop them from using the wrong one. But though we may be able to influence particular cases of speaking, it is impossible for us to eradicate a register we do not approve of. It is even arguable that the more successful we are at driving a word out of one register, the more it will stay alive in another.

Change

Register is important in both spoken and written language. Indeed, if you cast your mind back to the two examples of register that we have just looked at, the difference between men's language and women's language, and the use of register in poetry, you will see that the first applies mainly to the spoken language (men's language and women's language differ much less when written); whereas the second applies to the written language, since poetry, though it can make great use of spoken rhythms and expressions, is primarily written.

And register, like all else in language, is constantly changing. One of the changes is that words and expressions that used to belong only to the spoken have now found their way into the written. To illustrate this, let us take a look at loyalty cards. Large retail chains nowadays offer their customers a plastic card which records their purchases and then entitles them to reductions. Here is an extract from the leaflet accompanying one loyalty card:

> *Dear Mr Lerner*
> *I'm glad you've joined our loyalty card scheme. Here's your per-*
> *sonal loyalty card … On 16 May we checked to see how many*
> *points you'd collected and downloaded them straight onto your*
> *new, personal card …*
>
> *Remember you'll get a whopping 4 points for every £1 you spend*
> *in our shop … We've even included a leaflet with this letter,*
> *which gives you some great ideas about how to spend your points!*

If this had been written fifty years ago, it would have been in a very different and more impersonal register. You might try to list the usages which show the more informal and even chatty register of today. I have counted at least thirteen in this short passage.

Most strikingly, it uses the first person, so the leaflet comes not from an organisation, but from someone who signs herself *Jane Smith, Loyalty Card Manager*. Not only that, but she writes as if she knows me and is sharing her feelings with me: she is *glad* I've joined the scheme, and the information about how many points I get is introduced with a colloquial imperative: *Remember*. This belongs to spoken, not written, English, and on at least two occasions she is very colloquial indeed: a *whopping four points* and *great ideas*. I confess to finding *whopping* slightly ridiculous here – I might ask for a *whopping great helping* of ice cream if I wanted to make fun of my own greed, but I have difficulty in seeing an abstract transaction like points on my card as *whopping*. Even *downloaded*, which is after all the correct term for what they did, is meant to have a personal ring about it. The company *transferred* the points to my card, but since they are reminding me that it is my *personal* card, they have also replaced the accurate but abstract word *transfer* with a verb that sounds up to date, and also gives the impression of someone actually performing the task.

But since the purpose of the letter was not only to sound friendly but also to give some factual information, they have added an insert, printed in a square frame, which simply says: *Your points balance is 127 as of 16th May*. No chattiness here: they have even used the rather legalistic double preposition *as of* instead of the more usual *on*. This is the businesslike part of the message, written in rather formal English, clearly separated from the rest, which may have reminded you of the Sun English we discussed in Chapter 4.

If I were being prescriptive, I would now go on either to praise the firm for dropping their impersonal stuffiness and showing that they are real human beings who treat us as individuals; or to denounce them for false bonhomie, pretending that they care about our feelings when all they really want is to persuade us to spend more in their shops. That could open a fascinating and even heated argument about the nature of modern capitalism; but I'll be prudent and stay descriptive, pointing out that our consumer-centred culture has led to great changes in the register of customer relations (a term which was unknown fifty years ago).

Slang

Register, then, is choosing your language to fit the company. The extreme example of this is slang.

An experience we have almost all had is that of finding ourselves among a group of people who know one another well, and feeling like an outsider: perhaps when we were still at school, among a group of children from another and very different school, or a gang to which we didn't belong; perhaps among a group who are all ten years older than we are, or (later in life) all ten years younger; or perhaps an occupational group, of medical students or soldiers or footballers; or a group who live apart from others, like rough sleepers or criminals. What makes an outsider feel like an outsider in such a group? The answer is, above all, their language: their use of special terms, or of ordinary words with special meanings.

Since the main function of language is to enable us to communicate with one another, such group languages combine this purpose with the opposite: they enable the group to communicate inside itself by shutting others out. There is a sense therefore in which they use language partly to prevent communication. The two traditional terms for such group languages are *cant* and *slang*. *Cant* comes from the Latin word for 'sing', and was traditionally applied both to the language of beggars (perhaps because of their whining speech), and to the language of religious sects, full of moral uplift and moral disapproval. This latter is now the usual meaning: we speak of the language of a preacher or of anyone who considers themself holier-than-us as being *full of cant*. For the more general meaning, referring to the special language of any group, we now use *slang*.

What groups are particularly concerned to keep outsiders outside? Perhaps the tightest groups, those most anxious not to be infiltrated, are adolescent boys and girls, criminals, and soldiers. Let's begin with soldiers. Military slang serves a double purpose: it keeps outsiders outside, like all slang, and it also serves to evade unpleasant realities, as when killing civilians is referred to as *collateral damage* (this is discussed in the next chapter). As a specimen of military slang serving the purpose of group language, we could take this sentence by an American pilot: *I don't know if the bogie was chasing him, but I locked him up, confirmed he was hostile and fired a missile.* This is not really euphemistic, since the one piece of violence, *fired a missile,* is not evaded but openly named; but it is certainly group language – did you know that a *bogie* was an enemy aircraft? Outsiders might understand *lock on* as fix one's aim to a target electronically, but to change it to *lock up* can only serve the purpose of not being understood by you and me.

The criminal underworld wishes, for obvious reasons, to remain as unnoticed as possible. Professional criminals operate outside the law, not only in the sense that they commit crimes, but also in the sense that they try not to lead a legal existence: they tend not to have bank accounts, or to own houses, or to appear on any legal records. And they tend to live as far as possible outside the standard language too, using their own slang for almost everything that has to do with crime and the law. When the police search the house of a suspect they *spin his joint*; to plead guilty is to *duck your nut*; a bank can be a *jug*; to hijack lorries is to *jump up*. But like Samuel Johnson, who could not visit the caverns of miners to learn their special language, I did not learn these terms at first hand: I got them from a book by Laurie Taylor, a sociologist who managed to make friends with a gang of criminals, and so I have no idea whether they are still current or if they have passed out of use by now. As for the terms that have passed into the general language (*the Old Bill* or *the Bill* for the police, *verballing* for a policeman attributing a – usually false – statement to a criminal, *nick* for prison, *fit up* for construct a false case against someone), I suspect that these have now dropped out of criminal slang. But how could we possibly know?

Try as they might to keep their language special, even secret, such groups can never fully prevent it from spreading: a slang term may suddenly become fashionable outside the group. That is a main reason why slang is so unstable: the best way to keep terms from spreading outside the group is to keep changing them, and members of a group – ex-convicts, teenagers, soldiers – are quick to notice that an outsider trying to use their slang has not got it quite right, and has betrayed the fact that they are an outsider. When slang terms do find their way into the wider world, they are naturally still felt to be vulgar, and not to belong to Standard English. When this happens, the fact that the word began as part of the special language of a group will be forgotten, and by calling it *slang* we simply mean that it is undignified, and that when speaking 'properly' we would not use it.

For an example of slang finding its way into general speech, let's take *cool*. This is now over fifty years old, and though still used mostly by the young, is understood by everyone. What does it mean? Originally, *cool* was used about jazz: it praised a piece of music for being restrained and relaxed; but by now it has become a general term of praise. But we already have *warm* as a term of praise, and the two words seem to coexist quite peacefully. (*Hot*, too, can be a term of praise among those who say *cool* – but I have never heard anyone say *cold* as praise!) We praise people – or language – for being *warm* when they are emotionally charged and friendly, for being *cool* when they are fashionable, self-possessed or socially acceptable. There is a difference in meaning, but the main difference is one of register: different groups use the two terms. If a teenager gets on well with his grandmother he might well describe her as *cool* – I know a grandmother who proudly informed me that one page of her address book contained the sentence *Granny is cool*. But if she were praising the grandchild who wrote it, she would be more likely to call him *warm*.

Slang belongs to the spoken language, but novelists and playwrights who want to include low-life characters in their work will naturally want to make their speech authentic, and the obvious way to do this is to make them speak in the slang of their subculture. Such written slang is never likely to be completely authentic, simply because true slang changes so rapidly, and a literary work is written in the hope that it will last. So the slang of Dickens' cockneys, though it often has the feel of being genuine, is not likely to be accurate (we have already seen that this is true of attempts to show their pronunciation – see page 69). Since the readers of such novels seldom belong to the social groups depicted in them, and since members of those groups don't often read novels, this inaccuracy is no doubt inevitable.

Jargon

I defined the purpose of slang as being to keep outsiders out. The word can still be used to denote a group language, but that meaning has pretty well disappeared from what is now the commoner use of the word: any form of casual and colloquial language that is vaguely disapproved of, often by the very people who use it. Jargon too begins as the language of a group, but its aim is not so much to keep outsiders out as to denote the expertise which that group has.

Jargon does not have to be a term of disapproval – someone writing about law or music or accounting might use a necessary technical term, then add that the word is jargon, and explain it. But in ordinary speech the term is nowadays almost always used disapprovingly, to mean an unnecessary departure from plain speech, an attempt to blind us with technical terms. Anyone who apologises for using slang is thinking of the social situation, that they are being more populist than they perhaps should be; anyone who confesses to (or, more often, accuses someone else of) using jargon is thinking of the use of technical or pretentious language instead of plain English.

If you hesitate to say someone is *mad*, or even that he is *eccentric*, you can resort to slang, and call him *cuckoo* or *nutty* or *a nutter* or *a nutcase*, or *a fruitcake*, or say he has *bats in the belfry*, or is *batty* or just *bats*, or is *off his rocker, has a screw loose* or is *screwy or a screwball* – that is a small selection of the slang expressions for 'mad', some rather old-fashioned. Or you can describe him as *outside the range of normal behaviour* or *not within the parameters applicable to sanity* or *requiring institutionalisation on account of an abnormal behavioural syndrome.*

Here we have the difference between slang and jargon, and we can see that, although I have been pointing out their similarity (the special language of a group), they're utterly different in practice. The slang expressions are probably spoken, though since these examples have been around for a long time now they are quite likely to find their way into informal writing; the jargon is almost certainly written. Slang, we see, is full of colourful metaphors, jargon of abstract nouns – and we all prefer a metaphor to an abstraction. (That does not mean that abstractions are always to be condemned: we can't even denounce *abstraction* without using an abstract noun!)

To identify jargon, we need to point to the specialised area from which it has entered general usage. Space travel, for instance, has provided us with *countdown, lift-off, in orbit, splashdown, all systems go*; cricket has provided us with *stumped, googly, sticky wicket, a good innings, knocked for six* – and lots of others (cricket suffuses English culture). All those are examples of what was originally jargon, and is now more or less standard in English. If we identify jargon by where it comes from, what are we to say about the first set of examples above, the terms for *mad*? They come, clearly, from the world of administration (the Civil Service or hospital administration or health insurers), and we can see immediately that administration, by its nature, uses abstract nouns; it does not have the rich store of technical processes that enables other specialised fields to offer much livelier jargon. In fact a great deal of what is usually attacked as jargon is just one special kind of jargon: that of administrators. That is the jargon in which a police officer told us that the police don't need to be organised like the army: 'Operational situations requiring a military-style organisation and command structures are comparatively few'; and in which a lorry driver becomes a *transport equipment operator*. I don't know whether it was a civil servant or a politician (though I'm sure it wasn't a doctor), who in America referred to deafness as *a decrement in auditory acuity*. Or perhaps I'm not so sure – see the next section.

Jargon often has particular grammatical tricks: here are three of them. First, instead of *difficult cases*, a policy statement or a regulation might say *cases of a difficult character*; instead of *more urgent repairs, repairs of a more urgent nature*. Why? It's tempting to say it's because administrators like using as many words as possible, but perhaps we can be more precise. All adjectives classify: when we say *red shirts* we are classifying some of the shirts under the heading 'red'. This is so obvious that no one would bother to point it out by saying *shirts of the category 'red'*. But administrators spend a lot of time categorising, and probably find it hard to break the habit of doing so explicitly, making it clear that they are classifying the repairs as more or less urgent. An annoying habit, perhaps, for the rest of us – but understandable.

The second grammatical trick is the double negative. Double negatives in speech are of course famous – or rather infamous. We all know that the uneducated say *I haven't got no money* or *I don't know nothing*. If you have a logical mind, you might want to point out that two negatives cancel each other out, so that *I haven't got no money* actually means 'I have got some money.' But everyone knows that it doesn't mean this, that the double negative is used informally for emphasis (though not by careful speakers). I pointed out in the first chapter that those who like to correct your usage tend to have a few favourite examples, and this is certainly one of them. But there is also a perfectly logical form of the double negative, where the two negatives really do cancel each other out, and this is very popular in official jargon: *I am not unwilling to admit that you may have a strong case.* This 'genuine' double negative is occasionally used in speech (*I shouldn't be surprised if he doesn't turn up*), but not nearly as often as in legal or official writing, where it gives the impression that the writer is unwilling to concede too much, as in *It is not impossible that such an application would be favourably received* – or, just to be extra cautious, *might be favourably received.*

A slight digression here. In language, as in so much else, bad habits are sometimes the abuse of something genuine: the double negative of caution can be the expression of genuine feeling, perhaps by someone who is both sensitive and honest. Once again Philip Larkin provides a good example. *Talking in bed ought to be easiest* is the opening of one of his careful, sad poems, which goes on to admit that it's not at all easy

> *To find*
> *Words at once true and kind,*
> *Or not untrue and not unkind.*

The third grammatical trick beloved of jargon is using nouns as verbs. My local supermarket, testing a new parking arrangement, announced that it was going to *trial* it; a sales group or a production team will *target* a certain figure or result; a recording engineer will *position* the microphone carefully. Why are these verbalised nouns preferred to the already existing verbs *test, aim at* or *place*? I don't find that easy to answer. No doubt the parking directorate, the sales management or the recording engineers want to sound like experts, but is it the use of nouns that suggests expertise (do they feel that nouns are somehow more technical than verbs?), or simply the unusual use of a word, which marks them out from laymen like you and me? Perhaps it would be cruel to begrudge them their gloss of expertise, but there is no need for the rest of us to imitate them.

Some jargon is useful enough to pass into the language and be welcomed. *Loss leader* is a term most shoppers are familiar with nowadays: something sold at a loss in order to tempt customers into the shop so that they'll buy other things. The phrase is short, clear, and avoids abstract nouns, and I can't think of a neater way to say it. A more complicated case is *desirable residence*, which is estate agent's jargon for 'nice house' (estate agents never seem to use the term *house*, it's too ordinary). This has passed into the language in the form *des res*, which I suppose means more or less 'That's what an estate agent would call it, using his jargon.' The phrase is almost always ironic, and the rhyming abbreviation seems to me to catch the irony very neatly. We might as well enjoy our jargon – or rather their jargon.

Because jargon begins as more or less technical terminology, it may serve a useful function to start with, even if it makes us wince when more widely used. Let's take an example from social psychology. A psychologist trying to construct an 'exchange theory', analysing how two people interact with each other, writes: *One way of conceptualising a dyadic social encounter is as a sequence of 'utterances' or 'verbal behaviour units' taking place over time.* What this means is that when two people meet they speak to each other. Should we get impatient with a psychologist who writes *dyadic social encounter* for 'a meeting of two people', or *verbal behaviour units* when he means 'what they say'? Well, before getting too impatient, we ought to ask ourselves just what he is doing. He himself describes it as 'conceptualising', that is, trying to fit our understanding of everyday behaviour into a theory. His aim is to indicate what aspect of this everyday meeting is being compared with other, similar encounters, and for this he needs to use abstract nouns; such abstractions may make the ordinary reader wince, but he could reply that he is not writing for the ordinary reader. Technical terms, however, have a fatal attraction for the theorist, and there is often a strong temptation to use them when they aren't really necessary, in order to show that one is an expert – and one may need to be an expert in order to judge whether this is happening! Here is another passage from an exchange theorist:

> If one member of a dyad seeks to increase the degree of intimacy in the relationship between himself and his partner, the equilibrium of the relationship is temporarily threatened. He may (intentionally or not) signify this desire for increased intimacy by increasing his proximity to his partner.

We're all familiar with this situation: the boyfriend begins to sit too close. Obviously the young woman is not actually going to say to him *You are threatening the equilibrium of the relationship*, even if she is a psychology student. (If she does, that may be the best way to decrease his proximity!) I don't find it easy to decide how much of this jargon is necessary: to call the young man out on a date *one member of a dyad* is probably useful, since it enables the psychologist to compare this with other dyadic situations – and writing *dyadic* is shorter than writing 'involving two people'. But can we defend *increasing his proximity* on similar lines? The psychologist is not, presumably, measuring proximity, finding out how many centimetres there are between different couples! Here technical terminology seems to have found its way into the sentence just out of habit. Even this habit could be defended: the sentence was not written for ordinary people to read, and since so much of the study is already in the jargon of social psychology, it might be disconcerting to keep switching into ordinary language. Jargon, in other words, is sometimes necessary among experts, and sometimes just a habit, which does no great harm as long as it stays inside the field of expertise. What makes the rest of us wince is when it wanders into writing (or even speech) addressed to the outside world. Fortunately, the psychologist who invites his girlfriend to the cinema is not likely to say *May I increase my proximity to you?* But there is nothing to say in defence of the psychologist in my university who once proposed a form for writing reports on students containing the heading *attitudinal approach*. Why did he prefer that to *attitude*? It is hard to believe that he held a theory which distinguished *attitudinal approach* from *attitude* – and even if he did, the unfortunate teacher filling in the form would have no idea what the difference was!

The jargon with which I personally am most familiar is that of literary criticism. Novel readers shouldn't have much difficulty in knowing what *first person narrative* is, even if they wouldn't naturally use the term; they might be slightly more puzzled by *omniscient narrator*, but they would have no difficulty in realising that most Victorian novelists tell us what is going on in the minds of their characters. Poetry readers don't need to know what an *iambic pentameter* and a *heroic couplet* are in order to enjoy Pope's lines:

Like the vile straw that's blown about the streets,
The needy poet sticks to all he meets

– though those terms are useful if you want to talk about the lines. These are examples of harmless and useful jargon, and they have long been part of the literary scholar's terminology. More recent literary criticism, however, under the influence of structuralist and deconstructive theory, expects more of us:

> *Thus there emerges in Daniel Deronda an account of the determining connections between the referential function of language and its conservative and performative functions. Its inexorable referentiality prohibits the narrative from claiming authority either as a genuine fact or as a genuine act, for the referent itself constitutes the fact and the act and remains extralinguistic, necessarily excluded from the discourse that inevitably refers to it.*

To explain this passage would take us a long time, since it is clearly based on some very sophisticated and difficult theories (my computer's spelling and grammar check queried three of the terms). That in itself might not be to its discredit – to explain a paragraph about nuclear physics might require a three-year course in the subject. So I will just make three comments on it. First, the audience it is addressed to is very different from the audience that *Daniel Deronda* was – and is – addressed to: literary criticism for this author is not meant to help us read literature, but to set novels in relation to some (rather difficult) theories. Second, the general nature of the theory should be clear enough: it is concerned with the nature and functions of language, and the ability (or inability) of language to refer to the world outside itself. And my third comment is best put as a question. We do not object to the jargon of nuclear physics, because we know that it has to be difficult, and that it must be true (or else there would be no lasers, no moon flights, no nuclear power stations). Have you a similar confidence in the truth and coherence of post-structuralism that would justify learning its jargon?

Writing Upp

No, that is not a spelling mistake. This short section is about something very similar to jargon. Jargon emerges from the special language of a particular group of experts, and I have tried to show that it is sometimes necessary but often just a way of being pompous and obscure. Pomposity and obscurity can also occur when someone who doesn't belong to the group of experts is trying to impress them.

Talking down and *writing down* is a familiar idea: experts talk down to the general public, parents or teachers talk down to their children, policemen or soldiers might talk down to those to whom they are explaining the rules; a scientist or a philosopher, trying to explain difficult ideas to the general public, might be seen as writing down to them. If what you wish to say is too complex for the audience you have in mind, you make it simpler for them; if you are anxious to get their co-operation, you might speak slowly and patiently and explain all the difficult words; if you are trying to bring a technical subject to the lay public, you write simply. This is something that can easily backfire. First, your attempts to simplify may lead you to oversimplify, so that what you write is untrue, or only partly true; and second, the tone of what you write may sound condescending, so that it becomes clear to readers that you have a low opinion of their intelligence. If this makes them resistant, they may not attend fully to what you are saying, may not even hear it. *Writing down* or *talking down* have therefore become expressions that carry a flavour of disapproval.

The opposite situation can also arise: you may think your audience is cleverer and more demanding than you are, so that your natural way of writing will not be good enough for them. You therefore set out to overcomplicate, to use a style that does not come naturally to you but that (you hope) will cause you to appear cleverer and more sophisticated than you really are. Your motives may be good or bad – good if you are genuinely humble about your abilities, bad if you want to show off – but in either case the result can, in my view, do even more damage than writing down. I don't know any convenient expression for this, and to preserve the balance with *writing down* I would like to call it *writing up*, but that expression already has a meaning. A scientist *writes up* the results of his experiments, a journalist *writes up* an account of an interview she has conducted: to *write up* is to turn into a written account some material you already have in a different form. So I am resorting to something I have managed to avoid so far in this book, twisting an existing expression to

131

fit the meaning I want but which it does not actually denote, and as good a way as any to do this seems to be to spell it wrongly.

Who goes in for writing upp? Students, mainly, afraid that *The cat sat on the mat* looks altogether too naïve, and tempted to replace it with *The feline animal occupied a sedentary posture on the carpet.* That example, which I have just made up, is fictitious; let's have real ones. I was astonished at how reluctant my American students were to call anything *simple.* It seemed to them more dignified to say that a poem or an argument is *simplistic*; though *simplistic* means 'too simple' or 'over-simplified', they used it as a term of praise, clearly feeling so sure that the extra syllable added dignity that there was no need to look it up in the dictionary. Explaining what sort of songs/stories/ poems he prefers, a student begins 'For me personally I much prefer those which …'. Since *for me* means the same as *personally*, this sentence has been written in the belief that what is told us twice must be twice as impressive as what is said only once. Another student writes about poems dealing with 'things that were not part of the normal scope of everyday life, and as such used a different diction'. (He was writing about poems, but the same sentence could have been written about stories or spoken remarks.) It's good to see someone who knows what *diction* is, even if he doesn't believe that once is enough to say something: *normal* in this remark is simply repeated by *everyday*, *scope* adds nothing and *as such* is quite unnecessary, so if this person were not writing upp he could just have said *things that were not part of everyday life, and so used a different diction.*

What I'm calling 'writing upp' can overlap with jargon, since students are not the only people who go in for it. Let us take this splendid statement by one of Ronald Reagan's doctors, trying to control his short-sightedness, that 'previously documented decrement(s) in auditory and visual refractive error corrected with contact lenses were evaluated and found to be stable'. (I owe this gem to Walter Nash's splendid book *Jargon: Its Uses and Abuses.*) Some of this is medical jargon (*visual refractive error*), which is perhaps forgivable; some of it, however, is just writing upp: even doctors can feel that the occasion is too important to use ordinary English.

The mark of writing upp (and of talking upp) is the fear that one's words are not long enough, so that an extra syllable or two will add to their dignity. The greatest sufferers from this are, inevitably, monosyllables, and none more than the word *now*. Shakespeare's *Richard III* begins with Richard announcing that the wars are over:

> *Now is the winter of our discontent*
> *Made glorious summer by this sun of York.*

A good actor can do wonders with the single monosyllable that begins the speech; but would a modern politician be content to begin with such a tiny word? We all know politicians who prefer *at this moment in time*; and I have even known of one who said *at this moment in time which we are now at*. Airlines in America also feel that *now* does not sound important enough, and so ask their passengers to fasten their seat belts or put up their trays *at this time* – just as they don't like the bluntness of *our flight to New York*, preferring *our flight with service to New York*.

Well, it could be worse. It might be an aerial transportation experience envisaging as goal a locational shift to New York. Perhaps it will be, one day.

Netspeak

The electronic revolution involved no bloodshed and toppled no governments, but it has had an enormous effect upon our lives – and upon our language. Have you got a computer? Do you use it for email and for the internet? Have you got a mobile phone? If you say 'No' to all of these, you are certainly old-fashioned – which of course you have every right to be, but it does bring you some practical disadvantages. And if your answer is 'Yes' to all of them, then you have had to grow familiar with a new variant of English, the English used in email, in chat rooms and texting, and on the web. I shall call this language *Netspeak* – other names are possible, but this one is neat, clear, and (almost) accurate. It has 'dialects': there are expressions used in chatting and texting but not on websites, and there are differences between informal websites posted by individuals and those of official bodies like the Government or the BBC or *The Times*, which are in Standard English.

Because change is so rapid, it is difficult to be sure of what has already happened to Netspeak, and impossible to predict how it will change in the future: everything we write about electronic language is likely to be out of date in five years, and may well be wrong already.

'The language problem but you have to try,' wrote William Empson in 1935, in a poem about a love affair with a foreign woman; Netspeak can be at least as unpredictable as a foreign lover, but we have to try.

There are plenty of guides to electronic language, telling us how to write it. They tell us two main things. On the one hand that we should be inventive and playful, welcoming new words and new constructions, and using what they sometimes call *voice*:

> *Not the clear-but-oh-so-conventional voice of Standard Written English. Not the data-drowned voice of computer trade journals. And not the pureed voice of the mainstream press. The voice of the quirky, individualist writer ... welcome inconsistency, ... play with grammar and syntax. Appreciate unruliness.*

Such – and much more – is the advice of Hale and Scanlon in *Wired Style: Principles of English Usage in the Digital Age*. How do you respond to such advice? Does it seem liberating and encouraging, or does it simply leave you bewildered? If we are careful and consistent by nature, urging us to be inventive and unruly may be asking the impossible; no doubt if we are inventive and playful by nature, it may make us feel encouraged to do what we like doing. But can this advice be called a *principle* of usage, if it asks us to ignore principles? Creativity and originality cannot, after all, be taught: it is one thing to encourage them, but quite another to expect people to produce them to order. If Netspeak is wild like playful speech, or creative like poetry, it cannot be taught, and we cannot find rules for it. Are they guidelines if they tell us not to be guided?

And, on the other hand, we are often reminded that much of the material on the internet is permanent in a way that speech isn't; what we type and send may be there years later to embarrass us. There is, of course, a difference between permanent websites and the evanescent chat that takes place between individuals or in chat rooms; much of what is sent as emails is likely to fall somewhere in between. An email to your girlfriend will be in very different language from a job application. It is the possibility of permanence, and of what we write being read by strangers, that leads some style manuals to give us advice that is almost the opposite of that of *Wired Style*, urging us to be careful because what we send cannot be recalled or destroyed.

These two contrasting views of electronic language can be related to the fact that it exists somewhere between speech and writing. Speech, especially informal speech, is much more likely to ignore the rules formulated in grammar manuals and be casual; writing, because it is permanent, is usually more careful. When electronic language is most like writing, it will probably be in Standard English; when it is most like speech, it will be furthest away.

We all know the old image of a message put into a bottle and tossed into the ocean for anyone to find. If instead of one message found by one person only, and possibly sinking before anyone finds it, we think of a message that will never be destroyed and can be found and read by anyone, then we have the web. Email, in contrast, is addressed to one person, or at most to one person with copies sent to others. Clearly the web is like the situation of written language, and email can vary between the written and the spoken situation. If we want to see Netspeak at its most informal, most like spoken language, we must look at texting and chatting.

They are not quite the same: *texting* is normally used of messages sent by mobile phone, and *chatting* usually denotes an exchange between two or more people who are logged on to communicating computers. (I said 'two or more people' but we could almost say 'two or more teenagers' – though no doubt some adults also chat, especially perhaps those looking for a new partner.) Chatting usually takes place in real time – that is, one chatter's message appears immediately on the other's screen; in texting the incoming messages will only appear when the phone is switched on – but this difference is not important. In both cases, the language used is informal and colloquial, and full of abbreviations and even rebuses. (A rebus is a kind of visual pun, representing a word or part of a word by means of a picture or symbol, as in *b4* meaning 'before'.) Since a mobile phone screen has much less space than a computer screen, abbreviations and rebuses are clearly more useful there, but the texters obviously enjoy using them, so they are just as likely to occur in chatting. So since they both use much the same informal language, I shall now use the term *texting* to cover chatting as well.

Here are a few of the millions of text messages that are sent every day:

What is chris's and dk's and shaun's surnames?
Oh and richard
Hey an at the back of the queue- will try and get on the bus-.
Dave

Hey how r u? Just thought id say happy birthday n I hope u
have had a great day! When u off back 2 bristol? Tb sarah

Just thought I would let u know im home n will c u in the
morning 4 breakfast so give me a knock. Luv sarah ps have a
good nite.

It isn't difficult to list the most striking features of these messages. First, the accidental mistakes ('typos') have not been corrected: it would not be cool to go back over the message and change *an* to 'am'. This cavalier attitude to spelling may be a way of saying that spelling doesn't matter, but Dave has spelt *surnames* and *queue* correctly, and Sarah has spelt *thought* and *breakfast* correctly, and the spelling *nite* for *night* is quite widespread and clearly deliberate. It is in little words that are easy to spell that the mistakes most often occur, so the message may be not that spelling doesn't matter, but that the message being written doesn't matter, that it is not important enough to need the spelling corrected.

Second, the rebuses and puns (*c u* for 'see you', *4* for 'for') are there not so much to save effort but because they are fun – as I, if I were texting, might have written *444* instead of *4 for 'for'*. Most of them are standard – it is not after all easy to think up new ones – but I suspect that anyone who did think up a new one would be pleased and would use it.

Next, they are full of abbreviations: *tbh* for 'to be honest', *lol* for 'lots of laughs' (or, to some texters, 'laughing out loud'), *bf* for 'boyfriend'. These are not rebuses, and would probably not be understood by someone who had not learnt them; such abbreviations might be confined to a particular group of texters, or might be more widespread.

The chatters do not correct or even judge one another's language, and it would certainly be considered out of place to try to do so; but they clearly enjoy the playing with words, and such appreciation always has a judgement built into it, in the sense that to feel delight at an elegant bit of word play must imply that a less successful bit would be less enjoyable. Here are four (fairly widespread) abbreviations: *l8r* (for 'later'); *I can't member* (for 'I can't remember'); *borin as eva* ('boring as ever') and (a less common one) *bibi* for 'bye bye'. A teenager who is chatting is not, of course, likely to pause and judge any of them, but if they claim (as they obviously would) that using language like this is fun, then it must be possible to find some uses more successful and others less so. So let's step back and ask what we think of these.

Using the letter *i* for the vowel in *bye* is a kind of rebus: our first impulse on seeing *bibi* would probably be to pronounce it 'beebee', then we realise that we are meant to use the name of the letter and not its expected pronunciation, and we get a mild shock of discovery. That's where the fun lies. The pronunciation of *8* is exactly right for the second sound in *later*, so here too we have made a discovery. When speaking quickly we do swallow, partly or even completely, the first syllable of *remember* in saying *I can't remember*, so once again there is some accurate observation behind this misspelling. I am not quite sure about *borin as eva*. The *ng* at the end of *boring* does not represent two different sounds of which the second might be dropped in hasty speech; it represents one nasalised sound. But there may be teenagers who pronounce it 'borin' – a pronunciation long associated with upper-class sportsmen who go in for *huntin, shootin and fishin*. There is perhaps a nice irony in this meeting (or should I say *meetin*?) of two very different cultures. As for *eva*, it is a kind of parallel to *bruvva* as a spelling for 'brother', though one might expect it to be spelt 'evva' – especially if one's name was *Eva* and one did not consider oneself to be at all boring. I find this one less satisfying than the others – but perhaps I'm being prejudiced here by my belief that the most boring people are those who keep finding things boring!

Now in case any teenager should happen to read this, I'd better say that this discussion is of course quite different from actually texting. My aim here is not to join in the fun (and not to spoil it), but to unpack what is meant by finding it fun to use language in this way.

Those who chat online usually make up a name for themselves – and this too can be fun: fancy calling yourself *cybrid longtail*! Some chat programs limit the length of such names, but others don't; and in the chat I looked at, some of the names were very long. One participant called himself *Radebe Radebe Radebe Radebe* (I forget how many repetitions, but at least six); another called herself *Send me an angel – prostitution is not an occupation it's a hobby*. Are those names? (Even if we call them mottoes, they are certainly behaving like names, appearing on every message to identify who it's from.) In real life, names cannot be very long because that would make speech too awkward, and people called Elizabeth or Montgomery usually get called Liz or Monty; but in chatting on the internet, neither party has to utter the name or even to write it – they just press a key and it appears – so there is no practical objection to it being as long as they like. (*Radebe* is a footballer who had just retired from the team this lad supported, and the repetitions presumably showed his admiration; as for the quotation about prostitution, I have no idea where it comes from.)

Teenage language has its slang, of course, that finds its way into texting; and like most slang, it is used by people who are not very good at explaining just what it means. What exactly is an *emo*? I asked one or two teenagers, but am not at all sure that the explanation I was given would enable me to recognise an emo. I was told that in the first place it is a kind of music, then a hairstyle, and finally a kind of person: 'someone who sits in corners and cries and is allllways depressed. They are quite hot looking but are not very nice people.' I'm sure that Send-me-an-angel etc., who supplied this 'definition', feels sure she can recognise an emo when she sees one, but that is not the same as explaining to others what it is. Little Jack Horner also sat in a corner, and those suffering from depression are 'always depressed', but the 'definition' is clearly not meant to apply to them. In fact the more I look at it, the clearer it becomes that it is much more concerned with Send-me-an-angel's feelings than with what emos are actually like: the four l's of *allllways* do not mean that the emos are more often depressed than those with only three l's, they mean that Send-me-an-angel is tired of being told how depressed they are. To push my inquiries a bit further, I asked just what was meant by *hot* in this sentence, and was given four synonyms: *fit, good-looking, sexy, spunky*. I asked a couple of other teenagers, who added *pretty*, but it was clear that the word is generally understood. I am still not sure how far *hot* is a term of general praise, and how far it has a specifically sexual meaning; the same doubt attaches to the term *sexy* itself, along with *sex up* (see page 163). No doubt this is a sign of the uninhibited world we now live in – or claim to live in.

Is texting an example of written or spoken language? My best answer is that it is written language doing its best to be like spoken. Now one of the main differences between written and spoken is that spoken language has intonation, facial expression and bodily movements, which are all ways of modifying the impact of the words to take account of the feelings of the speaker and the human situation between speaker and hearer. That seems to be the one element in speech that neither texting nor any other form of writing can include.

Or can they? It is precisely to deal with this lack that smileys or emoticons have been developed. *Emoticon* is a compound word made up of *emotion* and *icon*. *Icon* (a term familiar to computer users) is a picture with a fixed and even recognisable meaning, though it is often necessary to be familiar with the conventions to recognise it. If we want to convey the idea of 'smile' or 'happiness' in alphabetic writing, we write the words *smiling* or *happy*, but we all know the drawing of a simplified face with the mouth curving upwards – and the contrasting drawing with the mouth curving downwards, which means 'angry' or 'miserable'. These are emoticons, since they represent emotions, and some chat programs have developed a few dozen similar icons to mean 'I'm being ironic' or 'I'm angry' or 'I love you', or 'I'm eyeing this warily'. Turning emotions into words is always a delicate task, and turning them into icons will usually seem clumsy to anyone who feels a particular shade of emotion, but we can see their attraction: they are an attempt to give to texting – a written medium – some of the quality of speech.

'Last year's words belong to last year's language,' wrote T. S. Eliot in a poem in 1942, 'And next year's words await another voice.' Of course he did not literally mean 'last year' and 'next year': he was thinking of the sort of change in sensibility that takes place over a generation or even longer. But now, suddenly, a year seems a long time. Language change as we have always known it, and as we discussed it in an earlier chapter, has the speed of a glacier – you don't see it moving. Netspeak, however, sometimes seems to change overnight, as we pant to keep up.

You will have noticed that it is not necessary to use Netspeak in order to discuss Netspeak. It can be discussed in Standard English (as can almost anything, if it is not too technical); and inevitably there are sociologists, even linguists (who should know better), who discuss it in jargon. So here to conclude is a sentence about Netspeak which seems about as far as can be from the subject it is discussing:

Text-based asynchronous interlocutors employ unconventional symbolic representations such as emoticons to facilitate expressiveness in the medium.

The language problem but you have to try.

CHAPTER EIGHT

Mind Your Language

Your visitor looks anxiously round the hall. *Where is the ... um ... the ...*, she begins. You smile understandingly and say *First door on the left*. She nods gratefully and disappears through the door; then emerges soon after, looking relieved. As we'd expect, since she has *relieved herself*.

Not many visitors, perhaps, are as coy as this one; she was probably a very nervous old lady, perhaps talking to a young man. But all the same, communication was perfectly efficient, though the conversation avoided naming either the room or what your visitor intended to do in it.

This chapter is about the language we use in such delicate situations, and is therefore a continuation of the discussion of register. We saw in the last chapter that our language is determined not only by what we are saying, but also by the company we are in. And there are some situations which can seem particularly delicate, and in which our choice of words can very easily shock or distress the listener, so that we might feel a strong need to tread carefully.

We can begin with two comments on the episode that we have just looked at. First, most visitors would not find the situation as agonisingly embarrassing as my imagined old lady did. They would not be afraid to name the room they were looking for: *the toilet, the loo* and *the lavatory* are the most likely terms in mixed company. But they would be much more hesitant about naming what they were going to do there, and the contrast in register between the various terms they could use is very striking. Whether the visitor says *relieve myself, have a wee* (or *a pee*), *urinate*, or *piss* – or none of these – will depend on the company, and on the visitor's normal habit; and on most occasions they will not use – or need to use – any of them.

What are those situations – those, that is, when there is a danger of shocking our listeners? Let's make a list, to start with: bodily functions concerned with evacuation, as we've already seen; politics, especially racial and sexual politics; money; jobs; death; and – above all – sex. These are all topics about which we might have strong feelings, and in which we have a wide choice of terms, some of which might arouse equally strong feelings in the listener. They are all linguistic minefields, and the language has developed ways of treading carefully through them, so that the mines won't explode. Unless, of course, we want them to.

Never Say Die

Let us begin with death. We are all going to die, but unless we are ill or depressed we don't want to, and often we don't want others to die either; though we cannot avoid the subject, we might wish we could. So we need another, similar, area of vocabulary we can draw on instead, and for this there are three obvious candidates: sleep, journeys and religion. The parallel between dying and going to sleep is obvious, and can be comforting, since sleep is on the whole pleasurable, especially when we're tired or in pain; *fell asleep* is therefore especially apt for the death of someone who was in distress. It is often seen on gravestones, and is also, of course, appropriate when talking to children, explaining why a grandparent is no longer there: he's *fallen asleep and won't be waking up*.

There is also the parallel with a journey, death being a journey from which we do not return; so a child can be told that grandma has *gone away* and *won't be coming back*. In the case of religion, the expressions *gone to heaven, gone to God, gone to join his/her wife/husband, in Heaven, with Jesus,* and the now old-fashioned but rather charming *in Abraham's bosom* could be literally true for the Christian who believes them. But such phrases are often used by those who don't believe them to be true, and perhaps even more often by those who half-believe, or wish they could believe; and in such cases their function is to make an unpleasant reality more acceptable.

And should we use them? You will no doubt take your own decision on this. My advice (it's no more than advice) is that there's nothing wrong with the expressions, but there is no need for them to drive out the words *death* and *dying*. To say to a child *Grandma died last week; I'm afraid that means she fell asleep, but in a way that means she won't wake up again* seems as good a way as any of saying what is, inevitably, hard to say.

There are other ways of not saying *death* or *died*, some of them belonging to particular situations. Condolence cards normally prefer terms like *sad loss* or *great sorrow* or (rather old-fashioned now) *great affliction*. Life insurance salesmen like to say *If you get knocked down by a bus*, which at first seems to serve the very opposite purpose, making death more, not less, unpleasant – but it has two advantages. First, it has the meaning of sudden death when still comparatively young, which is of course what life insurance is for; and second, it may well cause the listener to think how unlikely this is (*Bus drivers are careful, and I always look when crossing the road ...*) and so serve the purpose of removing any uncomfortable thought.

One of the commonest terms is, of course, *pass away*; everyone knows what it means, so using it is simply a way of avoiding the word *die*. Yet the word *die* is not indecent, and it is not easy to say why it is sometimes avoided. We are not avoiding mention of the fact that grandma is dead when we say that she *passed away*; it may be that there is something blunt about the monosyllable *die*, that a single short word doesn't sound gentle enough when we wish to be delicate. Less common than *pass away*, but somehow more interesting, are *pass over* or *pass over to the other side*. These sound religious, but are hardly Christian. Ancient Greek mythology had the dead person ferried across the river Styx by Charon, the boatman, and that must be the origin of this expression, which is sometimes used in all seriousness by Christians. This seems to tell us that religion is not just a matter of what you believe, but of a feeling of reverence that may not always take much notice of exactly what is being claimed. *He's passed over to the other side*, then, may express a reverence that is felt as religious, without too much concern with exactly what belief is being stated.

And are there, in contrast, deliberately blunt terms for dying, terms that could shock if used in the wrong circumstances? We say *kick the bucket, pop off* and (usually in the past tense) *snuffed it*, or *bought it*. None of these is likely to be used of someone we know (unless we disliked them!), and of course they could be out of place

– not so much embarrassing as offensive – if wrongly used. What of *pushing up daisies*? (In French you *eat the dandelions by the roots*, in German you *bite into the grass*.) It is clearly not religious, and per-haps a touch irreverent; it indicates that death is a matter of bodily decay, and perhaps nothing else, and it may have had its origin in an attempt to be deliberately pagan and irreligious. My impression is that it's most likely to be used of one's own death when that isn't felt to be imminent. There is nothing softening about the expression itself, but to use such an expression in a relaxed or light-hearted way is clearly to imply that death is not an immediate problem.

Illness and death clearly belong together, so I will here add that there is a similar range of register about illness. You can have a *weak heart* or, more colloquially, a *dodgy ticker*. When would this collo-quialism be used? Usually of your own weak heart, since its casual-ness seems to make light of the ailment, in a way that would sound insensitive if used of the person you are talking to – unless you knew them very well and knew that they often talked of their own illness in that light-hearted way. Perhaps the most interesting of the illness-evasions is the word *condition*. If our heart doesn't function properly, we have a *heart condition*; if we have difficulty breathing, we have a *lung condition*. Any of our organs can be in a healthy or unhealthy condition, of course, but we use the term only to mean 'unhealthy condition'. It is interestingly similar to the use of *problem*, as when we speak of having a *drink problem* or a *drug problem*, but with a difference. Troubles that are not under our control are *conditions*; those that are – or ought to be – become *problems*. To say you have *a drink problem* instead of saying that you – or others – drink too much is a way of shifting responsibility away from yourself, but not completely; we accept at least some responsibility for our problems, but none for our conditions.

Euphemism

We now need to introduce a term that will help in the discussion. *Euphemism* literally means 'speaking favourably' or 'fair speaking', using a favourable or at least neutral term because the usual term is considered offensive or denigrating. It can be described as the deo-dorant of language. Thus, as well as saying *fall asleep* for 'die', we say *bathroom* or *comfort station* for 'lavatory', *let someone go* for 'dismiss them (from their job)', *hostess* or *call girl* or *sex worker* for 'prostitute' or 'whore', *with learning difficulties* for 'mentally retarded', *leave the room* or *use the bathroom* for 'defecate' or 'shit', and *liquidate* for 'kill'. (These examples are not all the same kind of euphemism, as the discussion will show.) Older books on English language paid little attention to euphemisms, but it has become clear nowadays that they are a politically sensitive way of dealing with politically sensitive issues. It's a hot topic, so there is much to say about them.

The opposite to euphemism is, strictly speaking, *dysphemism*: speaking foul as contrasted to speaking fair, using an unfavourable, hostile or contemptuous term. But hardly anyone except professional linguists uses the term *dysphemism*, or even knows what it means. This is not because we are all so good-natured that we seldom speak foul of one another; it is rather because 'speaking foul' is usually directed against people, people we don't like or feel hostile towards, and we have a familiar term to denote that: we insult them. So euphemisms and insults form a kind of balancing contrast. In between comes plain speaking.

Language is constantly changing; I have said that before, and it is now necessary to say it again, very emphatically. Much of what follows may be out of date in ten years, some of it may be going out even as I write. The principles are not likely to change much, but the examples will. Many euphemisms, and most insults, belong to the spoken language, and since spoken language changes much more rapidly than written, some of these examples look as if they won't keep still even long enough to be studied. This is especially true of insults, since insulting someone is often a way of showing off, and there are few better ways of showing off than displaying the richness and inventiveness – and the newness – of our vocabulary. There are many tales of colourful and flamboyant men who are able to insult their victim (often a hotel porter or train attendant, sometimes a sexual rival) for ten minutes – in extreme versions for half an hour! – without repeating themselves. These stories never include a list of the actual insults, and I feel sure that such speakers have cheated – most probably by switching from one language to another, or by inventing new insults as they go on. Inventing insults must, after all, be rather easy: just list all the things your victim is not able to do.

A common way to express contempt is to use the name of a

neighbouring nation. We take *French leave* or show *Dutch courage*; if we are mean with money we could be accused of being *Scottish* or a *Jew*; venereal disease was often called the *French malady*. It is difficult to separate the moral issues here (should we insult our neighbours?) from the linguistic. What makes this practice comparatively harmless, it seems to me, is the fact that it is mutual; we take *French leave*, the French say *filer à l'anglaise*; we use *French letters* (or we did until the term *condom* became universal), the French use a *capote anglaise*. This seems less offensive than racial abuse, where there is a more deep-seated assumption that the other group is inferior. For that reason I find it more offensive to associate financial meanness with Jews than with the Scots, since in the former case it invokes the long ugly history of anti-Semitism.

These national insults are very changeable. Sexual disease used to be associated with the Italians in the sixteenth century, then with the Spanish, then with the Dutch and the French, and no doubt by many of these nations with the English. This suggests that they are not based on any objective knowledge, but on who we happen to be at war with, or in the habit of visiting as tourists.

Euphemisms, too, tend to be unstable but for a rather different reason, which I shall call the euphemism trap. Suppose you have one leg shorter than the other, or some other physical injury that prevents you from walking properly. For a long time you were called a *cripple*; then when people began to feel offended at what they felt to be a contemptuous term, it became *disabled*; then that too was felt as offensive, so *physically challenged* was introduced. *Old* began to seem a rather blunt and uncomplimentary term and so was replaced by *elderly*, and *old-age pensioner* by *senior citizen*. After the Education Act of 1944, those pupils who failed the eleven-plus exam went to a *secondary modern* school; this was felt to be a more favourable term than the old *senior* school. But it too began to sound offensive, so was changed to *secondary school* – not a very accurate term, since the grammar schools were also secondary, but euphemisms sometimes sacrifice accuracy to sensitivity.

The euphemism trap is that if you replace an offensive term by a new and harmless one, the new one is very likely, before long, to acquire the same taint. This is very clear when it comes to racial terms. This topic is so sensitive that even finding the right language in which to describe it is difficult. *Nigger* has always been an offensive term in America (as has *kaffir* in South Africa), and as open racism became less acceptable the word was replaced first by *Negro* or *coloured* (or, in South Africa, *African*), then later by *black* and most recently by *African-American*. If we are narrating this change, which words do we use? To write 'Negroes began to prefer the term *black*' means we are using a term (*Negro*) that is no longer acceptable. But to write 'African-Americans began to prefer the term *black*' is anachronistic, even misleading, since *African-American* was not in use at the time of that change. The linguistic traps seem inescapable.

The current preferred term, *African-American*, places those Americans on an equal status with all the other groups descended from immigrants (Italian-Americans, Swedish-Americans, etc.) For this reason, *African-American* is preferred to *Afro-American*, since the former appears to lay stress on cultural heritage rather than on race – though at the same time the more racially oriented term *people of colour* has become acceptable. The general movement – to root out offensive terminology – is clear; but total consistency is more than we can ever expect!

The person you employ to bury your dead relative is an *undertaker*, or rather it was; the term has now grown slightly old-fashioned. In America he became a *mortician*, and in both America and Britain he is now often a *funeral director*. I remember reading in my school textbook (many years ago!) that *mortician* is a euphemism, and we should not use it. This is odd, because it is actually less of a euphemism than *undertaker*; *mortician* does contain the Latin root for 'death' (found also in *mortal*), whereas *undertaker* simply meant someone who undertakes to do any task before it narrowed its meaning to the one task of burying. Clearly we have here another example of the euphemism trap: *undertaker* began as a euphemism but took on the associations it was trying to avoid, so had to be replaced by (in this case) a less evasive term.

So euphemisms are by their nature unstable; whatever word is substituted for the offensive term is likely to need replacing after a while. This may not be an argument against euphemisms – after all, we do not refrain from washing because we are going to get dirty again. But it does add yet another complication to language change, and even well-meaning people are likely to feel bewildered, or to find

147

they have inadvertently given offence. It is not easy, especially for older people, to keep changing one's language habits; but then we all know that to be well-meaning, in a delicate situation, is not easy.

So our list of subjects where we feel we need to be careful not to offend is a list of the areas in which we tend to use euphemisms. We began with death, and the next step can be killing, especially the form of organised killing which we call war. We looked at some of the vocabulary of war in our discussion of slang, and saw that the slang of soldiers can often serve the purpose of being euphemistic. So can the more official language of military reports and the more evasive language of politicians. A retreat can be a *strategic withdrawal*, killing all the insurgents can be *pacifying the region*, and Anthony Eden declared in 1956 'We are not at war with Egypt; we are in a state of armed conflict.' I called war a form of organised killing, but the many euphemisms it generates try to pretend that it isn't. So instead of enemy soldiers being killed, they are *taken out*; and the killing of civilians, in a euphemism that has become notorious recently, is *collateral damage*. Equally notorious is the euphemism *friendly fire*, which means being killed – or at any rate shot at – by your own troops or (more usually) the troops of your allies. To call your own troops or those of your allies your *friends*, given the rivalries that obtain among allies, may not be very accurate; but it is not altogether a misuse of the word. What is shocking, because it seems a kind of gruesome humour, is the suggestion that the shooting itself – the *fire* – is somehow 'friendly'.

War is of course not the only kind of organised killing; killing all members of a particular group – a racial or a religious group – can take place in peacetime. It used to be called a *pogrom*, a Russian word adopted into English, and most often used of the killing of Jews. The modern (and very recent) term is *ethnic cleansing*, which in a sense is not at all euphemistic, since it seems to accept the assumption that the minority who are being got rid of are unclean. But for me the most chilling euphemisms of recent times derive from the Nazi persecution of the Jews, and are therefore in German. Most notorious is *Endlösung*, literally translated as *final solution*, which meant 'killing all the Jews'; though the word I personally find most repulsive is the term used to denote a region where all the Jews had been removed or killed. This is *judenrein*, which literally means 'clean of Jews' or 'purified of Jews'; the ability of the German language to join two concepts in a single adjective seems to make the word particularly and horrifyingly matter-of-fact.

But perhaps the most striking thing about military and political euphemisms is how ineffective they are – once we have emerged from the assumptions that generated them. Is anyone deceived when a government *liquidates* its political enemies, or when an army *strategically withdraws* instead of retreating?

Employment

We live at a time when many people, especially professional people, are identified by the work they do; two strangers getting to know each other are likely to begin by finding out what their occupations are. We sometimes think of our job as the most important thing about us, and this means that it provides a rich field for euphemisms.

We can begin with the word *job* itself. No one knows the origin of the word, but we do know that its original meaning contained an element of condescension or even disapproval; a *job* was a small task and often one you would not stoop to do for yourself. The character in a play of 1627 by Thomas Middleton, who said 'I cannot read, I keep a clerk to do those jobs', clearly thought reading was a task beneath his dignity. This is, incidentally, the earliest recorded use of the term, and we still have this meaning in the expression *odd jobs*. In politics, a *job* used to – and still can – suggest corruption. Today the word has largely shed these negative associations; if a diplomat or a surgeon is asked what job she does, she will probably not feel insulted, though she herself would call it her profession.

Because our job, then, is so important to us, to lose it is not merely a financial loss; it can be a loss to our self-esteem. So we need a euphemism, and the usual one (American in origin) is to *let go*. Instead of *I'm dismissing you* (or, more familiarly and bluntly, *sacking* or *firing you*), the boss explains that he is *letting you go*, thus implying that the decision is yours and he is acquiescing in it – but it would be no use responding *I don't want to go. Your services are no longer required* is a little less euphemistic, since it contains no suggestion that the employee's own wishes are being consulted, but any expression which omits a direct verb for the employer's action – *fire, sack, dismiss, discharge, get rid of* – must contain an element of evasiveness.

Nowadays with the growth of freelance work (by management consultants, computer specialists and troubleshooters), being dismissed may have become less traumatic; the consultant who is *let go* may even wish to go. But the profession where this is least likely to be the case is probably acting. It is in the nature of acting that employment is temporary, and because there are more actors than there are parts for them in the professional theatre, only the really successful will come to the end of a run without a certain amount of anxiety about what comes next. The euphemism that has developed to cover periods of forced unemployment is *resting*, and it has now become so familiar that it is as likely to be used jokingly as seriously.

Employment, like so much else in British life, is impregnated with class differences, and *letting someone go* applies mainly to white-collar work; the equivalent for manual occupations is *giving someone their cards*, which is perhaps already old-fashioned. It is a euphemism when the employer tells the worker that they can *get their cards*, but possibly a sign of independence when the worker defiantly demands them. But losing your job is not simply a matter between you and your employer, depending on how well you are doing the job; it is also dependent on the general economic situation, and the term that indicates this is *redundancy*. To be *made redundant* is to lose your job because of outside pressures – technological change (you have been replaced by a machine) or economic recession (the firm cannot afford to employ so many workers). The fact that *redundant* is now so widespread a term is perhaps an indication that we are all now aware of wider economic forces.

A few euphemisms current in the workplace include *brownie points*, for something that will earn you favour with the boss (suggesting that competitiveness in the workplace is as innocent as in a children's scout or guide troop) and *feather-bedding*, a rather more colourful term for a giving someone a *sinecure* (a position with rewards but no duties). A sinecure is more likely to be official or semi-official, while feather-bedding suggests that the firm is being indulgent towards the individual.

The euphemisms concerned with employment differ in one way from those concerned with bodily functions. As we shall see in a moment, the latter are intended to avoid embarrassment; but those concerned with employment are more concerned with anger. We might be embarrassed by the bluntness of being *sacked* or *dismissed*, but we are more likely to be angry. And if – as often happens – a whole lot of employees have been *made redundant* together, the anger will be shared, and we may go on strike. When that happens, we may no longer care about the terminology.

Politics

Politicians have always had the reputation, justified or not, of telling lies, or at least (to use a now familiar euphemism) of being *economical with the truth*. So it is not surprising that political language is rich in euphemisms.

If you take a cynical view of politics, you will be pleased to learn that the original meaning of *politician* was 'a trickster, a clever and dishonest person'. Thomas Nashe wrote in 1592 that 'the Devil was so famous a politician in purchasing, that Hell, which in the beginning was a small village, is now become a large city' – a remark that one can easily imagine journalists gleefully seizing on and quoting today. In fairness, however, I must add that our modern, more neutral use of the word also dates from the sixteenth century, and *politics* (from much the same date) has usually been a more or less neutral term, as it is today – usually but not always, as we can see from the national anthem *God Save the Queen*. Not many people know the second stanza, which deals with the opponents of the monarch, and asks God to 'frustrate their politics, and confound their knavish tricks' – not much doubt about the unfavourable view of politics there! We must of course distinguish between taking a cynical view of the activity, and claiming that the word itself implies that view; to say today *Most politicians are corrupt* or *Politics is a nasty business* is to express an opinion, not just to explain the meaning of the word.

What are the politically sensitive issues in our society? First, there is the distribution of wealth – the fact that some are rich, others poor. Has this had any effect on the words *rich* and *poor*? We still freely use the word *poor* as an adjective, both literally (*My sister is so poor she can't afford a television*) and in a transferred sense (*He's a very poor tennis player*), but do we use it as a collective noun, speaking of *the poor*? We are more likely to say (if we think statistically) *the lower-income groups*, or (if we think politically) *deprived* or *disadvantaged*. If you are deprived of something, that seems to imply that you once had it; if you are disadvantaged, that seems to assume that everyone ought to be on equal terms. So are *deprived* and *disadvantaged* attempts to smuggle in an egalitarian or left-wing agenda under cover of a concern for the language? You can be deprived not only of what you once had but of what you are entitled to have; and the view that everyone ought to have equal chances is – more or less – accepted in modern democratic societies. So there is certainly a case to be made for using terms such as *disadvantaged* or *deprived* instead of *poor*, but it is a political case, not a linguistic one. Since, as we have seen, one of the great virtues of language is that it can be neutral between warring parties, it seems more honest that this discussion should be conducted openly as a political discussion, not disguised as being only about language.

The same situation obtains when we turn to international politics. There are rich nations and poor nations, but they are not often called that. The more usual term is *developed* for the rich nations, or else the name of a grouping of rich countries they belong to (*the G8 group*); and we describe the poor nations as *developing* (which has replaced the earlier *underdeveloped*) or, occasionally, *deprived* or (similar to saying *the G8*) *the South* (since almost all the rich countries are in the northern hemisphere).

The most important thing about terminology is that it should be accepted, not that it should be accurate. Everyone knows what is meant by the *working class*, and no one really thinks it implies that teachers, bank managers and scientists don't work, so there is no need to wish that term changed; if *developed* and *developing* have now become accepted terms, then they must be accepted. I have to say, however, that terminology in this area is so volatile, it is easy to imagine these words giving way to others. So there may be a case for questioning them, and questionable they certainly are.

There is a small but troublesome problem in the fact that the words *developed* and *developing* are so similar: they differ only in their last syllable, which is unstressed. I have heard an excitable speaker (and international economics is a topic that generates excitement!) gabble the words so that it was very hard to make out when he said *developed* and when *developing*. More serious, perhaps, is the fact that most of the developed nations are on the whole developing economically much more rapidly than the *developing* ones; a really poor nation may not be developing at all.

The policy of this book is to set forth the arguments in controversial cases, but that does not mean that I shall never state a preference, and in this case my preference is very strongly for using the terms *rich* and *poor*. They are not value judgements: to be rich is not a virtue, to be poor is not a vice (nor is the opposite true). They are old words, to which the language is well accustomed, and they have equivalents in most other languages. To wish to eliminate them seems to me a form of mild linguistic paranoia, and I hope it will be resisted.

So much for wealth: next, to intelligence. There are great differences of intelligence in the human population, though how great they are, how far they are inherited, and how far they correlate with other abilities, are all hotly debated questions. Should we use intelligence tests in our society, and what should we use them for? Those are questions for psychologists, and perhaps for politicians; it is not a linguistic issue, but as long as we use such tests we shall need terms to describe the results. If they show some people to be of high intelligence, they will show others to be of low intelligence. In the more or less impersonal world of intelligence testing, the likely terms are *intelligent* and *unintelligent*, along with the variants on *high, low, quick, slow*, and even *good* or *bad*. Outside that world, the less formal terms will come in, and that is where the arguments begin. The usual words for those who are good at using their brains are *intelligent, brainy, gifted, clever, bright* and *able* – and there are plenty of others. And of course they have opposites: *unintelligent, backward, dull, stupid* and, more colloquially, *thick* are probably the commonest. What do you say to a group of children gathered together for a remedial class who ask *We're the thick ones, aren't we?* Do you rebuke them for their political incorrectness? Do you lie to them? Do you just correct their terminology? And if so, if you say *We don't use words like thick*, how do you answer the question *Well, what word do you use then?*

The least acceptable term is probably *stupid*; so let us ask when – if ever – it is acceptable to use that word. The most offensive use of *stupid* is to apply it to children. Differences of intelligence are as marked in childhood as they are among adults, so the objection to calling children stupid is not that it is inaccurate but that it is offensive: indeed, it is not so much the children who are likely to object as the sensitive adults who do not want to hear the children being put down. And can we then use it of adults? What are the more acceptable uses? The one adult it is perfectly acceptable to call stupid is of course yourself. We use it when we are paying a compliment, as in *How clever of you to see that, and how stupid of me not to see it myself.* Or we say *I'm stupid at mathematics, I'm afraid.* People who say that seldom or never think that they actually are stupid: they are more likely to be admitting to a particular limitation that perhaps they are not particularly ashamed of, and they may even be implying that they are quite competent in other fields. And what about calling other adults stupid? We use it, of course, when we have lost our temper or are setting out to insult someone, as in *You stupid wally.* And apart from that? The interesting thing is that we seldom use it of people with really low intelligence. We say, for instance, *That was really stupid of you,* or *Professor X has written a really stupid book about that.* The first of these is of course a rebuke, and is most likely to be delivered to someone we think of as usually intelligent; the second is not actually claiming that Professor X is of low intelligence, but that he has adopted some very misguided theories. We might even claim that the theories, though we consider them stupid, are held by very clever people.

Perhaps this is the place to glance at one of the most widespread and controversial euphemisms, which is *challenged*: it is now quite common to say *mentally challenged* for the unintelligent, *physically challenged* for the handicapped. The motivation behind such variants is worthy, but here too they raise difficulties. The best example of someone being physically challenged is probably the Olympic athlete trying to knock a few seconds off his or her time; and of being mentally challenged would be, surely, the brilliant researcher solving a problem, or the poet trying to find the right words. But that is not what *mentally challenged* is meant to suggest.

To feel sympathetic towards those who are poor or unintelligent is certainly admirable, but the problems they face will not go away simply because we are careful about our language. We could draw a parallel here with a doctor who finds that a patient has cancer, or is likely to die within six months. There is a medical and scientific issue – is the diagnosis correct?; and there is an issue of language – how should he tell the patient? He will get the first right if he is a good doctor, and the second right if he has a good bedside manner and knows how to use the language sensitively. Of course one would like him to get both right, but they might not go together; the expression *bedside manner* was coined to denote a doctor who establishes a good relationship with his patient, and so would know how to break bad news. It denotes a quality quite distinct from being skilful at diagnosis and treatment, though of course it is quite compatible with such skill; but it is also possible to use *bedside manner* in a derogatory way, to indicate that a doctor is better at breaking bad news than he is on strictly medical matters – as one might say of a politician that he is a good speaker or a skilful debater. We might say that of politicians we admire, but also of those we don't!

In the same way, we need to distinguish the moral and political issues concerning poverty or intelligence – or other sensitive issues – from questions of language. To try and do away with the words that might cause distress to those who are disadvantaged is like improving one's bedside manner: an admirable aim, but it should not deceive us into thinking that we have actually tackled the substantive problems.

We have now entered on the subject of the next chapter: political correctness. The term is an interesting one, since it concerns not so much the questions that are obviously and traditionally political, but rather those (illness, intelligence, race relations, relations between the sexes) that have traditionally been seen as non-political, even as part of the natural order of things, but that we are now being urged to regard as political – and therefore subject to change. There will be much more to say about this; but for the rest of this chapter we shall take a long look at the areas in which minding your language has always been central and unavoidable.

Bodily Functions

Everything we do involves a bodily function, and bodily functions are of course natural. But the two expressions *bodily functions* and *natural functions* as usually employed are euphemisms, and refer to those bodily functions that cause embarrassment and even distaste, along with shame (and more pleasure than we often admit). Feeling a *call of nature* never refers to being hungry and wishing to eat; to call something *natural* is usually to defend it against the view that it is somehow improper, so there is little doubt which natural functions are being meant, and what nature is calling us to do. The neutral terms for them, accurate and a little stiff, are *urination* and *defecation* (or *evacuation*), along with more or less medical terms for the products: *urine, faeces* and *excrement.* Of course we have what are often called the four-letter words or Anglo-Saxon monosyllables, blunt and indecent: *piss* and *shit.* What is perhaps most striking about this terminology is the lack of ordinary acceptable verbs; we find ourselves having to choose between rather stiff medical terminology and vulgarisms that in polite company might offend. The Anglo-Saxon monosyllables are of course more acceptable today than they used to be, but still embarrassing to many speakers, especially when both sexes are present. It is no doubt for this reason that, instead of naming the action, we prefer to name the place where it happens, and speak of *going to the lavatory* (or *the toilet* or *the loo*). The evacuation of wind also seems to have no 'respectable' term except for the roundabout *break wind,* and since there is no special room to which we go in order to *belch, burp* or *fart,* our usual policy is not to mention them at all.

Since we are much more at ease naming the place where we relieve ourselves than we are naming the action or the substance evacuated, we have several terms for it in current speech, and it is striking how many of them are euphemisms. Returning to euphemisms for *lavatory,* the old term was *privy,* which of course simply means a private place. It was then replaced by *lavatory,* which has been softened to *toilet.* I say 'softened', because *toilet* seems to be considered more euphemistic, even though *lavatory,* literally 'a place where one washes', was already a euphemism. In American English (and in the speech of guides and hotels catering for Americans) there is a rich crop of euphemisms for the euphemisms: *powder room* (only for women of course), *bathroom* (though it has no bath), *restroom* (though one does not go there when tired), and the perhaps more accurate though also more comic *comfort station.* (I once heard a Portuguese guide tell his party 'If you want comfort, it's round the corner to the right.') Euphemisms for the place lead naturally to corresponding euphemisms for the action, like *Do you want to wash your hands?* (This has produced the joke of the guest replying *No thanks, I've already washed my hands behind a tree.*)

Perhaps the only non-euphemism for *lavatory* in current speech is *bog,* a term that is likely to sound vulgar in mixed or polite company, but it can be freely used by a man who is talking to another man;

as is always the case with questions of register, the company we are in is crucial. In this as in other fields, there may be no term which will always cause embarrassment – even the Anglo-Saxon monosyllables are quite at home in a single-sex conversation and among people who feel themselves to be uninhibited.

The commonest colloquial term in Britain today is probably *loo*. No one is sure what its origin is. The two favourite theories are either that it comes from 'Waterloo' (presumably because of the link with *water*, though I like to think that successful evacuation is being thought of as a victory), or that it comes from the French. Even here there are two theories – that it is from *lieu*, 'place', or from *l'eau*, 'water' – and it is certainly the case that one French term for it is *le water*, pronounced like a French word.

Since *toilet training* (another euphemism) is important in bringing up children, there are of course lots and lots of childish expressions for both the action and the place: *number one* and *number two*, *perform, sit down, do a wee-wee* or *a poo*. Families often have their own terminology for this, and you will perhaps be able to add a few other terms, either well known or quaint. That is to say, if they were used in your family, they will seem well known; if they weren't, they must be quaint.

I was once in the men's lavatory in a university when a student came in with his three-year-old son. 'Do you want to shit or just piss?' the father asked; I forget what the son replied, but I remember being startled by the language. I feel sure that the young father thought he was being uninhibited, and was bringing up his son to speak openly and without embarrassment about bodily functions; he did not believe in 'family terminology', or in varying the language to suit the occasion. If I had said to him 'Mind your language', he would have thought me an old fuddy-duddy; I am not sure what he would have said if I had started to speak to him about register, but it seems likely that he wouldn't have thought the matter important. He was teaching the child – not explicitly but by example – to use only one register when talking about bodily functions. I would love to know whether that caused problems for the boy as he grew up.

To set against that student, here is a comment by Bertrand Russell which seems to me to show great sensitivity to register. He was once asked in an interview to what he attributed the fact that he was a happy man, and he replied 'Defecating twice a day with unfailing regularity.' No doubt he believed this, but obviously he also wished to be mischievous, since the interviewer probably expected him to say how important philosophy was in his life. Setting out to shock by giving a very ordinary reason, he was careful not to shock by his language; his choice of the rather abstract, indeed medical, term seems a way of indicating that he meant what he was saying. He knew more about register than that student did.

The Language of Sex

One bodily function deserves – and needs – a section to itself. Sex is important in our lives, associated with great joy and, sometimes, with shame. It is inevitable that such intense emotions should develop a rich and emotionally charged vocabulary.

What terms do you use to speak about your sexual organs? Broadly speaking, you have four choices: nursery words (*willy, down there,* and – in at least one nursery – *cherub*), scientific terminology (*penis* and *vagina*), vulgarisms (*prick* and *cunt*), or metaphors (*the rod of life* and *love's channel,* his *tall pine* and her *Cyprian strait*). For the sexual act there is of course no nursery term, so the choice is threefold: scientific terms (*sexual intercourse, copulate*), vulgarisms (*fuck,* or the more recent and less offensive *bonk*), or metaphors like *make the beast with two backs.* Should we add a fourth possibility, straightforward and neutral terminology? The most neutral term is probably *have sex,* which can be used without embarrassment in a calm discussion; but when I once heard a young American discuss the question of date rape, and he spoke about the importance of telling your date that you'd like to 'have sex' that evening, I could not help wondering if that was the term he actually used – and if so whether it sounded so neutral that it killed all desire in the young woman.

In a subject so highly charged as sex, the question of register is unavoidable, and the use of the wrong register can produce awkward or embarrassing results. Scientific terminology is obviously appropriate when writing or speaking as a scientist, but can also be inserted into more casual conversation in order to amuse. Commenting on a likeable but very prim married couple, a friend once said to me 'One wonders whether they copulate', and the unexpected term produced an odd mixture of amusement at them and amusement at the curiosity we were showing – a typical example of how a shift in register can produce very complex effects. The vulgarisms are, of course, mostly used in informal, uninhibited, usually single-sex conversations – and sometimes also in the bedroom. Metaphor can be used to express our joy and wonder at the richness of sexual experience, and so, inevitably, it is often found in love poetry. Getting the register right can bring great satisfaction, perhaps even enhancing the joy of the sexual act itself.

Linguists distinguish between metaphor and metonymy: the difference, to put it simply, is that a metaphor replaces what you are talking about with something else that is like it, while metonymy replaces it with something else that usually goes with it. So if you are talking about your car you may refer to it as your *chariot* (a metaphor), or as your *wheels* (metonymy). What is easily the commonest term for sexual intercourse in modern English is not metaphorical but metonymic: *to sleep with*, or *to go to bed with*. Sexual intercourse usually takes place in bed and is often followed by sleep, but of course it does not have to; hence the many jokes on the lines of *Did you sleep with her? – No, we didn't get a wink of sleep all night*. Bed is such a central metonymic device when speaking of sex that it has yielded several common adjectives (*good in bed, beddable, bedworthy*, the last two both recent, that had not yet found their way into the *Oxford Dictionary* by 1928) and one very old noun (*bedfellow*) that dates from the fifteenth century. *Going to bed with* and *sleeping with* are of course euphemisms in origin, since they replace a direct statement about sex with some innocent activity that goes with it; but since they are now by far the commonest terms for sex, they seem to most of us simply part of Standard English rather than euphemistic. An older term, now largely replaced by *sleep with*, was *lie with*, which was a touch less euphemistic (it is after all slightly more accurate – though sexual intercourse does not have to be lying down!) As for the very widespread term *make love*, which for many people is now the normal term, it is not widely realised just how recent this is: well into the twentieth century, a man who *made love* to a woman was merely talking to her – courting, flattering, declaring his feelings. The earliest recorded use in the *Oxford Dictionary* of *make love* to refer to sexual intercourse is dated 1950.

159

Let's go back to Sun English, which you may remember I tried to survey in the chapter on Standard English. As we'd expect, it offers a large number of terms for sexual activity and sexually attractive people. In the one issue, I found the verbs *romp, tumble, date, canoodle, pick up* (some of these can have milder meanings, depending on context, but they seem quite plain here); the nouns *nookie, fella,* and *babe magnet*; and the adjective *spicy*. I also found a striking use of *make love*, in a letter from a woman who described herself as 'addicted to sex', and gave an account of meeting a young man in a pub with whom she went into an outhouse full of empty beer barrels, and 'made love'. 'When it was over he grabbed his pint, went back into the pub and ignored me.' That is the most extreme example I can imagine of how this use of *make love* has nothing to do with love.

One rather old-fashioned way of describing what happened in that outhouse would be to say that the young woman was one of the man's *conquests* – though in this case she was so willing that the term is inappropriate. The sexual meaning of *conquest* is particularly interesting, for two reasons. First, because it is clearly based on the parallel between love and war; there are innumerable poems, going right back to ancient Greek and Latin, which see a sexual encounter as a battle. And second, because of the difference between how men and women have traditionally been seen. A man *makes a conquest* when he *enjoys* (*goes to bed with, seduces*) a woman; a woman makes a conquest when a man falls in love with her, and she is able to refuse to gratify his passion.

Since both human beings and animals have sexual intercourse, there are – inevitably – verbs that describe the sexual activity of animals, and others that emphasise the common element between animals and people. By far the commonest verb for animal sexual activity is *mate*, which is only rarely used of humans – though the noun is common enough. A man's *mate* could be another man, in which case it is his friend or a companion at work, or a woman, in which case it is probably his sexual partner. In the case of animals, *mating* sometimes involves a permanent partner and sometimes not – we must be the only species with such enormous variety of sexual practices, both between cultures and between individuals. We do not often use the verb *mate* for humans, and when we do we more often refer to a permanent union than to the sexual act itself. This would make us like some animals but not others, but I doubt if any comparison with animals is intended when *mate* is used as a verb. The noun *mate*, however, is used both of humans and animals for a sexual partner, and does, I think, often suggest a resemblance between us and those species which stick to a single partner – as if we fit into nature, but into the nature of ravens rather than of sparrows or lions.

There are plenty of other verbs for sexual intercourse: *have, screw, enjoy, get laid,* and even more followed by prepositions: *have it off with, have one's way with, make it with* – many of them suggesting conquest, hostility, even violence as much as love. How do we guide anyone through this maze of terminology? Fortunately, we usually don't need to, for we usually don't need to tell people about register; if we are sensitive to the social situation we are in, we will use the right register. But – to revert to one of the ongoing themes of this book – register changes as society changes, and no field shows this more clearly than the language of sex. If this book were being written forty years ago, it would have been necessary to write *f*ck* or *pr*ck*; forty years before that, the words would have been written in Latin, using the decent obscurity of a dead language to avoid offending the reader, so that a discussion like the present one would not have been possible. Today many men above the age of 50 or so, and many women of all ages, still feel uncomfortable about using the words, and some (though fewer) about hearing them.

The difference between the spoken and the written language is crucial here, and is well illustrated by a moment in Graham Greene's novel *The Heart of the Matter*. Scobie, the middle-aged unhappy hero, is having an affair with a young and innocent war widow, Helen. When Helen learns that Scobie's wife is returning, she writes him a letter to say that she realises she has no claim upon him, though she loves him. One sentence runs 'My dear, my dear, leave me if you want to or have me as your hore if you want to.' Scobie then thinks to himself 'She's only heard the word, never seen it spelt: they cut it out of the school Shakespeare.' It is a touching moment, in which Helen's innocence is illustrated by the fact that she can't shift a word from the spoken into the written language without making a mistake. In 1948, when the book appeared, *whore* belonged almost entirely to the spoken language, and mostly to the informal spoken language; even Scobie, who no doubt used it freely among men, may never have written it and seldom seen it written. How much has this changed today? Ask yourself how often you have heard the word, and how often seen it written.

Change of register usually causes a shock, since it is a signal either that the social situation has changed, or that the speaker has decided to treat it differently. And it can be a wonderful opportunity for a writer; exploring what can and cannot be said and in what circumstances provides one of literature's finest pleasures, and if the situation is changing the writer has more to explore. Here is an example from the American playwright Edward Albee. In his play *All Over*, a woman is telling her lover, in careful, languorous prose, that it was not their affair that hastened the death of his wife, but his divorcing her:

> *It wasn't* us *that did her in – our ... late summer ... arrangement: there had been others. Our ... mercy to each other, by the lake, the city ... that didn't send her spinning back into the animal brain; no, my dear; fucking – as it is called in public by everyone these days – is not what got at her; yours and mine, I mean.*

The whole play is written in these elaborate sentences, full of sophisticated language and carefully chosen abstract nouns to refer to their love affair (*arrangement, mercy to each other* – excellent examples of euphemism through abstraction), and into this elegant language the four-letter word intrudes with a shock. The shock, of course, corresponds to the contrast between their sophisticated lives and the directness of the sexual act. It is a triumph of style on Albee's part, and it could not have been written before the four-letter word could be spoken on stage. The character's claim that it is called *fucking* by everyone these days is of course not quite true; we are meant to feel a certain shock as we hear the blunt word crashing into the elegance of what the character says. In another fifty years that effect may no longer be possible.

It is foreigners learning English who need to be guided, just as we need to be guided when we learn a foreign language. Learners of French often need to be told to be careful of the word *baiser*, meaning 'kiss'. It can be used as a noun, and even as a verb in phrases like *baise-la-main*, 'kiss the hand'; but by itself as a verb it doesn't just mean 'to kiss'. They seldom have to be told this twice.

And what about the words *sex* and *sexy* themselves? A fascinating verbal development of the last ten years or so is the extension of these words into areas which have nothing to do with sex. A document can be *sexed up*, that is, 'made more interesting'; a report can be *sexy* if it catches our attention, and makes us want to read it. When the British government was accused of exaggerating the danger of Iraq's weapons in order to justify the invasion, the term that was regularly used was that they had *sexed up* the intelligence reports. This seems to me a sign of how completely the taboo on mentioning sex has now faded in our society. From a situation in which mention of sex had to be disguised as something else, we have moved to one in which discussion of something else can be made more interesting by being compared to sex – though we haven't dropped the first situation either. Films and television programmes dealing explicitly with sex are still called *adult*, while a lively discussion of some difficult political issue that only interests adults can now be called *sexy*.

Homosexuality

This chapter would be incomplete if we did not add a word about homosexuality. It is only about forty years since male homosexuality ceased to be illegal in England, and the transformation of attitudes in that time has been enormous – though most homosexuals will tell you that homophobia is by no means over. As long as hostility exists there will be a term for it, and *homophobia* seems to be established as the standard term, though it has an oddity. *Phobia* actually means 'fear of' rather than 'hostility to' or 'prejudice against', though it is easy to see how one drifts into the other; *francophobia* can mean either 'fear of the French' or 'intense dislike of the French'. As for the *homo* in *homosexual*, it does not come from the Latin word for 'man' (as in *homicide*), but from the Greek word for 'the same' (as in *homonym*, a word which sounds the same as another). So, strictly speaking, *homophobia* should mean 'fear of what is the same' – but no one speaks strictly in this area!

What about the person who is homosexual? The usual term for a homosexual female is *lesbian*, which dates from the nineteenth century and is now Standard English; and for a homosexual man the now more or less universal term is *gay*. Everyone knows that it means 'homosexual', and it has now almost completely displaced the earlier *queer* – though *queer* seems to have had a revival recently. Since *gay* is used only of male homosexuality, instead of saying *gay and lesbian* it is possible to use a single word and speak of theoretical discussions of homosexuality as *queer theory*. This might at first look ambiguous: does it mean that the theory itself is queer, as a belief in witchcraft or in spontaneous combustion could be described as *a queer theory*? The indefinite article is important here: *a queer theory* is a theory which is queer, whereas *queer theory* is theory about homosexuality. I suspect that some fashionable queer theorists might be mischievously pleased at the possible ambiguity.

You will often hear complaints that the new meaning of *gay* has deprived us of a perfectly good, even a very valuable adjective; that we can no longer exhort the guests at a party to enjoy themselves and be gay, or refer to *gay Paris*. It is difficult to be sure if this complaint contains a touch of homophobia along with hostility to language change. If it comes from a poetry-lover, he may well quote Yeats' poem *Lapis Lazuli*, a passionate plea that art, including tragic art, should give pleasure, and which insists that 'Hamlet and Lear are gay', and that the 'ancient wrinkled eyes' of the old Chinese sages listening to 'mournful melodies' are gay. He may even claim that this poem has now been spoilt for him.

A sexual meaning for *gay* is not new. One of its original meanings was 'keen on social pleasures', and from this it easily came to mean 'sexually promiscuous'; in the nineteenth century a woman who was *gay* was a prostitute. This meaning died out before the twentieth century, and was presumably forgotten when the word came to mean 'homosexual' around the mid-twentieth century. The meaning 'homosexual' is now standard, and is understood by everyone; does that mean that *gay* can no longer be used with any other meaning?

Ambiguity exists in every language, and speakers and writers soon learn to handle it. You can be a *head of department*, a machine can build up a *head of steam*, a glass of beer can have a *good head* to it, you can walk at the *head of a procession*, you can have a *fine head of hair*, a boat can *be head of the river*, you can *keep your head* when others panic and lose theirs, discontent can *draw to a head*, and so on for page after page of the *Oxford Dictionary*. None of this troubles speakers of the language. Knowing a language means being able to negotiate our way through such ambiguity; poets and punsters enjoy the opportunity for verbal suppleness that this gives them. When one of the meanings is sexual we are usually able to shut it out without difficulty, though the opportunity for suggestive wordplay is there; a girl's school can employ a French *mistress*, an injection can give you a little *prick*, a birdwatcher can invite us to look at her *great tits*, without fear of misunderstanding, until someone decides to snigger at it. Many of our commonest verbs, like *have* or *come*, can have a sexual meaning, and of course this offers an opportunity for jokes in doubtful taste (*Mary had a little lamb – and all the doctors were surprised*). But in ordinary speech and writing this does not worry us; if it did, we would hardly be able to speak without sniggering.

So why need there be a problem about *gay*? Why can't the meaning 'male homosexual' exist alongside its other meanings without intruding, as the sexual meanings of *come* or *have* do not intrude unless we invite them in? This is a fascinating and difficult question; the answer may be that the meaning is new and we are not yet quite comfortable with it. Homophobia, like all prejudices, dies only gradually, and plenty of people are not only upset by homosexuality, but also feel distressed at the fact that they feel upset. Here it can be informative to look at the term used when it is revealed, by someone else, that someone is homosexual: he or she has been *outed*. Using a preposition as a verb is not completely unknown in English (we encountered *up* meaning 'raise' in Sun English, and we can *down* a drink), but it is unusual enough to sound odd. So the fact that we do not *announce* or *reveal* or *betray* or *tell the world* about John Doe's homosexuality perhaps indicates that the act of revealing it is highly charged with complex and not fully understood emotion; an awkward action needs an awkward word. Is it not this awkwardness which has prevented us relaxing about the word *gay* as well? Only when most people feel quite relaxed about male homosexuality itself will they feel equally relaxed about the word *gay*. That, at any rate, is my explanation. Perhaps you have another?

Marriage – and Non-Marriage

The frontier between being married and not being married has grown fuzzier in our time, and this has, of course, had consequences for the language. A man and a woman who lived together as if married, but who had not been through the ceremony, were described, until recently, as *cohabiting* (a more or less neutral term) or as *living in sin*. This latter expression clearly indicated moral disapproval, but was sometimes used by the couple themselves, either ironically or quite seriously, to show that they did not accept this moral prohibition.

An interesting example of how changing customs change the language is the disappearance of the concept of *conjugal rights* and the rise of the concept *marital rape*. *Conjugal rights* usually meant the right of a husband to demand sex from his wife: this right has now virtually disappeared from the law and the term in consequence has disappeared from the language. *Marital rape* is a term that until recently would have seemed like a contradiction, but is now gradually being recognised in law. *Demanding one's conjugal rights* and *committing marital rape* refer to much the same situation, and the change in terminology indicates very neatly the change in the moral and legal position.

As often happens when an important social change has taken place, especially when there has been strong resistance to it, some of the political struggle is displaced onto the language: conservatives object not only to the new practices but to new terminology, while radicals seek to change not only what happens but the language in which we talk about it. This is what lies behind most of the arguments about political correctness which will concern us in the next chapter.

In the case of marriage, the terms that have had to be rearranged are of course those for the practice and those for the two people. Some that have arisen in America sound quaint to British ears: *significant other, live together arrangement* (sometimes shortened to *LTA*), *spouse equivalent*. Sometimes it is difficult to be sure if these are still current, or already regarded as quaint; even, sometimes, whether they are being used seriously or in jest. The question *Are you (Is your son/daughter/sister, etc.) married?* has now become much more complicated than it was; the answer *No* might mean that the person is cohabiting or is single. *Are you attached/unattached?* seems to cover both possibilities, but if the person has old-fashioned sexual principles, they might be attached to someone they intend to marry but not be cohabiting or even sleeping with them.

Some of the ambiguity over marriage can also be seen in the use of *affair* (a shortening, of course, of *love affair*). When two people are *having an affair* that always means that they are not married to each other, and almost always that it is being kept secret. Fifty years ago the expression could be used when both of them were single, but today it would almost certainly mean that one or both of them is married, since a permanent sexual relationship between two unmarried people no longer has any stigma attached.

But there is still a good deal of uncertainty about the terminology. The traditional words for a more or less permanent sexual partner to whom you are not married were *lover* and *mistress*. Perhaps the most famous of Shakespeare's songs is *It was a lover and his lass*, a simple celebration of young love 'in spring time, in spring time, the only pretty ring time'. The song does not tell us, and the word *lover* does not tell us, whether their love was consummated or not; but since the lover in this case has a lass, he is clearly male. A lover, in earlier centuries, was usually male (though one could speak of a pair of lovers, in which case the word applied to both sexes); today both man and woman can speak of *my lover*. Modern students writing about Elizabethan poetry often refer to the poet and his lover, an expression that would have puzzled the Elizabethans themselves; the poet is the lover, and addresses his love poems to his mistress. (And a *mistress* as the recipient of a love poem could be, but need not be, a mistress in the commoner sense. That is, she might or might not have slept with the lover.)

Those days are past; so what are the equivalent terms today for the person with whom you cohabit or have a regular sexual relationship? By far the commonest is *partner*, which seems by now to be displacing all the alternatives – *lover, mistress, friend, girlfriend, companion*. The problem (a typical one when social arrangements are changing and vocabulary has not yet caught up with them) is that every possible term has other meanings. *Partner, friend* and *companion* all have non-sexual meanings. This only poses a problem if those meanings are likely to intrude and cause confusion. A married woman who made furniture had a business partner, and at an exhibition of their work she was talking to a customer who remarked that he had just been talking to her husband about the furniture. 'That's not my husband, that's my partner', she responded, whereupon the customer gave a slightly embarrassed laugh and said 'Well, we don't worry about these niceties nowadays, do we?' The example is a genuine one, but it is perhaps sufficiently unusual to be a story worth telling, which is to say that the danger of such confusion is very small. *Friend* is so likely to be ambiguous that it would cause endless confusion if used in this sense; but it is worth remarking that in German, where nouns denoting people often have gender-indicating terminations (so that the word for male friend is different from that for female friend), the term *Freundin* (female friend) used by a man is very likely to mean sexual companion. *Companion* has the attraction that it has a certain accuracy, since its literal meaning is 'someone who eats bread with you', but this will be noticed only by those who are sensitive to etymology. So *partner* it is likely to remain.

And since a sexual union can produce children, the term for your partner and children has also changed. The traditional term was of course *family* – which is ambiguous. In the narrow sense it means 'nuclear family', so the question *Has he a family?* meant *Has he any children?* But in the wider sense everyone has a family, because everyone has parents, ancestors, and (in most cases) aunts and cousins. Now the term often used is *loved ones*; in fire or flood or earthquake, survivors are anxious about the fate of their loved ones. Of course this gives an opportunity for cynicism (*Loved ones? I can't stand them!*) but that is an inevitable – and fortunately minor – consequence of the wider social shift we are looking at, using a term denoting the emotional rather than the legal relationship.

To conclude this chapter, here is a rather speculative historical note. In exploring the language of sex we have, inevitably, looked at the way it can be used to shock or to be offensive. In earlier centuries, the most shocking terms belonged not to sex but to religion: people wrote *d**n* (or said *darn*) instead of *damn*, or *G*d* instead of *God*, because they took the Third Commandment seriously ('Thou shalt not take the name of the Lord thy God in vain'). Is it odd that the same area of meaning should provide what we revere and also what we use for cursing? It looks like an example of the paradox often pointed out by anthropologists, that the sacred is closely connected with the unclean. We can see the same paradox in ordinary language if we look at the way we use the word *swear*: we *swear at* to express hostility, we *swear by* what we most revere.

But religious oaths have lost much of their power for many people; those who say *God* or *Christ* as swear words do not usually feel they are saying anything very shocking. Many would say that this is because religion no longer looms so large in our lives. If that is so, what has replaced it? If swearing is taken as evidence, it looks as if the answer is sex; the sexual terms now have more power to shock than have religious terms, and instead of writing *G*d* for *God*, we took to writing *f *ck* for *fuck*. Does that mean our feelings of reverence have been transferred from religion to sex?

But we have more or less lost our inhibitions about the sexual terms as well; we write them in full and, as I've tried to show, we use them much more freely. Does that mean we no longer have any terms whose use is inhibited by reverence? Because we have no reverence? Has our secular society begun to lose all feeling for the sacred?

Too big a question for a little book on usage to tackle. But you might like to think about it.

CHAPTER NINE

Political Correctness

The English language is full of contempt for women. It's not only that there are so many words that denote women of loose sexual morals (*hussy, harlot,* and more recently *slut, tramp, broad,* and more recently still *slag* or *slapper*), or women who are malicious, bad-tempered or empty-headed (*shrew, scold,* and more recently *bimbo*) – it is difficult to keep such a list up to date, since these terms change so quickly. Things are much worse when we look at the history of such words. *Hussy* originally just meant 'housewife'; *harlot* was originally applied to men, then extended to apply to women, and now refers only to women; *tramp* still has as its main meaning 'a person with no fixed home' but was extended in the twentieth century to mean a sexually promiscuous woman; *broad,* from referring simply to a woman, took on the meaning of a sexually loose woman. The story is much the same with the second group, the words that denote bad-tempered women: *shrew* was originally applied to men, then to women as well, then only to women; *scold* comes, strangely enough, from a Scandinavian word for a poet, then probably was applied to poets who made fun of their subjects, and finally developed its modern meaning – the noun applying mainly to women; *bimbo* originally just meant 'baby' (no doubt from the Italian *bambino*), and now means a pretty but empty-headed woman.

What does this history tell us? First, it reminds us that our language is constantly changing, so that a discussion of political correctness needs to deal with both the past and the present. Indeed, they cannot really be separated, because most of the words from the past are still with us: language consists of the past that has accumulated, as well as the latest additions. Then, when we look at the history, it

170

tells us that terms expressing contempt which originally applied to men and women often come to be applied to women only; and further, that terms which simply denote 'women' come to mean 'sexually loose women'. History, as often, tells us something important: it shows the direction in which the language has changed. And as far as women are concerned, that direction is downwards.

Contempt for women is not, of course, the only kind of bias in our language. There's a good deal of racist contempt, too, and often the racist insults are even more abusive, just as racist violence has often been more savage than sexist violence. (Of course there's been plenty of violence against women, but it has usually been against individual women, whereas racist violence has often taken the form of riots, pogroms and lynchings.) When we compare racist insults with sexist insults one striking difference emerges: that women are usually insulted by being placed in a sub-group that is clearly disapproved of (usually prostitutes), whereas black, Asian, Jewish and sometimes Mediterranean people are insulted simply for belonging to that racial group (*nigger, wop, yid*). Racist contempt is often undiscriminating, as we can see from what is probably the commonest of racist terms, *wog*. No one is sure of its origin, but one theory is that it's an abbreviation of *golliwog*, a soft fabric doll with a black face, popular in the early twentieth century. It is impossible to attach any precise meaning to *wog*, since it seems to have been used to denote any racial group except Northern Europeans. We can see its looseness of meaning from the British saying *Wogs begin at Calais*; indeed, looseness of meaning is probably central to racist contempt. The racist is not interested in what group his victims belongs to, he simply wants to make the point that they're not part of his own group.

And what can we do about all this hatred and contempt? The old answer was that we can do nothing: words are just words, and we have no power over them. But here we once again encounter the contrast between description and prescription, the prescribers now being a very different group from the Fowlers and their followers who believe the language is going to the dogs. Now it is the feminists and other reformers, looking towards the future not the past, who tell us to watch our language, to be careful what we say (or write) when there is a danger that our choice of words could give offence, or reinforce undesirable stereotypes. So it is now time for us to take a deep breath and confront the issue of political correctness.

And immediately we find ourselves in the midst of argument, for even the expression I have used as the title of this chapter is controversial. It is not difficult to define *political correctness* in a more or less neutral way as, say, the avoidance of terms that denigrate disadvantaged groups; but the term is not usually neutral. It is most likely to be used by the politically incorrect, to whom it conveys the idea that they are being asked to conform to fashion. Fashion? That too is a loaded term. People are happy to be thought fashionable when it comes to dress, but for one's use of language to be described as fashionable suggests that it is irrational and won't last long; so we are much more likely to hear people boasting that their language is unfashionable than that it is fashionable. We are not going to be able, in this area, to avoid controversy.

For the ardent feminist, or other keen reformer, and the indignant reactionary do not disagree only about politics; they also disagree about usage. Reading a provocative piece of writing, we can correct its spelling and its punctuation without fear of argument, but to try and correct its usage is likely to lead to as fierce a discussion as its content would. In this section I shall be as objective as I can, but there is no doubt that what I say will arouse some disagreement.

The movement for politically correct language began with gender, and that remains the most important area, for two reasons. For most people, sexual politics is more important than racial politics. It is possible (depending of course on where one lives and who one mixes with) to avoid much contact with people of another race; but it is obviously impossible not to encounter the other sex. And as well as this, gender, as we shall now see, lies at the heart of language. English has freed itself from the gender distinctions that other European languages have retained: in French the sun is masculine and the moon feminine, in German it's the other way round. We don't need to worry our heads about such differences: for us sun and moon are both *it*. But though we may have shed grammatical gender, we still have plenty of other ways in which gender impinges on language. So we'll begin with that.

From all directions nowadays we are urged to avoid sexist language: not to say *he* when we mean 'he or she'; not to refer to the *chairman* of a meeting, who might be female; not to refer to Charles

Dickens as *Dickens* but Jane Austen as *Jane* – the list of examples is endless. Many organisations – firms, trade unions, government offices – now issue guidelines to their members, telling them what terms they should avoid, and (usually, not always) what these should be replaced by. We'll look at one such set of guidelines later in the chapter. Let us start with the commonest example, and the one that arouses the most indignation: the use of *man*. This can mean 'man, not animal' or it can mean 'man, not woman', and therein lies the problem. Darwin's book *The Descent of Man* appeared in 1871, and *The Expression of the Emotions in Man and Animals* in 1872; they aroused plenty of indignation, but no one thought of objecting to their titles. Today his use of *man* might get him into as much trouble as his theories did then.

Man is a good example to begin with, since it enables us to take a glance at other languages. English is not the only language in the world, though sometimes the reformers seem to assume that it is. Latin, for example, has two words for man: *homo*, which means 'not animal', and *vir*, which means 'not woman' (though it must be confessed that the usage is not always consistent). But German is consistent: *Mensch* ('not animal') is kept distinct from *Mann* ('not woman'), and so German women do not feel excluded by it.

The sexist use of *man*, then, is not found in every language. Does this matter? Well, it depends on what the reform campaign is saying. If it is claiming that sexist usage contributes to or reinforces sexist oppression, then we need to ask whether Roman society was, or German society is, less patriarchal than ours – and the answer to this is certainly 'No'. Of course it is always possible to claim that the linguistic activity itself is seen as oppressive, even if it is not evidence for other oppression, and in that case we come off worse than the Germans; but this is rather a weak claim. Women would probably not bother to object to sexist terminology if they had not suffered from other, more serious, forms of oppression.

I feel fairly confident that this is true, because of the case of left-handed people. Our language has almost as much prejudice against the left-handed as it has against women. A *dextrous* person is being complimented for their manual skills, a *sinister* person is mistrusted; but originally the two words simply meant 'right-handed' and 'left-handed'. If you are *gauche* you are clumsy (socially more often than physically), but the word simply means 'left'. And of course *right* is perhaps our most inclusive term of approval: answers, conduct, actions, opinions, and thinking can all be right. Yet despite all this unfairness in the language, left-handers have not found it necessary to complain, and do not ask us to watch our language when using these terms. Surely the reason must be that they are not kept under politically or discriminated against socially to anything like the same extent as women have been, so this prejudice in the language is not seen as part of a wider oppression. Being only linguistic, it does not upset them.

Back, then, to the use of *man*. Avoid using it unless you are re-ferring specifically to males – that is the recommendation of those wishing to remove gender-bias from the language, and it seems a good policy for English speakers. But nothing is quite simple in lan-guage, and there are two difficulties that we ought not to ignore. One is how we deal with the past (this is discussed on page 194). The other is that *man* is such a pervasive term in English: the number of occasions when it crops up in idioms and compound words is astonishing. We *man a stall*, and we *man the barricades*; criminals commit *manslaughter*; artists have a *one-man show*; to finish the job on time the firm needs more *manpower*; a barrier can be natural or *man-made* – the word is everywhere.

This makes the task of avoiding it daunting, but not impossible: it means that we must be vigilant when using the language. Using lan-guage is always a mixture of habit and vigilance; most of our words come to us almost automatically, but some require careful thought. And of course the more formal the occasion, the more careful the thought needs to be. To the feminist it will seem no bad thing that speakers should pause to take thought in order to use gender-free language; it can be welcomed as compensation for many centuries of unthinking male dominance. But it will of course mean that not all speakers will come up with the same solutions; and some cases will be easier than others. It is quite easy to turn the *one-man* of *one-man show* into *solo*, or else to say *one-man* or *one-woman* as appropri-ate; it is quite easy to *mount* or *defend* the barricades, to *run*, to *look after* or to *manage* a stall (*manage* has nothing to do with *man*, but comes from the Latin word for 'hand'); it is usually easy to replace *manpower* with *labour* or *workers* or *staff*. When the Anglican church

174

modernised its marriage service, the priest no longer declared the couple to be *man and wife* but *husband and wife*; the couple can still, if they wish, be married with the old form of words (in which the wife also promises to 'obey') but hardly any choose to do this.

What of *chairman*? One favourite among the politically correct reforms is replacing this with *chairperson*, but it has been found that it is usually a woman who is called the *chairperson*; a man is still called the *chairman*. For this reason, *chair* seems to me a better solution. Indeed, my preference (you may not agree) is to avoid *person* altogether; the word has now got itself a reputation as coming from the unthinking and unsubtle feminist, ignoring linguistic sensitivity in the interests of the crusade, and it usually alienates potential allies. I have even heard the expression *to person the stall* – and the sniggers it aroused certainly did the campaign for equality no good.

The use of *chair* instead of *chairperson* is, however, a kind of solution not available to us in the case of *layman*. This originally meant someone who was not a priest or clergyman, but has also come to mean someone who is not an expert (not a lawyer or a scientist, for instance). Here the choice is simply between continuing to say *layman* and announcing one's political correctness by saying *layperson*. If one chooses the latter, my preference would be to write it as two words (*lay* is then an adjective, and this form is probably less offensive to the diehard).

Manslaughter is trickier. It is a technical term in law, and non-lawyers can hardly alter it without causing confusion. There is an alternative available – *homicide* – but that could not enter legal terminology without the agreement of the profession.

There are also some difficulties that are more narrowly linguistic. For instance, the uses of *man* which it would be most awkward to get rid of are those where it comes in the middle of a word: we praise a politician for *statesmanship*, a tennis player for *sportsmanship*, an artist for *craftsmanship*. Most hearers probably do not even notice the *-man-* in the middle of these words. There are no readily available synonyms for them, in any case; and it would be a pity to lose these words from the language.

Though the use of *man* may be the best-known example of sexist language, it is of course not the only one. There is, for instance, the use of feminine suffixes: *poetess, actress, manageress*. Many women feel the feminine suffix to be a put-down, implying that poets, actors and managers are the real thing, while poetesses, actresses and manageresses are an attempt by women to imitate it. So there is a case for dropping the suffix – in English at any rate. Once again we can notice the contrast with German, where the feminine suffix *-in* (*Schauspielerin, Verwalterin*) is normal, indeed universal, and not felt to be demeaning. Indeed, there are advantages in always using a different term for the female version, as we can see when we look at those English examples where it is always retained: *princess*, for instance, or *countess*. It would seem a rather clumsy joke to refer to Prince Charles and Prince Anne. What this shows us is that language has random humps of obstinacy – words that seem so odd when politically corrected that there is virtually no chance of their being changed.

The case of *priestess* is interesting. Its commonest use is for the priestess of Apollo, the woman who went into a trance and delivered the words of the oracle at Delphi. If it has other uses, these are almost certainly for non-Christian religions. Of course this is partly because Christian priests (including Protestant ministers) have always been male. Now that several of the Protestant churches ordain women, there seems to be no tendency to give them a female suffix. Again there is a linguistic complication here: *priest* is usually reserved for Roman Catholic priests (though it is used by High Anglicans as well), and there is no sign of women being ordained in the Roman Catholic church. If they ever are, it will be interesting to see if they are called *priests* or *priestesses*.

Pronouns

Next, pronouns. Along with the use of *man*, this is the commonest issue raised in language reform. *Everyone is entitled to his opinion*, we used to say; if it was objected that *everyone* includes women, this was met with the reply that in English usage the male embraces the female. No one is likely to make that joke today. Half the world's population is female, so everyone is entitled to the opinion that we should not pretend otherwise, even in English usage. So what do we say instead of *his* opinion?

This turns out to be awkward. Should we say *Everyone is entitled to their opinion*? *to her opinion*? *to his or her opinion*? How at this point we might envy the French, for whom the words for *his* and *her* are the same! Or let us take another sentence: *Everyone is inclined to think too highly of himself.* In that case it is tempting to be mischievous and suggest that this sentence can stay as it is, since it's usually men who have too high an opinion of themselves. But mischief won't solve our grammatical problem, so once again we are faced with the choice between *himself, themselves, herself,* or *him- or herself.*

Whichever solution we choose, there will be objections to it. Let's begin with the plural: *Everyone is entitled to their opinion*; *everyone is inclined to think too highly of themselves.* This frees us from the need to choose between masculine and feminine, and so is often recommended by language reformers; and there is also an argument, which is interesting ideologically, in favour of using the plural. Do we say *woman's writing* or *women's writing, woman's art* or *women's art, woman's psychological make-up* or *women's psychological make-up*? There has been a shift, among the politically sensitive, from singular to plural here. *Woman's writing* suggests the kind of writing appropriate to womankind, while *women's writing* suggests what women have actually written. The singular has a generalising, even idealising effect, so that the speaker who feels hostile to stereotyping, and is aware that women do not all write in the same way, is likely to prefer the plural.

But there are objections to using the plural. One that you will quite often hear (perhaps from the same people who object to *hopefully* as a sentence adverb) is that *everyone*, since it contains the word *one*, is obviously a singular, so we should not of course allow ourselves to slip into the plural. I have a sneaking sympathy with this objection, since it encourages us to be aware of the make-up of the words we use; but logic alone seldom wins a battle against usage. A more serious objection is that quite often the sentence is not about the plural but about the singular, and might even be emphasising the singular: *Every single one of them must make up their own mind* sounds decidedly odd to my ear. On occasion, using the plural can even be misleading. Here is a piece of good advice offered by a marriage guidance counsellor: *If you and your partner are having difficulties, tell them about your worries.* Who does *them* refer to? It sounds as if the partners are being urged to get outside counselling, that *them* refers to the members of the counselling service the troubled couple should turn to. No doubt that could on occasion be wise, but it is not what is intended in this case: the partners are actually being urged to talk to each other. So do we not need a singular here?

Here is an eccentric suggestion that would solve the problem of *themselves*, but not, unfortunately, the problem of *them*: we should say *Everyone has to choose for themself*, or *is inclined to think too highly of themself*. After all, if we want to give the word a singular meaning, why not give it a singular form – and *themself* was a normal English word until the fifteenth century. I have never heard anybody say it, but I would be delighted if the word was reborn.

So much for using the plural pronoun; let's turn to the next possibility. Here is a remark about what scientists do: *A scientist can study the behaviour of objects under certain conditions. She can describe what happens and offer explanations without paying any attention to ordinary people's ideas.* This was written by the American academic Jonathan Culler, who chose to replace the usual *he* not with *they* but with *she*. The result is a sentence which most people will read with a slight shock of surprise: the majority of scientists, surely, are still men, so why use the feminine? The answer, of course, is that producing this shock was precisely the author's intention. Since *he* is the usual way of being inaccurate, Culler chose the opposite in order to make the reader think. Making the reader think is, surely, a benefit to be seized on – though it means of course that he(!) will start thinking about sexist language instead of the actual topic, in this case the relation of science to common sense. There is a price to pay for everything.

There is also a milder and rather ingenious form of this strategy, which suggests that if a man is writing he should continue to use *he*, whereas a woman writing should use *she*. This, in a way, is an even more attractive solution, but it would of course mean that only women could strike a verbal blow for equality.

So we have *they*, and we have *she*; the next possibility, which is widely used, is *he or she*. This is undoubtedly the fairest and most truthful alternative, and there is nothing to be said against it except its clumsiness. But who can doubt that it is clumsy? And if Culler's paragraph continued *He or she is responsible only to the truth, and ordinary people have no reason to object to his or her explanations …,* we would soon grow irritated with the verbosity. If it caught on, we would probably learn to live with the clumsiness, even, after a while, to stop noticing it; but until that happened I would probably not be the only one to feel uncomfortable at what was happening to our beautiful language.

I can predict with some confidence that this problem will eventually solve itself, as one usage becomes established and so begins to seem natural to us. When that happens, any awkwardness or illogicality we now find in that usage will melt away, and it will become Standard English. What I cannot predict is which will be the winning form.

Avoiding Offence

Now we need to draw a distinction. The movement for political correctness in language has more than one aim. Our discussion of the use of *man* and of pronouns was concerned with what we can call gender-bias: the assumption built into the language that it is only really necessary to talk about men. I began the chapter, however, by pointing out that there is also a good deal of contempt for women built into the language. This is not the same thing as gender-bias, though the two are obviously connected: we are likely to despise those we ignore, and ignore those we despise.

So let us turn now from ignoring to despising. Here the aim of politically correct language (or 'verbal hygiene', as Deborah Cameron prefers to call it in her book of the same name) is, not to bring the forgotten into the light, but to avoid giving offence – to urge us not to use language to demean or insult. As a moral aim this seems wholly admirable, and our first reaction to it might be wholehearted approval. But if one approves of the injunction, is one concerned with language? Could we not simply say 'Do not demean or insult'? This question is certainly worth asking, and the reply of the defender of verbal hygiene might be that racist or sexist language does more than just insult someone, it insults him or her in a peculiarly insidious way, by suggesting that his or her offence is to belong to a particular group. If you insult someone by saying *you stink* or *you nasty little toad* or *you stupid reactionary*, or by calling them a *rat*, a *snake*, a *cow* or a *bitch*, you are just insulting that person, not placing him or her in a racial or sexual category and dragging the whole category down as well.

179

This seems to me a strong argument, and you may find it completely convincing. It is, however, the case that any common noun (*toad, reactionary, bitch*) describes a class, in this case of persons or animals, and when it is used as an insult the whole class is being dragged down. A staunch conservative might object to *reactionary* as a term of abuse, and an animal lover might protest indignantly that she loves toads or snakes. And if we look carefully at animal insults, we can notice a certain amount of imbalance between the sexes even there: to call a man a *bull* usually suggests that he is clumsy or hot-tempered, but does not express the same degree of contempt as calling a woman a *cow*. The fact that men are more often feared and women more often despised has left its trace in the language.

And now we have another difficulty, and one not easily disposed of. Who decides whether an expression is insulting? A once-famous cartoon showed two American men in what was probably a New York bar squaring up to each other with fists clenched; the caption ran 'Who are you calling an intellectual?' We should not underestimate the human capacity to feel insulted, to take offence at what to others seems harmless – or even, in this case, more of a compliment. If we felt it necessary to yield to anyone, or any group, who claimed to feel insulted by the wording we used, language would become a minefield.

Perhaps it already has – as in the question of how we refer to the handicapped. This is the third area (along with gender and race) which the movement for political correctness has concerned itself with, and because it is the most recent it is much discussed nowadays. We are sometimes told to avoid saying *the disabled* because it dehumanises people, and to refer to *disabled people* or *people suffering from a disability*; or not to say that someone is *a victim of arthritis* but *a person who has* arthritis; and even to avoid the word *handicap* because 'it carries connotations of *cap in hand*'. (These are all, of course, real examples.) The last is most easily dealt with. The origin of *handicap* is uncertain – and fascinating – but the most likely theory is that it comes from a form of gambling or contest in which the different parties put their stake in a cap (not 'cap in hand' but 'hand in cap'); there is no evidence that it has anything to do with begging or deference. Next, *victim*. There is not, I think, any objection to speaking of the *victims* of crime or of genocide, nor of the *victims* of

180

an earthquake or an epidemic; it seems to be only those who suffer from an incapacity or a disease who (sometimes) dislike the term. There is no doubt that the condition itself is unpleasant: everyone who has cerebral palsy or arthritis would rather not have it. Perhaps the objection to *victim* is to mentioning the unpleasant condition in relation to the person, as if that somehow taints them. In that case, it is an example of prudery – the belief that certain things are best not mentioned – and it is interesting that in a time when prudery is decreasing in relation to bodily functions and sex, it is increasing in relation to illness and disease.

As for *person who*, it seems to claim that using the definite article followed by an adjective is dehumanising. Is this true? Definite article plus adjective as a way of referring to groups of people is ordinary (and value-neutral) English usage, as we can see when we think of *the French* or *the Germans* – or indeed of *the gifted, the industrious, the smokers among you* – or *the men* and *the women*. Indeed, saying *the French* is recommended by some reformers as a good way of avoiding the sexism of *Frenchmen*. As for inserting *person* to show that you recognise the other as a human being, this seems to add to the reputation of *person* as a piece of reformer's clumsiness. Are socialists or Anglicans to become *persons who believe in socialism*, and *people who belong to the Anglican church …*?

The intention behind these exhortations to mind our language is of course wholly praiseworthy: to treat others as fully human, and not to demean them. But that intention has to be set against another criterion, which is knowing what an expression means. Such knowledge derives from the language community as a whole, not from a group who choose to feel offended – or flattered – by a usage which is not normally considered to be emotionally charged. Indeed, since feelings are so strong, and language is so complex, those who feel strongly about a usage are very likely to get things wrong, supporting their well-intentioned protest by offering a generalisation about language that is incorrect. I have, for instance, read a discussion of sensitivity in language that defended the use of *gay* because (it claimed) *homosexual* is a derogatory term. A doctor I once had asked all his patients if they were heterosexual or homosexual; although some patients may have resented being asked, as an intrusion on their privacy, I would be very surprised if any of them objected to the terminology.

An interesting borderline case here is *bourgeois*. Society can be divided (by a rather simple analysis) into the three classes of *aristocracy, bourgeoisie* and *proletariat*. The *bourgeoisie* (literally 'those from the towns') are the 'middle class' – merchants, manufacturers and possibly professional people. It is quite possible to use the word as a term of dispassionate social analysis. But it is often used to refer not just to a social class but to their values and way of life, and can easily come to mean 'stuffy', 'self-satisfied' – even 'sanctimonious'. So if one remarked that the WEA (the Workers' Educational Association) ought now to be called the Bourgeois Educational Association, since most of the students are now middle-class housewives or retired professionals, this could be intended as a neutral observation with no element of praise or blame. But it could be received as an offensive remark – made worse perhaps by the fact that the word sounds foreign! *Homosexual, bourgeois, handicapped, victim*: terms of classification, or insults? If the listener is quite free to decide whether a word is offensive or not, which of us shall escape whipping?

Questions of usage are not, of course, confined to single words, so I turn now to an expression which you may (or may not?) find objectionable: *women and children first*. Deborah Cameron claims that this is sexist because 'it belongs to a patriarchal discourse in which men are there to "protect" women and children – the women and children being by implication men's property, men's to control.' Such thinking belongs, of course, to a tradition of chivalry that goes back centuries. The belief that women are there to be protected is no doubt preferable to the belief that they are there to be bullied and exploited, and to that extent the feminist might regard chivalry as an improvement on what went before – but still needing to be improved on. We can, however, ask whether the expression is to be taken literally or more loosely. Its literal application is, of course, to a shipwreck or similar situation in which it may not be possible to save everyone's life, and in that situation it seems not so much chivalrous as biologically useful, since the group will survive best if we first rescue those most capable of producing the next generation. Most of us in modern Britain, however, do not expect to find ourselves in such an extreme situation, and we may therefore feel that *women and children first* is less a practical policy in an emergency than a looser expression of chivalrous sentiment that now belongs to the past.

Here is an even more controversial example. J. Penelope, writing about a scene in a television film called *The Billionaire Boys Club*, objects to its use of *consciousness-raising*. A young man in the film uses the term to describe his emotion on seeing his first dead body. Here is Penelope's objection to this usage: 'For us,' she writes, 'consciousness-raising was a profound, mind-altering experience that impelled us to change our lives', and she objects to the word being 'perverted' when used to describe 'a yuppy's shocked repulsion when he saw his first dead body.' Few of us, in our modern sanitised society, see dead bodies, and the shock of doing so (whether one is a rich young man or a poor old woman) may well be more deeply moving than Penelope seems to grant; but my concern here is not with the substance of what she is saying, but with her attempt to restrict a word (in this case *consciousness-raising*) to its original use. Suppose we compare it to the use of the word *conversion*. This was originally a religious term, referring to the turning of the sinner to God, or the turning of an unbeliever to a particular religion – its earliest use appears to have been for the conversion of Saint Paul. It later took on a wide range of other meanings, in logic, in mathematics and in astronomy, as well as the more recent meaning of any change of opinion (conversion to socialism, to capitalism, to democracy – even, perhaps jokingly, to a taste for wine or admiration for a film star). One can easily imagine a devout Christian objecting to this more frivolous use as a 'perversion' of what for them is an important concept, but they would have little chance of preventing it. Once a word has arrived, it belongs to the language, not to the group who first thought of using it.

Political correctness, as we have so far dealt with it, has a negative effect on language: it discourages certain usages. But it can also encourage other usages, as well as supporting actual changes in usage. A particularly interesting example is the replacement of *sex* by *gender*. The term *sex* (not in the sense 'sexual activity', but in the sense of the division into two sexes, male and female) belongs to biology. Now one of the hottest controversies which feminism has sparked off is that between biological and social explanations. Patriarchal authority, seeking to confine women within traditional 'feminine' roles, has always tended to support its arguments with appeals to biology. For instance, a contributor to the *Journal of the Anthropological Society* in 1869 claimed that 'there must be radical, natural permanent distinctions in the mental and moral conformation, corresponding with those in the physical organisation of the sexes', and that women are therefore 'incapable of receiving a training similar to that of men.' This expressed a view that was widely held throughout the nineteenth and early twentieth centuries, often by 'experts': the claim that too much study and intellectual activity would cause terrible physical damage to women. It was often put forward with all the authority of 'medical science'. It is understandable, then, that feminism has always tended to be suspicious of biological arguments, and has claimed that the traditional division into the roles of men and those of women is determined much more by society (and therefore changeable) and much less by biology (and therefore fixed). This battle is now more or less over, and has resulted in a victory for feminism: we now have female scientists, politicians and scholars in a way that was unimaginable two centuries ago, and it has not caused any of the terrible physical damage to women that 'medical science' predicted. Hence the preference today for sociological rather than biological explanations.

English vocabulary already possessed this important distinction: *male* and *female* are biological terms, *masculine* and *feminine* are social terms, *sex* is a biological concept, *gender* is a social concept. An enlightened feminist vocabulary could use (perhaps I should say 'could have used') this distinction to make us more conscious of what can and what can't be changed, by encouraging the use of *sex* when distinguishing 'male' from 'female' and *gender* when distinguishing 'masculine' from 'feminine'. But this has not happened. Most of us have filled in forms which asked whether our *gender* is *male* or *female*. An opportunity to mark a valuable distinction in everyday vocabulary has been lost, and in the new usage it is only animals, no longer humans, that are divided into two *sexes*. So the politically incorrect have yet another reform to complain of, and the new edition of Eric Partridge's *Usage and Abusage* places *gender* among the 'vogue words'.

Guidelines?

To be fair to the reformers of language I clearly ought to let them speak for themselves, so I have chosen as an example the guidelines put out by the Canadian Linguistic Association, a distinguished scholarly body from which we would expect reliable advice. Here are two of the guidelines from their website:

> *Avoid gender stereotyped or demeaning characterizations; e.g. presenting men as actors and women as passive recipients of others' actions. Men are frequently the agents, women the recipients, of violent acts. We recommend that the portrayal of violent acts be avoided altogether regardless of the sex or species of the participants.*

> *Avoid consistently putting reference to males before females. Not only does this order convey male precedence, in English and French it will put males in subject position and women in object position.*

I should say first that the guidelines include some good advice, such as to avoid using *he* or *man* 'except in unambiguous reference to males'; we have already discussed this. I should say too that I feel sympathetic to the anti-sexist aim of the guidelines as a whole. But what should we think of these two?

The first one seems to conclude with a recommendation that is not about language use at all, but about content; and seeing it standing naked as it does, I find it hard to know what it is saying. The exhortation to avoid *portrayal of violent acts* is defensible if rather old-fashioned if addressed to novelists, highly controversial if addressed to newspaper editors, and absurd if it concerns police reports.

The reasoning behind the second guideline is simply false, since it is quite easy to think up a sentence in which examples of an inferior category precede the superior ones: *There are a few good white footballers in the team, but none of them can match the brilliance of the all-black midfield group.* And it is not clear if *subject position* and *object position*, as used here, are grammatical or social terms; the grammatical subject need not be the one in a superior position (*The slaves were bullied by their masters*).

I can't resist quoting the oddest guideline of all, since its content is so interesting – and will probably seem tasteless to some readers. This is the one which reads: *Avoid sexist (or otherwise derogatory) content in examples (e.g. 'The man who beats his mistress will regret it sooner than the man who beats his wife' – slight revision of actual example).* I'd love to know what the actual example was before they 'revised' it – was it more or less sexist than their revision? Even more, I'd love to know whether the statement is true. The distinction between wife and mistress, like the term *mistress* itself, sounds rather old-fashioned now, but the sentence seems to be saying that it is in women's interest not to marry the man they are living with. If so, did the Linguistic Association object to the statement because it's true or because it isn't?

Why have I dwelt on this? Language is far more complicated and subtle than reformers, in their enthusiasm, always realise, so that the most well-meaning exhortations can be quite useless for reform purposes. Concern for the nature of language can be a cloak for male chauvinist prejudice; but it can also be quite genuine.

Why are verbal hygiene and political correctness resisted? It may be for political reasons, such as opposition to feminism or equality. This is not often explicit: there may be plenty of male chauvinists and racists in modern Britain, but they tend not to speak out in public, since their views are unfashionable, and widely disapproved of. So we are not often told directly that we should say *chairman* because the person presiding at a meeting ought to be a man, or *Everyone has a right to his own opinion* because it is right and natural to think of everyone with an opinion as male. The common reason for resisting these changes is that the proposed form is awkward, or inelegant. Finding a proposed form inelegant can no doubt be a way of avoiding the change itself, serving as a disguise for one's conservative opinions. I say this in the interests of honesty, since I have raised so many of the objections to proposed changes, and in the hope that I have not myself been guilty of the offence, either in what I have already written or in what follows.

That words have favourable or unfavourable connotations is of course unavoidable – words like *good, bad, nice* or *nasty* have little meaning except for their favourable or unfavourable connotations. For that reason they are unlikely to change much. But as our values and social attitudes change, the words that have a familiar meaning and also a favourable or unfavourable flavour are likely to reflect this change – but not in a straightforward way. As we can see if we compare what has happened to *aggressive* and to *dialogue*.

These two examples could have been discussed in 'On the Cusp of Change' in Chapter 3, but I have treated them here because these changes show something of the complexity of our political attitudes, and how they are changing. The basic meaning of *aggressive*, 'likely to make the first attack, hostile', or (with unfavourable associations) 'discourteously hostile', has not changed. What is new is its use with favourable associations: an advertisement in the Situations Vacant column of a newspaper is now likely to say *We are looking for someone with an aggressive attitude to selling* (or *expansion*, or *competition*). Similarly the basic meaning of *dialogue* has not changed: 'a conversation of a more or less formal kind between two or more people'. Probably its most frequent use is as a literary term, as when we distinguish between the *dialogue* and the *narration* in a novel. In recent years, however, it has been used more and more in a political context, as when we hope for *meaningful dialogue* between hostile groups, or speak of *Marxist-Christian dialogue*, and this usage almost always has favourable connotations. It seems odd that both *aggressive* and *dialogue* should have taken on a favourable association, since the two terms are in a sense opposites: if two hostile parties are engaged in dialogue, does that not mean that they are being less aggressive?

In a capitalist society, economic activity involves competition, and firms need to be aggressive. In a world where countries are closely involved with one another, war becomes more dangerous, and bystanders feel an ever-increasing desire to see it avoided. It should not surprise us, therefore, that in the modern complex world our vocabulary encourages us to favour being aggressive in one area of social life, and discourages us in another.

The ever-closer involvement of countries with one another has led to the idea of the *global village*, and has affected (or *impacted*? or *impacted on*? – see page 38) our vocabulary. Take, for instance, *ethnic*. The original meaning of this was 'heathen', and it was used to denote nations which were not Christian or Jewish – often, of course, with disapproval. With the rise of anthropology, the study of cultures very different from our own, it became something of a technical term (*ethnology* is more or less the same thing as anthropology). Perhaps the most visible element in a foreign culture, certainly in a non-European culture, is dress. As global contact has led to remote cultures becoming more visible, and as we have become less *ethnocentric* (less convinced that our own tribal customs are superior to all others), people are now more likely to wear *ethnic costume* or *ethnic jewellery*, to learn *ethnic dances*, even to cook *ethnic dishes*. Of course the clothes which the British wear every day, or everyday British customs, could be described by an Asian observer as *ethnically British*. But we are not very good at seeing ourselves as others see us, so to most people *ethnic* now means 'foreign' – in practice, 'very foreign', since ethnologists, until recently, studied only remote cultures. So whereas foreign food might have seemed distasteful to our grandparents, and African dances might have seemed barbarous to their parents, *ethnic cooking* and *ethnic dances* are now politically correct.

Irony

Another complication now – and one that takes us to a central feature of language. We do not always say what we mean. *Very clever*, we say to someone when we think their joke has fallen flat, or was too laboured. *Oh thank you*, we say when we feel insulted. *Very generous*, we say when someone has given too small a tip, or made too small an offer. The term for this is, of course, *irony*, and those simple examples were all from the spoken language; if we heard them, we would have no difficulty in realising, from the tone of voice, that the speaker means the opposite of what they have said. Here is an equally simple written example: *I posted the letter on Monday and it didn't arrive till Saturday – isn't our postal service wonderful?* And here is one that is rather more complicated: *No doubt the Creationists will find some way of refuting the geological evidence.* This is not a Creationist speaking, is it? The phrases *no doubt* and *will find some way* seem clearly to indicate that an outsider (possibly a scientist) is here writing about Creationism, and writing sceptically. And incidentally, it is important in this sentence to realise that *refuting* is being correctly used – that is, to mean 'finding valid arguments to disprove', not simply 'rejecting'. If instead of *refuting* the writer had used *rejecting*, the statement would be less ironic and probably less effective; if it had been '*disposing* of the geological evidence', it would be a slightly different form of irony, since *disposing* of could here carry either meaning.

All these examples can be seen as ironic if we just look at them, or hear them. Very often, however, we need to know the context in order to recognise irony. Context can include tone of voice in a spoken utterance, and knowledge about the author, or what is said elsewhere in the book, in the case of something written. Irony is sometimes very easy and sometimes very difficult to recognise.

An anthropologist, asked what an anthropologist is, replies *Oh, it's just a fashionable name for nosy parker.* (*Nosy parker*, now rather old-fashioned, is slang for someone who is inquisitive about things he ought to leave alone; it is said to derive from someone who spied on courting couples in the park.) By using the term here, and by adding the word *just*, the speaker suggests that anthropology is nothing more than vulgar curiosity pretending to be a science (*fashionable* adds a further touch of mockery). There is obviously some truth in this: anthropologists systematically study customs that are often regarded as private, such as courtship. If the sentence were spoken by an outsider, especially a rather cynical outsider, it might be meant straight, that is, without irony. But the speaker was herself an anthropologist, and it is difficult to believe that she can have been quite so cynical about her profession. We can safely assume that the remark is ironic, but how ironic? Is the speaker a passionate believer in her discipline, pretending to be dismissive, or using irony to express some of her own uncertainties? To answer this we'd have to know a good deal about the situation – and about the speaker. Spoken irony of this kind can be recognised, but will contain subtleties which it's difficult for the outsider to be sure about.

Irony is everywhere, and in tightly coherent groups it is impossible to eradicate. A friend of mine worked one summer in the local vegetable market and, describing the situation to me, he remarked that social intercourse there was based entirely on insults. I'm sure a lot of them were politically incorrect insults. This showed that the stall-keepers were relaxed in the way they spoke to one another, though it is not impossible that there were rivalries and tensions also being expressed. Any study of language and its uses must concern itself with irony; my reason for discussing it in this chapter is that its interaction with questions of political correctness can be tense and complicated. It is so easy to defend insults or politically incorrect remarks by claiming that they were 'just ironic' that we clearly need to ask ourselves how we recognise irony. Almost anything that can be said straight can also be said ironically, and many an ironic remark may be heard as straight. Let us look at a few examples.

African-Americans sometimes call one another *nigger*. Clearly what they are doing is appropriating an offensive term and using it as a mark of solidarity among themselves. This strategy is not unknown among oppressed or insulted groups. The early followers of George Fox were contemptuously called *Quakers* after a magistrate mocked Fox for telling him to tremble at the name of the Lord; the name caught on, and after a while the Friends began to call themselves Quakers. As long as they were consciously copying what they realised was an insult, they were being ironic; but now, of course, it has become an accepted alternative name for the Society of Friends. Will the same happen to the word *nigger*? Will its ironic use as a term of comradeship among black Americans become more and more widespread until it begins to lose its irony and turns into a normal term? This seems unlikely, since the word would have to lose its offensive quality for this to happen; but very unlikely things have happened in language, and it is always rash to predict.

Now suppose it was a white man who called a black man a *nigger*. Traditionally this would of course be a simple example of racist language, but suppose the two men were friends and were used to making jokes at each other's expense. The black man might say in reply something like *So the slave-owner's blood still runs in your veins!* It could be very difficult for an outsider to judge the exact shade of irony in a conversation like this. The better the two know each other, and the firmer their friendship, the more confident they can be of maintaining the ironic tone; but they are skating on thin ice, and we can be sure that if the conversation does go wrong, and the black man is offended, it will not sound very convincing for the white man to claim *I was just being ironic*. Since irony relies on <u>not</u> saying what you really mean, its effect is ruined when we have to say explicitly *That was ironic.*

Let's take a more complex example. Two wealthy and powerful young men are talking, and one says *But that's like woman's reasoning – you can't mean it*. The other smiles and says *I didn't know you were a male chauvinist pig, John*. Which of them (or both, or neither) is being ironic? It's not easy – it may not be possible – to answer that without knowing a good deal about the situation, and about the two men. We'd want to know if the first – or the second – was smiling as he spoke, if anyone else was present (and if so, whether it was a man or a woman), and above all we'd want to hear them, since intonation is one of the commonest ways of indicating irony in the spoken language. And we'd want to know something of the background: perhaps they have taken part in other conversations in which one of them has been accused – or has accused someone else – of male chauvinism. We might well decide that only those in the know can be certain of the mixture of irony and sincerity; we might even decide that the mixture of irony and sincerity is so subtle that they themselves are not sure about it.

Should we be surprised that such a simple sentence can grow so complicated when we examine it? (Indeed, we could probably un-cover even more complications if we probed further.) My answer is 'No': there is nothing surprising about finding such depths of am-biguity in everyday speech, for colloquial language in emotionally charged situations is perhaps the most subtle and complex that lan-guage can get – no wonder it fascinates novelists. That is why irony is such a pitfall for the language reformer. The simple instruction that we should avoid certain terms because they are offensive takes no account of irony. But the easy defence, that every time you use an offensive term you can get out of trouble by claiming that you were being ironic, is (like all easy solutions) often unconvincing. This does not, of course, mean that language reform is impossible, but it does mean that it is often trickier than the reformer realises.

We have looked at the problems irony can cause for the politi-cally correct, since this chapter is, after all, about political correct-ness; but it would be wrong to leave the matter there. I now want to say a few words in praise of irony; for it is one of the great joys of language, and the problems it causes are the consequence of the rich-ness and subtlety that it offers us. Here is a recent example that is so neatly topical that it makes me wince. In his *Online Dictionary*, Andy Ihnatko defines the *real world* – that is, the world outside the virtual reality of cyberspeak – as 'that which cannot be accessed via a key-board. A nice place to visit, and a good place to swing by when you're out of Coke, but you wouldn't want to live there.' We could spend a long paragraph unpacking what this is saying: the *real world*, which for most of human history has included everything we experience, is now defined negatively as what's left over when one's not sitting at one's computer. We're told we 'wouldn't want to live' precisely where we do live; this asks us to reflect on what we mean by *living*. It's not easy to decide just how ironic Ihnatko is being here, and just how uneasily we're meant to smile when we read it. Despite (or perhaps because of) its relaxed colloquial style, this sentence is very delicately written.

But simply because of this delicacy, irony can be dangerous. When the danger of hijacking first caused screening of air travellers to be introduced, notices were placed at the screening barriers saying *NO JOKES*, and warning passengers that anything they said would be taken seriously. This is very revealing. It tells us that in tense situations we tend to resort to irony (no doubt lots of people had been saying things like *You'll find the bomb in my left-hand pocket*), but that if the situation is really urgent, we abandon irony. You never hear such remarks now.

Here is an example where not the speaker but the author is being ironic. When Mr Collins, the pompous and self-satisfied clergyman in *Pride and Prejudice*, proposes to Elizabeth Bennett, she refuses him. This does not discourage him, since, as he explains to her, 'it is usual for young ladies to reject the addresses of the man whom they secretly mean to accept, when he first applies for their favour', and he therefore assures her that he is 'by no means discouraged by what you have just said, and shall hope to lead you to the altar ere long.' Elizabeth is taken aback by this, and repeats her refusal more emphatically, whereupon he assures her just as emphatically that 'I know it to be the established custom of your sex to reject a man on the first application, and perhaps you have already said as much to encourage my suit as would be consistent with the true delicacy of the female character.' Mr Collins has probably never used the word *irony* in his life, and perhaps never uttered an ironic remark; and it is this very naivety which makes him so comic when he accuses Elizabeth of not saying what she means, since he is in effect accusing her of being ironic. In a rather broader sense of the term it is of course Austen who is being ironic here, but her irony does not take the form of a particular remark: it resides in the way she presents the whole situation. And in this situation what possible answer can Elizabeth make, except to insist that she does mean it? She did not, of course, know the slogan that feminists scrawled on walls two hundred years later: *Whatever we say, wherever we go, yes means yes, and no means no.* But if she had, she would surely have been tempted to quote it.

It is, of course, no accident that this couplet deals with sex, since

192

there is perhaps no situation in which the possibilities of irony are richer, and its dangers greater. The couplet is in fact saying 'We're not being ironic: we mean what we say', and it assumes a situation more urgent than Elizabeth's – that of being raped, not just of receiving an unwanted proposal. Since date rape is an all-too-common reality, and is often justified with the argument that 'she really wanted it, though she said No', I cannot help sympathising with that couplet; but on the other hand, a sexual situation is one in which, very often, not everything is said which is meant. That this can lead to the temptation to interpret 'No' ironically is illustrated by the folk song 'Oh, no John', in which the girl is told by her father, or her absent husband (there are many different versions) to say 'No' to any seducer. She does so, but in the end she yields, still saying 'No, John, no' – either sighing it out ironically, or singing it in response to a question like *Can you resist me any longer?* – in which case of course the irony belongs not to her but to the song. The political incorrectness of this song is so striking that I asked a keen folk singer whether she or her friends had any qualms about singing it. I was told that folk singers love political incorrectness, singing songs about seduction and about wife-beating with great gusto, and groaning if told that they shouldn't.

What then is the relation between what we sing and what we do, between the way we represent life, and the way we live it? On the one hand, there would be no songs about wife-beating if wives had never been beaten; there would be no song about 'No, John, no' if women in sexual situations always said exactly what they meant. Jokes, songs and stories grow out of life, not out of pure fancy. But on the other hand those who sing songs about wife-beating almost certainly do not beat their wives today. Both extreme positions – that the way we speak (or sing) about delicate situations has nothing to do with real life, or that it merely echoes real life – are oversimplifications.

This forces me to end the discussion of irony in a thoroughly unsatisfactory way. To assert that every joke, every ironic remark, every song must be judged morally and politically and condemned if it offends anyone is the extreme of dogmatism. To claim, on the other hand, that we can say what we like as long as we add that it was 'only a joke' or 'meant ironically' is the extreme of licence. In between is the difficult, complex, unsatisfactory position we all have to work out for ourselves. As complex and unsatisfactory as life.

Legislation cannot deal with irony. Social situations cannot banish it. Language reformers cannot deal with it in their rules. Offenders will often use it as an excuse. This does not mean that language reform should be abandoned, but it does mean that it's not easy. And the more sensitivity to the presence of irony the reformer shows, the better chance that the reform will succeed.

The Past

So tricky can it be to handle the issues raised by verbal hygiene in the world we live in, that to worry about the world that has passed away may seem to be looking for unnecessary trouble. But language belongs to the past as well as to the present. We inherit the language from those who went before us, and will pass it on to our descendants: language is meaningless except as a tradition handed on. Every sentence we utter depends on what the language has been as well as what it now is. This is true of all speech, and especially noticeable when we quote. Asked what we mean by democracy, we often say it is *the government of the people, by the people, for the people*; asked for our moral principles, we might say *an eye for an eye, a tooth for a tooth*; or, with a different morality, *love your enemies*; asked about the individual and society, we might say that *no man is an island*. We may forget, perhaps even not know, that we are quoting (Abraham Lincoln, the Old Testament, the New Testament and John Donne, in these four cases). Told (or reminded) of the fact, we would probably feel strengthened in our view, recognising that there is a long tradition behind our beliefs.

But do we want to say *no man is an island*? Shouldn't it be *no person* or *no man or woman* or *nobody*? There are plenty of other ways of putting it, ways we might prefer. But John Donne wrote (understandably in 1624) 'No man'. If we want to quote him, if we want to show that this admirable sense of social solidarity has been with us for hundreds of years, we can't pretend that he said something different. We can change it, of course, and add a remark like *as he would no doubt say nowadays*, but that is a slippery path to venture on. This is what Donne wrote (in his *Devotions Upon Emergent Occasions*):

No man is an island, entire of itself; every man is a piece of the continent, a part of the main; if a clod be washed away by the sea, Europe is the less, as well as if a promontory were, as well as if a manor of thy friends or of thine own were; any man's death diminishes me, because I am involved in mankind; and therefore never send to know for whom the bell tolls; it tolls for thee.

That is, I must confess, not exactly what Donne wrote: I have modernised the spelling, to make it seem less remote and more accessible. That seems a fairly uncontroversial change, not very different from printing a modern edition in a nice clear typeface. But *No man or woman is an island*? That is a different kind of change, surely, since it changes the content of what he wrote. Suppose an Indian reader were to complain that Donne is being Eurocentric: Asia is also the less if a clod is washed away. Suppose a modern radical were to remark that there are class assumptions in the writing: it seems to assume that we move in circles which own manor houses, and perhaps also have servants – 'send to know for whom the bell tolls' probably means 'send your servant'. And even if we confine ourselves to removing the sexism, are we going to change *mankind* as well – to *humanity*? to *all humanity*? to *all men and all women*? There are so many ways we could rewrite it. We could, of course, add a disclaimer: we could say *I'm sure if Donne were alive today he'd have said 'no human being' rather than 'no man.'* But what would it mean to make this claim? Everything Donne wrote is the work of a man who lived from 1572 to 1631. *If he were alive today* is, when we think about it, an odd thing to say: who is *he*? What elements in his writings do we decide to apologise for? His theology? His belief in Hell and damnation? His old-fashioned astronomy?

I once heard a distinguished professor of the Hebrew Bible (it is no longer called the Old Testament in academic circles) reading from the Psalms during a discussion; the passage sounded slightly odd, and I realised that instead of saying *Sing unto God, sing praises to his name*, he was saying 'sing praises to God's name', not using the word *his*. Since I know no Hebrew, I asked if there were no personal pronouns in Hebrew; he explained that he was saying *God's* instead of *his* in order to avoid the assumption that God must be thought of as male.

Is that verbal hygiene? I think it more accurate to say that he was mistranslating. To think of God as male is, arguably, wrong in the twenty-first century: I think it is, though many traditional Christians do not. But to pretend that God is not spoken of as male in the Old Testament is, quite simply, to mislead. The aim of professors of Hebrew, as of all scholars, is to tell us the truth.

What we write is what we write. Others can struggle with it, interpret it, be inspired by it, regret parts of it, find ways of explaining it, even of explaining it away. But the one thing they must not do is pretend that we wrote something different. To cut ourselves off from the past, by never quoting, never drawing on tradition, is to be less than human; to rewrite the past is to lie; to struggle to use the past honestly, wrestling with what has changed and what has stayed the same, is to be human.

The Power of Language

How much does linguistic hygiene matter? We have touched on this, but perhaps a fuller discussion would be helpful. It is parallel to the question of how much politeness (or manners, or courtesy?) matters. There is on the one hand the view summed up in the old rhyme 'Sticks and stones may break my bones, but names will never hurt me': the view that it is no doubt desirable to talk in a non-hostile way, but it does not really matter very much compared with what we actually do. Against this is the view that language is itself dangerous because it influences our thoughts and, through them, our actions: that we should not dismiss 'unhygienic' language as trivial, because it is a symptom – even a cause – of what we actually do. Let us call the first the 'sticks-and-stones view', and the second the view that 'language is power'. Which is the truer view?

If we are looking for moral advice, rather than truth, the answer is easy. We should hold the sticks-and-stones view when we are the offended party, and the case concerns the language used by others towards us; and the language-is-power view when we are ourselves speaking, and the case concerns the feelings of others. On a practical level, the argument could stop there, but I will indulge in a little theorising before leaving the subject – or rather, allow George Orwell to do a little theorising. The most famous – and frightening – modern view that language is indeed very powerful is George Orwell's account of 'Newspeak'.

Newspeak is the name he gives to the form of English that has become the official language of the totalitarian state in his very influential novel about the future, *Nineteen Eighty-Four*. In the frightening totalitarian society that Orwell imagines, Newspeak is the main instrument of thought control:

> *It was intended that when Newspeak had been adopted once and for all, and Oldspeak forgotten, a heretical thought – that is, a thought diverging from the principles of Ingsoc – should be literally unthinkable, at least so far as thought is dependent on words … To give a single example. The word* free *still existed in Newspeak, but it could only be used in such statements as* 'This dog is free from lice' *or* 'This field is free from weeds'. *It could not be used in its old sense of* 'politically free' *or* 'intellectually free', *since political and intellectual freedom no longer existed even as concepts and were therefore of necessity nameless.*

The state that Orwell imagines can see into your home (by two-way television) and can spy on everything you do; most frightening, according to Orwell's view, is that it controls language itself, and thus thought. *Nineteen Eighty-Four* is of course a nightmare rather than a matter-of-fact prophecy, but the danger of Newspeak seems to be presented to us quite seriously, and so I would like to offer some reassurance. Orwell's account of spying and torture is certainly frightening, but the account of how language controls the inhabitants is so implausible that it is nothing to be frightened of. The crucial ambiguity in the account of Newspeak is whether the state controls language by direct exercise of power, or whether it has discovered some linguistic means of control. The first of these is nothing new: forbidding people to use certain words and expressions is always possible, and indeed is very old. (In the Old Testament it is forbidden to utter the name of God, and hence he is usually referred to as Adonai, the Lord.) Laws to forbid blasphemy, and customs that forbid obscenity, have always been with us, although they have never been completely successful and are perhaps weaker today than they have ever been. As we saw in the discussion of register, such linguistic prohibitions have usually resulted in the forbidden words leading a vigorous underground life. There are even examples of entire languages being forbidden: in South Africa after the Boer War, Afrikaner children were sometimes forbidden to speak Afrikaans in school or even in the playground; there are similar tales of the treatment of Welsh children, or of Catalan children in Fascist Spain. If these prohibitions had any effect, it was probably to encourage the spread of the language. Whether the state in *Nineteen Eighty-Four* would be so much more efficient that it could catch and punish anyone who used the word *free* to mean 'intellectually free' is not a linguistic question at all, but a question of how effective we think state power can ever be.

Orwell then adds what can be seen as a genuinely linguistic point, the claim that a heretical thought would be 'literally unthinkable', but on this he is so vague that it is difficult to know just what thought processes he has in mind. It is certainly not true that we are unable to think thoughts unless the words for them are already available: if it were, there could be no new ideas. Orwell probably had something like this in mind when he added the clause that destroys his whole argument, 'at least so far as thought is dependent on words.' To this we have to say that thought is not, in that way, dependent on words. Darwin invented the idea of natural selection, Saussure the idea of language as a system of differences, and Einstein the idea of general and special relativity – ideas that in a very real sense did not previously exist, and the terms for which did not exist either. That did not prevent these thinkers inventing the ideas, and once this had been done they simply had to combine existing words, or give them new meanings, or invent a new word.

Language is powerful, but not, fortunately, as powerful as that.

CHAPTER TEN

Our Two Vocabularies

This chapter begins with an example; the theory will come later. So let's begin by reading these two passages.

When midway through the shadow, his rudder swished up sickle-shaped, slanting his body. His hindlegs touched stones, he sprang. The scales of the two fish coming straight towards him in the darkness reflected only the darkness, but he had seen a hair of faintest light where the ream of a back-fin had cut the surface and glimmered with the moon-frosted slide. His teeth tore the tail of the leading fish, which escaped – his rudder lashed for another turn, his body screwed through the water, and struck upwards with teeth into the mullet's gorge. Tarka swam into moonlight and dragged the five-pound fish (despite its beats and flaps) on to a shillet heap under the spillway of the slide. He gripped it with his paws and stood over it and started to eat it, while its gills opened and closed, and it tried feebly to flap.

In the second century of the Christian era, the Empire of Rome comprehended the fairest part of the earth, and the most civilised portion of mankind. The frontiers of that extensive monarchy were guarded by ancient renown and disciplined valour. The gentle but powerful influence of laws and manners had gradually cemented the union of the provinces. Their peaceful inhabitants enjoyed and abused the advantages of wealth and luxury. The image of a free constitution was preserved with decent reverence; the Roman senate appeared to possess the sovereign authority, and devolved on the emperors all the executive powers of government. During a happy period, AD 98–180, of more than fourscore years, the public administration was conducted by the virtue and abilities of Nerva, Trajan, Hadrian and the two Antonines. It is the design of this, and of the two succeeding chapters, to describe the most important circumstances of its decline, and fall; a revolution which will ever be remembered, and is still felt by the nations of the earth.

The passages are of course about quite different subjects: the first is from the life story of an otter, and the second is from a history of the Roman Empire. They were also written at very different times. *Tarka the Otter*, by Henry Williamson, was published in 1927; *The Decline and Fall of the Roman Empire*, by Edward Gibbon, was published between 1776 and 1788. I have not quoted them in order to discuss the lives of otters or Roman history, but to draw your attention to their style. For I hope you were struck by the huge contrast between the way they use the language, and in particular by their choice of words. Why do they feel so different? It is not just a matter of the difference in subject matter, though that is important. You would not expect to find words like *comprehended, civilised, monarchy, abused* or *administration* in *Tarka the Otter*; or words like *sickle-shaped, hindlegs, slide, screwed* or *upwards* in Gibbon's historical study. What is the difference between these two kinds of word? It is not a grammatical difference, since both lists contain nouns and verbs and adjectives. It is not just the difference between familiar and unfamiliar words, since both lists contain both kinds. But it is a very important difference, which most English speakers are more or less conscious of, though they may not be able to explain what it is. In order to understand it, we'll need a bit of history.

A Spot of History

If we compare *one, two, three* with the German *eins, zwei, drei* or the Dutch *een, twee, drie*; if we compare English *milk* with German *Milch* and Swedish *mjolk*, and notice that *hand* is the same in English, German and Swedish; and then look at Latin *unus, duo, tres* or French *un, deux, trois* or at Latin *lac* and Italian *latte*, Latin *manus* and Italian *mano*, several things become clear. It is obvious that English resembles Dutch, German, and the Scandinavian languages quite closely, but is very different from Latin and the languages that derive from it (French, Italian, Spanish, Portuguese) – and it is even more different from Greek, Russian, Irish or Hindi. Yet all these were once the same language, spoken at least four or five thousand years ago, possibly in central Asia, which split up as different groups of its speakers migrated and lost contact with each other. For since languages are always changing, two groups that lose contact with each other – though they may originally have spoken the same language – will begin to speak differently; and eventually they won't be able to understand each other. So English, Dutch, German and the Scandinavian languages (which we can call the Germanic languages) must have been the same fairly recently – about two thousand years ago; and Latin began to split up into French, Italian and the other neo-Latin languages at about the same time. But the time when these two groups were the same as each other was much longer ago – and fixing a date for that is much more speculative. So we can think of German, Dutch and Danish as our sister languages, and French, Spanish or Portuguese as our cousins. As for Russian or Hindi, they are more distant cousins, and it was only through the work of nineteenth-century scholars that it was discovered that they too belong to the same family.

So when the Danes invaded England in the eighth and ninth centuries they spoke a language that was already quite different from English, but it is likely that if they listened to each other carefully they were able to communicate. Today Danish and German and Dutch have got further away from English – and from each other – but if we look carefully at the words we can still see the family resemblance. The famous last words of Goethe, for instance, 'Mehr Licht' (meaning 'more light'), sound the same in Scots as in German.

Nobody understands fully why languages change; we saw in an earlier chapter how English won't keep still, partly because the world is changing, but also because there seem to be processes of change within language. Sounds change, meanings change, and languages take words from other languages. This is usually called borrowing (though the 'borrowed' words are never given back!), and English over the centuries has probably been the greatest borrower of all.

When Britain was a Roman colony – from the first to the fifth century – the official language of the country was Latin, but most of the inhabitants spoke a Celtic language. Then, at about the same time as the Romans withdrew, a new set of invaders arrived, whom we usually call the Anglo-Saxons. The language they spoke was the ancestor of modern English. As they conquered the country, the Celtic language was driven into the western and northern fringes of the island, and became Welsh, Cornish and Gaelic. Cornish as a native language has now died out, but some of the Welsh (mainly in North Wales) and some of the Highland and island Scots still speak a Celtic language. Oddly enough, English took hardly any words from these languages; evidently the conquerors borrow much less from the conquered than vice versa. There are a few Celtic words in English, but they were taken in much later.

Once the Anglo-Saxons were settled in England, however, the story is very different. They had already taken in a few Latin words (probably from traders when they were still in continental Europe) like *wine, cheese, copper, pound* and *inch*, and they learned a few more from the Romanised people of the towns in Britain. The most prominent of these was the word for a town itself, *castra* (which originally meant a military camp in Latin); it is well known that any English towns which incorporate this word in their name (*Winchester, Manchester, Lancaster*, and of course *Chester*) were once Roman towns. The few English words deriving from Latin did not mark out the English of the sixth or seventh centuries as being very different from other Germanic tongues, but after that the borrowings began in earnest. First came the Danish invasion. After the Vikings had burnt and pillaged large parts of England they eventually settled in the north-east, which became known as the Danelaw. Hostilities finally ceased. Indeed, one or two English kings (most famously Knut or Canute) were actually Danish. As a result, English is full of words taken from Danish – *fellow, husband, law, root, skill, window, wing* and many other everyday terms; place names ending in -*by* or -*thorp*; and (most strikingly) the pronouns *they* and *them*. Languages usually take foreign words for new substances or customs acquired from the foreign nation, but they seldom change the words we think of as the core of the language. So the fact that the Old English *hi* was replaced by the Scandinavian *they* is a sign of how close the contacts between the two peoples must have been.

Then, and even more important than the Danish invasion, came the Norman conquest of 1066. The Normans were actually a Scandinavian people in origin but they spoke French, and for several centuries after the conquest French was the official language of England, spoken at court, and used in religion and law. English kings and most of the nobles spoke French as their mother tongue for the next three or four hundred years, and though English eventually reasserted itself, it was deeply marked by French. The most famous example of this marking owes its fame to Walter Scott's account of it in *Ivanhoe*: that the names of domestic animals when they are alive are Anglo-Saxon (*ox, cow, calf, sheep, swine, boar, deer*), but when they appear on the table they are French (*beef, veal, mutton, pork, bacon, venison*). It was English-speaking labourers who looked after the animals when alive, but their French masters who sat down to enjoy them at dinner. The *government* of the *nation, politics, legal questions,* the *noble class* of *dukes, duchesses, viscounts* and *barons, feudal customs* and *values* such as *chivalry, honour* and *glory, heraldry,* the *administration* of *justice,* the *courts, judges* and *juries, plaintiffs* and *defendants, crimes* and their *penalties* – all that was in the hands of French speakers, and every noun in that list is derived from French.

A Twofold Vocabulary

The result of this colourful history is that the vocabulary of English is of two kinds: Anglo-Saxon (I'll call it Saxon, for simplicity) and Latinate. Almost all our short ordinary words are Saxon: the common verbs, *be, go, come, do, walk, run, sit, stand, eat, sleep, lay, lie, can, may, must, fall, rise, sleep, wake,* etc; the names of everyday foods, *bread, milk, meat, fish,* etc; the common adjectives, *good, bad, big, small, high, low,* etc; the pronouns (except, as mentioned, *they* and *them*); most of the nouns that denote everyday objects, *stool, house, water, fire, wood, coal, tree, plant, stone, grass* and hundreds more. Learned words, however – scientific terms, abstract nouns, words associated with thought rather than with the physical world – are far more likely to be Latinate (and in the case of scientific terms, we should add Greek). There is no other European language, perhaps no other language in the world, which draws its vocabulary so thoroughly from two different sources.

Furthermore, the two sources overlap, as we often have both a Saxon and a Latinate term with much the same meaning. When that happens, the Saxon term usually sounds simple, concrete and everyday, and the Latinate term abstract, learned and theoretical. Even those who know nothing of the history of the language can usually feel this difference. Compare *height* and *altitude*, *fatherly* and *paternal*, *lovely* and *beautiful*, *neat* and *orderly* – in each case, the Saxon term, which comes first, is the more homely. Or consider the difference between *go, quit,* and *leave* on the one hand (all Saxon) and Latinate *depart*; between *come* and *arrive*, between *awkward* and *embarrassing*, between *think* and its Latinate equivalents *consider, cogitate* or *reflect*. Sometimes a clear difference in meaning has developed, as between *library* and *bookshop*. Quite as often the meaning is more or less the same, but the flavour or the context is different. *Diurnal events* are much the same as *daily happenings*, but sound much more official; *aquatic* means more or less the same as *watery*, but is more likely to be the term used in a scientific context.

English, then, has a duplication of its vocabulary; and as this is a rather abstract idea, we cannot easily say it without using Latinate words. We can replace the Latinate *double* with *twofold*, but there is no word *twofolding*, so we have to say *duplication*. And for *vocabulary* itself, the only Saxon word is the rather attractive but quite obsolete *word-hoard*.

And there is a further complication. Since French derives from Latin, there are two ways in which a Latin word can enter English: directly, or via French. Words taken from early contact with the Romans, words taken from church liturgies, and words brought into the language by scholars, usually come direct from Latin. Words used during the time when England was a bilingual country naturally come from French. Sometimes the same word followed both routes, so that we have such pairs as *dainty* and *dignity*, *double* and *duplicate*, *chamber* and *camera*, *count* and *compute*, *machinery* and *machinations*, *sure* and *secure*, where the first comes from French, and the second direct from Latin.

Here are some examples of a set of three words with more or less the same meaning: *ask, question, interrogate; rise, mount, ascend; take, capture, captivate.* In each case the first word, which is Saxon, is the most ordinary and the most frequently used; the second, which comes from French, is more formal but still an everyday word; and the third, which comes direct from Latin, and entered our language rather later, is the most formal and the furthest from everyday speech. But if we look at *quack, doctor, physician*, we can see that the Saxon word can take on a colloquial and (in this case) slightly mocking meaning, so that the term from French (*doctor*) has become the usual one.

And now of course we have the answer to our opening question about the difference between the style of *Tarka the Otter* and the style of *The Decline and Fall of the Roman Empire*: the former uses overwhelmingly Saxon words, while the latter uses lots of Latinate words. I chose the passages as representing the two extremes. Telling a story is usually more matter-of-fact than discussing a historical situation, physical movements are more matter-of-fact than ideas and generalisations, and the story of an animal will obviously contain much less in the way of thoughts than a story about human beings. So I chose *Tarka the Otter*, with its wonderful awareness of sights, sounds, smells and physical movements, as likely to represent the extreme point of Anglo-Saxon vocabulary. Gibbon is famous for his orotund, abstract and ponderous style, with long sentences and lots of abstract nouns (could one describe his style without using Latinate words like *orotund* and *ponderous*?), so I chose the second passage as likely to represent the extreme of the Latinate. To check that I had chosen well I did a word count on the two passages, and my conclusion (you might like to amuse yourself by checking it for accuracy) is that in *Tarka the Otter* six per cent of the words are Latinate, and in the Gibbon 45 per cent are Latinate. (I counted word-events, not word-types: if the same word occurs twice, I counted it twice, since that gives a truer picture of frequency.)

You will have noticed that even in the Gibbon, the score for Latinate words is less than half. This is because it is impossible to write English without frequent use of determiners (*a, the, that*), of conjunctions (*and, but, when*), of prepositions (*of, with, on, by*) and of the most common verbs, especially the verb *to be*. These are virtually all Saxon, and they occur frequently. (If I had counted word-types only, ignoring reappearances of the same word, Gibbon's score would have risen to 63 per cent.)

Now I have to admit that if we look carefully at the twofold nature of our vocabulary we could claim that 'twofold' is an oversimplification. I have already observed that there is a good deal of Scandinavian vocabulary in English, taken from the Danes who invaded and settled in the north-east part of the country; and in my count I included the Danish vocabulary along with the Saxon. Most of our Danish words have been so completely absorbed into English, and were so similar in the first place, that *bread, window,* and *husband* – along with many others – feel very like native Saxon words. The sentence '*They* both had the *same dream*: that *their sister* had *died*' contains no Latinate words, and sounds very like native Saxon, but the italicised words are all from Danish. As for our Latinate vocabulary, it is of course made up not only of words taken from French during the centuries after the Norman conquest, but of learned words taken directly from Latin in the sixteenth century, and later musical and artistic terms taken largely from Italian; and – the one factor that really undermines our twofold distinction – of words taken from Latin <u>before</u> the Norman conquest, which often sound completely English to us. 'There is a *dish* of *plums* in the *kitchen*, and a *cup* of *wine* I would walk a *mile* for' looks at first glance like a sentence of Saxon words, but in fact all the italicised words are from Latin, all taken very early into our language. Then there is the question of Greek words; modern science has taken far more of its special vocabulary from Greek than from Latin, so that a good deal of very modern-sounding vocabulary is made up of Greek roots. '*Heterosexuals* study *biochemistry* under *neon*, but the *metabolism* of *palaeolithic arthropods* was *autoerotic* if not *genetic*' that is a more or less nonsensical sentence with plenty of scientific words, and all the nouns and adjectives in it derive from Greek. Most of our Greek vocabulary has remained within the domain of science, but there are exceptions. An interesting one is *mega*.

Mega comes from the Greek word for 'big'. It came to be widely used in scientific terms in the course of the nineteenth century. Not many of these terms entered ordinary language, but some did: a *megaphone* magnifies sound, a *megalomaniac* has too great an opinion of himself, and a *megalosaurus* (or 'big lizard') is a kind of dinosaur. Notice, incidentally, that *magnify*, being quite an ordinary word, uses the Latin not the Greek word for 'big'; we don't often use Greek roots for everyday words. Then *mega* began to develop a more specific meaning: a *megawatt* is not just a large number of watts, it means 'a million watts', in contrast to a *kilowatt*, a thousand watts. *Kilo* comes from the Greek word for 'thousand', and, since scientists often need to measure large units, the contrast between *kilo* and *mega* (a thousand times and a million) has proved very useful: we have *kilobytes* and *megabytes, kilocycles* and *megacycles.* As long as such prefixes stay in the realm of technical language they have little wider interest. But while *kilo* has on the whole stayed there (except for our habit of using *k* to refer to salaries or other large sums of money, as in *50k*), *mega* has not. Almost anything can now be *mega* if we want to emphasise how large it is, or even, in a looser use, how good it is. I was told by a helpful clerk in the booking office that if I bought my train ticket before 9.30 it would cost *megabucks.* She could have said it would cost *a fortune*; but the combination of Greek and American seemed to her the best way to say that it was a very large fortune.

It's an oversimplification, then, to say that English has a twofold vocabulary; but only a slight one. Most words of Scandinavian origin sound much like Saxon words, and Greek words usually sound like a more extreme version of Latinate words, so I think we can continue to think of English vocabulary as twofold. This almost systematic doubling is probably the most important single fact about English vocabulary.

You may feel that my contrast between the Gibbon and the Williamson passages built a lot on only one example, and you may feel too that we need more modern examples. So here are two more passages, to act as a check (a bit shorter, but of course I cannot make them too short, or it would not be meaningful to calculate the percentages).

They were not exactly a family, the two women and their children, who were both in the same class at the William Blake Primary School. They had come together for convenience, after Frederica's flight from her husband and hard-fought divorce. Both were highfliers, although Agatha was the most obviously successful, rising fast in the hierarchy of the Civil Service, a woman with a solid place in the world, a secretary, a telephone, colleagues, an office. Her private life was secret.

It is a truism that historical writing is itself culturally determined, reflecting intellectual fashions, political preoccupations, and moral values at the time it is written. In the case of British history, this has resulted in a great diversity of perspectives both on the content of what is narrated and on the geopolitical framework in which it is placed. In recent times, the process of redefinition has accelerated under the pressure of contemporary change.

Both these passages were written in the last four years. The first is from A. S. Byatt's novel *A Whistling Woman*; the second is from the General Editor's Preface to a volume of the *Short Oxford History of the British Isles*. We would expect a modern novel about sophisticated people to use more Latinate words than a story about an otter, but less than a discussion of how to write history; and we would expect that discussion, if written in the twenty-first century, to be rather less Latinate than the highly oratorical style of Gibbon, writing about the ancient Romans. And sure enough, this is what we find. The Byatt novel scores at 27 per cent, and the Preface at 37 per cent. I suspect that *Tarka the Otter* (at six per cent, you will remember) has a lower score than any other book in the language – or can you find a lower one?

The contrast between Latinate and Saxon vocabulary is a simple opposition; but actual situations soon grow complicated. Take, for example, the question of whether or not you eat meat. We have biological terms for this, *carnivore* and *herbivore*, both Latinate; *carnivore* simply means 'meat-eater' (*carnal* meaning 'fleshy' and *-vore* as in *voracious* or *devour*). In everyday speech we say *vegetarian* (also Latinate) rather than *herbivore*, but there is no everyday equivalent to *carnivore* in British English (Indian English has the term *non-vegetarian*). Of course we could say *He's a meat-eater* (ignoring the complication of whether he eats fish), but we also tend to use a negative, as in *He's not a vegetarian*. Perhaps this indicates that vegetarianism is a concept – an 'ism', in fact – and so requires a more or less technical term, while eating meat seems to most of us merely normal, and so does not need a term. If it did, would we then use a Saxon or a Latinate term?

Some very powerful effects can be achieved by making use of the double vocabulary of English, and since poets are those who use the language most sensitively, poetry can, not surprisingly, do a great deal with it. Wordsworth's autobiographical poem *The Prelude* describes an episode when as a young man he roamed the mountains trying to trap birds:

> *Through half the night,*
> *Scudding away from snare to snare, I plied*
> *That anxious visitation; – moon and stars*
> *Were shining o'er my head. I was alone,*
> *And seemed to be a trouble to the peace*
> *That dwelt among them.*

This passage begins in purely Saxon vocabulary, even to using the rather unusual word *scud* for 'run like a hare'. The etymology is uncertain: it may be Scandinavian rather than Anglo-Saxon, but is certainly not Latinate. Using an unusual Saxon word is often striking, since it calls attention to the fact that we are going back to the roots of our language. When the poet's description of physical movement gives place to purpose and inner awareness, he shifts to the very Latinate terms *anxious visitation*. Then, when we move out from his consciousness to the peace around him we have more Saxon (and almost monosyllabic) vocabulary: 'moon and stars Were shining o'er my head.' Finally, returning to his consciousness, he tells us outright what his choice of vocabulary has already suggested, that he was a *trouble* (another Latinate word) 'to the peace That dwelt among them.' Inner consciousness is represented by Latinate terms; physical movement and external nature by Saxon. The only exception to this is *peace*, which, although a very ordinary word, is nonetheless from Latin *pax*. We simply have no ordinary Saxon word with that same meaning, the term *frith* having dropped out of use in the fourteenth century, so Wordsworth had no choice here.

There have been occasional protests against the Latinisation of English. William Barnes, the nineteenth-century poet who wrote in Dorset dialect, wanted to replace our Latinate nouns with Saxon ones, so that *electricity* would become *fireghost*, *vowel* would become *breath-sound*, and *fossil* would become *forestoning*. There is a kind of crazy integrity about this which can appeal to the heart of the English speaker, though it had no chance of success. A much milder version can be found in Otto Jespersen, perhaps the greatest scholar of the English language in the early twentieth century, who admitted that Latinate words had more international currency than Saxon ones, and were therefore more suitable for science, but also claimed

209

that 'national convenience should be considered before international ease'. Since he was Danish, he probably felt an affection for Germanic terms, and preferred *sleeplessness* to *insomnia*, and *wire* to *telegram* (but see page 25 for this last).

Latin Grammar and Latin Meaning

Do you get indignant when someone says *The media is to blame*? I pointed out in Chapter 1 that it is quite easy to predict which words or expressions will cause people to get angry, since there is as much fashion in linguistic indignation as there is in language itself. The use of a singular verb after *the media* rouses as much indignation as almost any other usage, and it is a consequence of the Latin element in our language.

Consider the four words *phenomena, data, agenda* and *media*. All are now current English words, and the last is one of the most commonly used words in the media – journalists and television commentators love to talk about themselves! *Phenomena*, which means 'things which are perceived', comes from Greek; the other three come from Latin. All four words are plurals in their original language, and were treated as plurals when they entered English. Now they are often treated as singular, as in *The data is clear on this point*, or *The agenda seems to be very long*. Let us look at them one at a time.

phenomena

This is the simplest case. The singular form, *phenomenon*, is found in English, and indeed is probably more common than the plural form. We speak about an interesting (or an extraordinary) *phenomenon*; literally, this means 'something we perceive', but we use the term very widely, even for something we can't actually perceive, to mean much the same as *happening*. If that is a mistake it is a mistake in meaning, rather than in grammar, and since loan words are always changing their meaning, we ought not to consider it a mistake at all. And since we have – and use – the singular form, there is no reason at all to use *phenomena* for the singular.

data

This means, literally, 'the things that are given' and it is of course a common and necessary term in science, where one has to distinguish the data from the conclusions. This one is slightly less straightforward, but the case for treating it as plural still seems strong. The singular form, *datum*, is found in English, though it is now rare, and is not used by scientists, who if they are looking for a singular form of *data* usually say *data point*. And on the whole we probably think of *data* as a plural, since it means much the same as facts: *His argument was supported by convincing lists of data.* It seems to me quite natural to turn that into *The data are convincing*, as we would say *The facts are convincing.* But I would not like to predict whether usage will in time overwhelm this argument, and *data* will be treated as a singular by everybody.

agenda

Literally, this means 'the things that ought to be done', and it usually denotes the list of what has to be discussed at a meeting. The things are plural, but the list is singular, and so the word has more and more grown to be treated as a singular. The case for doing this seems to me overwhelming, for the good reason that we need to be able to use it in the plural. If you have two meetings, you need to be able to say *Both agendas are very long* (or short, or tricky, or whatever), and there seems no other way of saying this without using a very roundabout sentence.

media

Here too we have a singular form, which we actually use, as when we speak of an *English-medium school*, or the telephone as a useful *medium of communication* (though in the second case *means of communication* is probably more common). Print, radio, television and the internet are of course the four great media of mass communication, shortened to *mass media* and, more and more, to *media*. Logically, this noun is in much the same situation as *data*, and the fact that we think of it having a plural meaning is made quite clear by the possibility of referring, as I just did, to the *four great media* of mass communication (nobody says *medias*). The logical case for treating it as a plural is therefore very strong, though it is perhaps weakened by the existence of the very similar term *the press*, referring to all the newspapers, which is unquestionably a singular. The fact that *media* is now so widely and frequently used as a singular is probably decisive in this case; logic has little hope against usage when the usage is so common. When defeat is inevitable, logic had better just lie back and think of English.

211

As well as Latin grammar, there is also the question of whether a Latin word retains its meaning when it is taken into English. As we know, there is no way to stop words from changing their meanings, but the process of change is not always smooth. Changes in meaning often begin as mistakes, but at what point does a mistake become so widespread that it begins to be correct? Once again, there is no substitute for using our judgement. Here are some borderline cases.

aggravate

This comes from the Latin *gravis*, meaning 'heavy'. It is not uncommon for a word meaning 'heavy' to take on other meanings: *lourd* in French also means 'clumsy', and *gravis* in Latin can mean 'unwholesome', or 'oppressive' or 'important'. In both French and English the main meaning of *grave* is 'serious'. To *aggravate* is therefore to make more serious – you aggravate a difficulty or a condition or a situation – always in a bad sense. It is understandable that when you complain that someone's behaviour has *aggravated* the situation you are expressing annoyance, and from this the word has come to be seen as meaning 'annoy', so that a person's behaviour might aggravate you. The more conscious you are of the etymology of the word, the more likely you are to dislike this shift of meaning. You won't say *I am aggravated by this use of aggravate*, since your annoyance is a sign that you don't use it in that sense. And since we have the perfectly good words *annoy* and *irritate* to cover the meaning, there is no need for us to aggravate the situation further.

original

The case of this word is rather different, because the original Latin meaning continues alongside the new meaning. As you should just have noticed. The Latin *origo* means 'beginning' or 'source', as does the English *origin*. If you paint a copy of the Mona Lisa, or translate a poem by Horace, we contrast the copy or the translation with the *original*. *Original* is here a noun, and we are not saying anything about the quality of Leonardo's picture or Horace's poem; we are simply contrasting the real thing with the copy. But if you write a book, and we are discussing the quality of what you have written, we may claim that it is a highly *original* work – meaning that it is very different from other books on the same subject. It is *original* in the sense that it does not look like a copy of any other book. From this it is a short step to saying that the books you write do not look like copies of anything else – they are so different from other works that we can immediately recognise them as yours. You are, in the modern sense, an *original* writer. This development of meaning is quite understandable, but as you have perhaps noticed it means that the new meaning is close to being the opposite of the old: an *original* writer, in the modern sense, is one whose works clearly have no *originals*. But this paradox does not seem to cause us any confusion.

pristine

The two Latin adjectives *priscus* and *pristinus* both mean 'belonging to former times, old-fashioned', and (perhaps most commonly) 'in its original state'. In English, *pristine* is most often used in connection with cleaning, as when a sheet or a handkerchief is *restored to its pristine whiteness*. From this, it has developed the meaning 'clean'; but this will be felt as a mistake by those conscious of the original meaning, and here too it is difficult to decide whether this new meaning has ceased to be a mistake. Once again, there is no need to exclaim *Look! It's pristine* as we take a sheet out of the washing machine; we have the word *clean*, and as an exclamation of delight we have the word *spotless*, which is much more common than *pristine*, and more clearly expresses our delight.

In conclusion, here is an exercise to torment yourself with. It is easy to write a sentence containing nothing but Saxon words: *The cat sat on the mat*, or the sentence that used to be a way of using every letter key on the typewriter, *The quick brown fox jumped over the lazy dog*. Can you write a sentence – a genuine English sentence – that contains nothing but Latinate words? Remember that *the* and *a*, the verbs *be, do, come, go* (and almost all our really common verbs), the pronouns and all the prepositions are Saxon. If you try this and find yourself frustrated, let me tell you that there is such a sentence in this chapter, so you might like to search for it as an alternative exercise. Whichever task you choose – good luck!

213

CHAPTER ELEVEN

Other Englishes

Four hundred years ago English was spoken by five or six million people, almost all of whom spoke no other language. Two hundred years ago it was spoken by about ten million in Britain, seven million in the newly independent USA, and a handful of colonists, mainly in Canada and South Africa. Today it is the first language of well over 400 million, and a fluent second language of at least a billion more.

Four hundred years ago there was great variety among the forms of English spoken in Britain; today British English is more uniform, but there is enormous variety in English around the world. The difference we are most familiar with is that between British and American English – both of these, of course, the English of native speakers. They both have considerable internal differences: we have only to think of how Londoners, Northerners, Scots and Irish speak, or of the differences between Alabamans, New Yorkers and speakers of the standard American English spread over much of the continent. There are further varieties, of course, in the Commonwealth countries, such as South Africa, Australia and the West Indies. The term we used for geographical varieties in an earlier chapter was dialects, but American or Australian English are more often called varieties, and dialect is used for varieties among native speakers within (or from) the same country.

American English

The variety that the British are most familiar with is, of course, American, since they have grown up with an awareness of American English, derived from watching American films and television and, more and more, through meeting Americans. It is also the variety about which many people (and not only the British) have strong feelings. A charming middle-aged Englishwoman, touring America in the footsteps of Dickens for a television programme, explained to an American she was interviewing that she believed the kind of English she herself spoke was – she hesitated a moment before bringing out the next word – 'better than the kind you speak'. This does not seem the best way to endear yourself to the natives, but the American did not seem offended. 'You're making a value judgement,' she replied, and then went on to claim that American English, in the time of Dickens, and perhaps subsequently, was more full of vitality than British English. (She did not explain whether that too was a value judgement.) This judgement – that British English is 'better' – is, in an odd way, often shared by Americans. I lived in Tennessee for a while, and people often said to me 'Gee, I could just listen to you talking all day long.' They clearly liked my accent, but their liking may have had a touch of condescension about it; they were finding it charming but quaint, perhaps not to be taken altogether seriously.

Let us take care to avoid value judgements for a while, to be descriptive, not prescriptive, and ask what the most noticeable differences are between British and American English. What strikes us first when listening is, of course, the pronunciation; it is not easy to describe it in writing without getting very technical, and since this book does not deal directly with pronunciation, I'll omit it. Next are differences in vocabulary: Americans say *truck* for lorry, *elevator* for lift, *cookies* for biscuits, *airplane* for aeroplane, *closet* for wardrobe, *yard* for garden, *maybe* for perhaps; they eat *chips* rather than crisps; they go to *college* rather than to university. A British person who visits America for the first time is often surprised to find how many everyday objects have different names. Suppose we need to fix a few things on our car – the boot or the bonnet doesn't lock properly, the gear lever rattles, or there is a crack in the windscreen. We say all this to the mechanic and he will understand us, though for him the boot is the *trunk*, the bonnet is the *hood*, the gear lever is the *gear shift*, and the windscreen is the *windshield*. Or we go shopping with our children. The baby needs a set of nappies and a dummy, the toddler needs a pushchair, the mother needs tights and father has decided to buy a waistcoat. This time I am not sure everything will be understood. No doubt much will depend on whether the shop assistant is used to hearing British English; he calls nappies *diapers*, the dummy is a *comforter*, the pushchair is a *stroller*, tights are *pantyhose* and a waistcoat is a *vest*. There may be a little giggling, but we'll end up with the right purchases.

There are of course a few well-worn jokes about Anglo-American misunderstandings, more often involving verbs, and verbs with prepositions, rather than nouns, since mistakes about concrete objects are not very difficult to sort out – you can usually point! We have no difficulty in understanding the American expression *do the dishes*, but most Americans are not familiar with *wash up*, especially since they use that to mean 'wash', so that the American hostess asking her British guests if they'd like to *wash up* might leave them a little surprised at American hospitality. Even more awkward is *knock up*. The English host who offers to knock his female visitor up in the morning is simply using a rather old-fashioned expression offering to wake her, but if she is American it may sound as if he intends to get her pregnant. And if she asks for the bathroom, and he tells her it's on the *first floor*, she will not climb the stairs unless she knows that her first floor is our *ground floor*, and our *first floor* is her *second floor*. And the English host might not have sent her upstairs if he'd known that the *bathroom* she wanted is known to him as the *lavatory* (or the *toilet* or the *loo*, depending on the term he normally uses – as we saw in Chapter 8). She comes back down the stairs when she is *through* – another Americanism which is by now quite well known in Britain, though it can still mislead if you are on the telephone and the American operator asks *Are you through?* If you say 'Yes' (because you are connected) you are likely to be cut off. Less well known, but quite as striking, is the difference in meaning of *momentarily* – 'for a moment' in British English, but 'in a moment' in American – so that when the pilot announces just before take-off that *we'll be momentarily airborne* the British passenger might be understandably alarmed!

We all know what *trucks, elevators* and *cookies* are; in fact all the items in that first list were chosen because they are well known outside America. They show how familiar American English now is to the British and to most other English-speaking countries, and many of them are now used in Britain. Vocabulary differences between

British and American English are not really different in principle from the vocabulary differences between English dialects, such as whether one says *girl*, *lass* or *maiden*, depending on which part of Britain one lives in, or the enormous number of different words for a little creature such as the newt, for which there may be a lot of variation within one county. As more and more of us move from one part of the country to another, and Standard English exerts more and more influence, these differences among English dialects tend to diminish – just as other differences flood in from the English of other countries.

It is clearly not possible to list all the Anglo-American vocabulary differences in a book like this, and there are now several good dictionaries of American usage and American vocabulary. But I must now add that it is not only in vocabulary that the two varieties differ. There are grammatical differences too, for instance in the use of tenses: Americans say *I would have told you that if I would have known* where the British say *if I had known*, and *He just arrived* instead of the British *He's just arrived*. This last example is particularly interesting, since it involves what is sometimes called the perfect tense, a tense that causes great difficulties to most Europeans. Although French and German, for instance, both use the auxiliary verb *have* to make a form of the past tense, they do not use it in the same way as English. That is why you often hear Europeans, even those who know English well, say *I have done it yesterday*. It is hard for them to grasp that our perfect tense is really a kind of present tense, and means something like 'I am now in the position of having done it', and so it cannot be used with a word like *yesterday*, which belongs to the past. This is one of the trickiest details in English grammar – and like all grammatical details, native speakers know how to use it, even if they cannot explain it. But it is easy to sympathise with the foreigner learning English when one observes that an already difficult grammatical usage is not quite the same on the two sides of the Atlantic.

We saw in our discussion of grammar that it is not always possible to separate questions of grammar from questions of vocabulary, and my next example illustrates this. It concerns the second person pronoun. As we all know, English has only one form, *you*, for singular and plural, for subject and object. German has five, so that *Du hast es, Ihr habt es*, and *Sie haben es* are all translated as *You have it*, with no distinction between singular familiar, plural familiar, and the polite form. When *you* is the object, *ich sehe dich, ich sehe euch,* and *ich sehe Sie* are all translated as *I see you*. This makes English easier to learn (though it is worth mentioning that ease or difficulty of learning a language applies mainly to the early stages; when it comes to mastering usage and idioms, all languages are difficult).

In some parts of America there is a plural form of *you: you all,* pronounced (and sometimes written) as *y'all.* It is found mainly in the southern states, but not unknown in other parts, and enables some Americans to distinguish between singular and plural, as with French *tu* and *vous* (though still not between familiar and formal), and gives the visiting British an extra pronoun to learn.

But such things never stay simple. Just as French and German use the plural form when addressing one person if the speaker wants to be formal, so *y'all* can also be used in the singular. But David Crystal, who has made a fascinating study of its use, points out that it is often used in the singular to convey warmth, so that *Y'all take care now* – addressed to one person – might be felt as more friendly than *You take care now –* the opposite to the French or German use!

My final example of Anglo-American difference concerns dates. When writing the date in figures only, as is usual when abbreviating it, British English puts them in the order 'day, month, year'. So also do other European languages (differences between languages disappear, of course, when it comes to figures). So the twelfth of March 2005 is 12/3/2005. This seems sensible enough, but although we say either *the twelfth of March* or *March the twelfth,* Americans almost always say *March the twelfth* – or even *March twelve.* And so when writing it in figures they write 3/12/2005 – which to a European would of course be *the third of December.* Many Europeans and most Americans do not know about this difference.

Or rather, they did not. What changed this was the eleventh of September 2001. Everyone knows about the attacks on New York and Washington on that day, and almost all of us know that the Americans refer to it as 9/11 – an all too appropriate abbreviation for them, since the emergency number on the telephone (999 in Britain) is 911 in the United States. Plenty of people in Britain now refer to the disaster as *nine-eleven,* though I feel fairly sure that most Americans do not realise that to the British the figures normally mean 'the ninth of November'. I sometimes speculate whether this is going to cause a change in our way of writing the date, but that seems unlikely. We still write the tenth of September as 10/9, and indeed we don't altogether think of *nine-eleven* as a date, rather as a name for the event itself. But time will show.

Time will show; and few things are more foolish than to guess what it will show. Noah Webster, the great American lexicographer, predicted in 1789 that 'in the course of time' North American English would be 'as different from the future language of England as the Modern Dutch, Danish and Swedish are from the German, or from one another.' This prediction was often repeated in the early nineteenth century by both British and American writers (the British usually with disapproval, the Americans sometimes with delight). 'The course of time' has seen two centuries pass, and there is no sign of this happening – though it is worth mentioning that when British and American usage differ, the British are far more likely to know the American expression than the other way round. The main reason for this is obviously films, followed by pop music, in both of which American performers have large British audiences.

All English-speaking countries have their own vocabularies, though the differences between British English and that of South Africa, Australia and New Zealand are mild compared with American English. In South Africa a *robot* is not an automatic servant but a traffic light, the *bioscope* is the cinema, and if you *stay* in Western Road that does not mean you are there temporarily but that you live there. In Australia if you are taking your *sheila* to the beach *this arvo*, and are reminding her to take her *bathers*, it is not difficult for us to guess that these are the terms for 'girl', 'this afternoon' and 'swimming costume'. The English-speaking territory whose English is so far from ours as to cause us real difficulty on occasion is probably the West Indies, where difficulties can result from their intonation and their many pidgins and creoles. To which I now turn.

Languages Meeting

What happens when languages meet? It has happened quite often that English has met another language. When the Anglo-Saxons were still on mainland Europe they encountered Roman traders, and took a few Latin words from them; when they arrived in a country that was not yet called England they encountered a Celtic people who spoke Old Welsh – and a few of whom no doubt still spoke Latin, since the Romans had only recently left. Neither of these encounters had much effect on the language; no one quite understands why the Anglo-Saxon invaders took hardly any Celtic words into their language. Then in the ninth and tenth centuries, when the Celts had been driven into what is now Wales and the highlands of Scotland, and the rest of the island was English-speaking, the Vikings invaded. These spoke a Scandinavian language, and occupied the north and east. And then, two hundred years after that, the Norman French conquered the whole of England; so, in the space of five or six centuries, English met three, even four, other languages. By far the greatest effect was produced by the last two encounters, those with Scandinavian and with French, as we have seen in our earlier discussions. Then, in the last three hundred years, English has met a lot of other languages – not in Britain, but because of English-speaking armies and traders, followed by colonial officials, as they entered and occupied and for a while ruled over what used to be called 'the empire on which the sun never sets'.

When languages first meet, the two sets of people obviously cannot understand each other; but sometimes they need to – if for instance they want to trade, or if one group is trying to collect slaves or indentured labourers from the other. In that case they will use a very simplified form of one language, or perhaps a mixture of both. This simplified language is known as a pidgin, and it is most likely to be based on the language of the dominant nation. The commonest pidgins are therefore versions of the languages of the great trading and colonising nations: French, Spanish, Portuguese and above all English. A pidgin is nobody's mother tongue, and if the two groups lose contact it may die out.

Perhaps the most studied pidgin is Tok Pisin, spoken in Papua New Guinea, which is English-based. 'I see you' and 'You see me' in Tok Pisin are *mi lukim yu* and *yu lukim mi*; the pronouns have no case endings, so the words for 'I' and 'me' are the same. 'My father' and 'our house' are *papa bilong mi* and *haus bilong mipela*; *bilong*, from English 'belong', expresses possession, and *pela*, from English 'fellow', expresses plural. Quaint to our ears, but perhaps not very difficult to learn.

Pidgins have fewer sounds and fewer words than normal languages, so it is often necessary to use a lot of words to say something quite simple. But this is not because the speakers are primitive people who cannot master complicated grammar or a large vocabulary. Speakers of pidgin already have a language of their own, which will have nothing crude or primitive about it; all linguists, in fact, are agreed that there is no such thing as a primitive language. Every human language goes back many thousands of years, and those spoken in countries most remote from civilisation often have very complicated grammar. The inhabitants of Papua New Guinea who use Tok Pisin come from a country with many hundreds of indigenous languages, any one of which we would find much harder to learn than they find English.

A pidgin arises naturally as a result of natural influences, but there can also be attempts to deliberately construct something very like a pidgin. Half a century ago, two philosophers of language, I. A. Richards and C. K. Ogden, devised what they called Basic English. They chose from the vocabulary of English about a thousand words which they thought would provide the most useful vocabulary, selecting the words not for their frequency or familiarity but for their usefulness in enabling speakers to express most of the things they would want to say. They clearly felt that to construct an artificial language within a natural language had many advantages over the purely artificial languages like Esperanto, and they even seem to have hoped that Basic English might become a world language, but of course it didn't.

The latest attempt on these lines is Globish, a simplified form of English which to a certain extent already is a world language. It is very common today for two speakers who do not know each other's language (a Japanese and a Brazilian, say, or a Bengali and a Finn – the number of possible encounters is enormous) to communicate in English. The English they use may have a very limited vocabulary, and may not be very idiomatic, but it works for practical purposes. It is not likely, however, to develop sayings and idioms of its own, since it does not belong to any identifiable group. That will happen when a new form of English grows up in a particular area, spoken by a group of people who are in regular contact with one another, as has happened in (for instance) Singapore or the Philippines. Singlish (or Singapore English) and Taglish (or Philippine English) have the kind of simplified grammar and mixed vocabulary found in pidgins, and they can produce some very colourful speech, and even writing. The only reason they are not quite the same as pidgins is that they are often spoken by people who can speak Standard English as well.

If two groups who can communicate only in pidgin begin to intermarry, their children may grow up with the pidgin as their first language. In that case something very interesting happens: the children speak the pidgin much more quickly, and it develops the same complicated grammar as any natural language. It is then known as a creole. If a creole derived from English is spoken in a country that, as it moves into the modern world, comes into contact with world English, we can get the odd situation that both English and an English-derived creole are spoken in the same place. In that case international English, being much more widespread and powerful, may gradually displace the language that derives from it. In Greek and Roman mythology Saturn, king of the Gods before Jupiter, devoured his own children; English can do the same.

Post-Colonialism

English is now spoken as a second language by far more people than those who are native speakers. That is what it means to be a world language. The highest proportion of fluent, non-native speakers is found in Europe, above all perhaps in Holland and the Scandinavian countries, where some could pass for native speakers. But if we count as 'English speakers' all who can make themselves understood in English, then India may have the largest number (far more English speakers than Britain has people).

To the inhabitants of Africa and Asia there may be no political development of the twentieth century more important than the end of the European empires: the German after the First World War; the Dutch, Portuguese, French and British after the Second. The independent countries have since had to decide what to do about the legacy – military, economic, political and linguistic – left by the departing powers. It is understandable that they should wish to shake off some of this legacy, including the linguistic. Indonesia has got rid of Dutch, Angola of Portuguese, and many of the French colonies in Africa seem to be getting rid of French – and learning English instead! For everyone is learning English. Almost every country in the world – perhaps every one – has English speakers; most countries teach English in school. Matthew Parris, writing in *The Times*, has described the fascinating experience of visiting a primary school in Ethiopia to listen to an English lesson. The school buildings were primitive, some of the children had sores or eye problems or were in rags, and the classes were large; but the teachers were dedicated and competent, discipline was perfect, and the children were learning enthusiastically and well. He was watching an unstoppable revolution, the spread of world English. Perhaps the most striking moment was when one of the pupils asked him what his own native language was – was he an Italian? He had taken part in the lesson, and helped them with their English, but the fact that he could do that did not, to the pupils, necessarily mean that he was English. This teaches us two things, surely. First, that being monoglot (speaking only one language), as most people are in Britain, is not necessarily a natural condition – all over Africa, people speak several languages. And second, that English no longer belongs to the native speakers: now that it has become a world language, anyone could be speaking it. One of the consequences of this is re-examining what we mean by a mistake.

When a foreigner who is speaking English uses words or constructions that seem odd to us, we normally distinguish between mistakes and variants. If English is their first language (if, for instance, they are American or Australian or Jamaican – or indeed Irish or Cockney) then differences from Standard English are variants; but if the speaker is French or Mexican then differences from Standard English will be considered mistakes. So when South Africans say *stay* not only for where they live temporarily but also permanently, we do not consider that a mistake but a variant. But when Ghanaians say *Yes please* and also, by analogy, *No please*, although the usage is quite logical, it is not idiomatic English. And because the speaker's native language is not English, but Ga or Twi or Ewe, we call it not a variant but a mistake. But English is now so widespread, and its relation to other languages can be so complicated, that this distinction sometimes breaks down. There are parts of the world where it is not even possible to be sure what some people's native language is. In Lusaka, the capital of Zambia, a good many people speak English and Nyanja, the African language which is spoken over the whole country, and also an African language spoken only by their own tribe.

Within the family they might speak either English or Nyanja, with their grandparents they might speak only the local language, in the market what they speak might depend on who they are talking to. If they are fluent in all three (as many are), it is not easy to decide what their native language is; and a situation like this is found all over Africa and in parts of India.

And even when it is quite clear that English is not their mother tongue, speakers might still be reluctant to regard their variants as mistakes. The case of India is the most striking here. Indians often use tenses differently from the British, and say *He is knowing the answer*, or use prepositions differently, and ask you to *pay attention on* what they are saying. Are those mistakes? Very few of India's millions of fluent English speakers could claim that English is in any sense their native language, but this does not prevent some Indians from arguing that they should not be required to speak Standard British or American English. They claim instead that British or American speakers, when talking to Indians, should be required to 'de-Englishise' or 'de-Americanise' their speech in order to communicate with 'speakers of new varieties of English', who have a right, as one defender of 'Indian English' writes, 'to say what they want to in essentially the way in which they want to say it.' It is almost impossible to imagine a Swede or a German claiming that departures from British or American English should be encouraged in their country because they have a right to say what they want to say in the way they want to say it. If fluent in English, they are more likely to pride themselves on speaking English without errors, and if any are pointed out, would be eager to correct them. What is the reason for this difference? It must surely be that Sweden and Germany were never British colonies, so that there is no political drive to regard British English as a relic of imperialism, and to resent its imposition.

When the newly independent colonies began to consider what language they should use, the same thing happened in many of them. In India, Hindi seemed the obvious choice; in Ghana, the Akan languages; in much of East Africa, Swahili; in Sri Lanka, Sinhalese. And in every country, there were minorities who did not speak this new 'national language', or even if they did speak it, resented it as an attempt to crush their pride and independence – indeed, as a sign of 'imperialism'. So those who live in the north of Ghana or in the south of India prefer English as the national language of their independent country, because it is equally foreign – or equally familiar – to everyone. When we add in the enormous usefulness of English as the language of trade, of science and – now – of the internet, it looks as if world English is here to stay.

For ever? Well, as we all know, 'never say never'. At the moment America is the richest and most powerful nation in the world, but this may not last. What will happen when the richest nation is Japan (or Germany or Brazil) and the most powerful is China (or India or whoever)? Will there be a new world language, or will English be so entrenched that the new leading nation will have to speak English as well as its own language? I have asked a lot of questions in this book, and tried to answer most of them, but this one I shall leave unanswered.

Instead, let us conclude on an issue that at first glance seems to have little to do with world English.

Spelling

I knew a young woman once whose surname was Ough. She pointed out, with a mixture of amusement and pride, that there were eight ways of pronouncing it. She was cheating slightly, since she included *lough* (pronounced with the same vowel as *lock*, but with a guttural rasp for the last consonant), which is really Irish, and *hiccough*, which is just an upmarket spelling of *hiccup*. But that still leaves six quite genuine pronunciations, as in *cough, bough, although, through, enough* and *thought*. She pronounced it to rhyme with *although*, but there was no way of guessing this.

That is probably the most extreme example of the irregularity of English spelling, but there are plenty of others: *c* can be pronounced as in *come* or *censor*, *s* as in *wise* or *waist*. And as well as different pronunciations of the same letter, there are different spellings for the same sound: *see, sea, piece, metre* and *Phoebe* (but perhaps the last is cheating, since it's really a Greek word); or *fate, wait, eight* and *lay*. You perhaps know Bernard Shaw's joke spelling of 'fish' as *ghoti* – *gh* as in *enough*, *o* as in *women*, and *ti* as in *station*. We can make up other joke spellings, like *mops* for 'miss' (*o* once again as in *women*, and *ps* as in *psychology*); great fun for word games, but crazy (surely) for our unfortunate schoolchildren. Italian schoolchildren don't have to learn spelling – why should we?

If you have been reading this book straight through you may have been surprised to reach the end without yet finding any discussion of our crazy spelling, or proposal for spelling reform. Every now and then a letter appears in *The Times* or another newspaper announcing that it really is time for us to clean up our spelling, and perhaps claiming (as Shaw did) that it costs us millions of pounds every week, because of the extra letters we have to type.

So have I deliberately kept the question of spelling till last, so as to end on a rousing call to action? To conclude by saying that since English is now a world language, the moment has come to do the one simple thing that will make it really worthy of its eminence, and make it easy for everyone to learn – reform the spelling?

Alas, no. I am not going to end on that clarion call, because the spelling reformers are urging us down a road to nowhere. There are three objections to their campaign, all of them so interesting that even without a call to reform they will make a good ending to our journey round the language. I'll begin with the least important.

It would not be easy. If we believe Shaw's calculation (which I don't) about the vast sums that our spelling costs the economy, we can be quite sure that during the transition period, changing the spelling would cost far more. Think of the chaos in schools where Class 1 is learning the new spelling just after Class 2 learned the old: if they had new reading books, would the old ones be thrown away? Would all our existing books be thrown away? Would a novel published in 2007 be as hard to read as a book published in 1507?

Of course we could be told that these are the time-honoured conservative objections to any kind of radical change, and that you can't make omelettes without breaking dictionaries. As I write, a very modest spelling reform is being tried in Germany, where the government has decided to do away with the symbol ß, the German way of writing double s. This small change is already being resisted, and may cause a good deal of disruption, although we shan't know until some time has passed.

I turn to my second objection: English spelling is not as crazy as we usually assume, and the contrast with Italian is rather misleading. The reason Italian poses no spelling problems is that it's such a uniform language: its entire vocabulary, except for recent borrowings from English, derives from Latin. But English, as we saw in the last chapter, has accommodated a constant stream of foreign words in its vocabulary, which have sometimes brought their spelling with them, and sometimes had English spelling thrust on them in a way that can't always be consistent. The *k* at the beginning and the *gh* in the middle of *knight* were once pronounced, and are a reminder that it is related to German *Knecht*, which still has five sounds, whereas *knight* now has three.

But that, you may feel, doesn't matter. It is interesting for a few historically minded scholars to be able to look at an English word and see its history in its spelling; but most language users care about the present, not the past. If they want to study the history of our words they can do so; they don't need constant historical reminders in everyday usage.

But the history embedded in words cannot, alas, be so easily pushed aside. Here's a simple sentence: *I adore international politics.* Eccentric, you might feel, but for the moment we're only concerned with the vocabulary. You might not share this adoration; you might be more interested in the political events in your own nation. Now say these three pairs of words aloud: *adore* and *adoration, nation* and *international, politics* and *political.* Do you notice the differences in pronunciation? The vowel at the beginning of *adore* is the neutral vowel we use at the beginning of *alone* or *again*; but at the beginning of *adoration* we give the *a* the same value as in *mad* or *sad.* The *a* of *nation* is the vowel used in *fate*, in *international* it is pronounced like the *a* of *fashion.* And in the middle syllable of *politics* the vowel is once again neutral, whereas it takes the stress in *political* and is the same vowel as in *lit.* So if English spelling were reformed, and the same sound were always written in the same way, these pairs of words —*nation/international, politics/political,* and *adore/adoration* – would all be spelled quite differently from each other, and it might not be clear that they are variants of the same word. Three examples, but there are hundreds more.

And which is more important: that our spelling should be an accurate guide to pronunciation, or that it should be a logical way of making words look alike because they belong together? After all, we don't often read aloud. If we *sign* our name, that's our *signature*; but if we *sein* our name, would we feel so sure that's our *signacher*? We

227

surely want written English to help us understand how the words are behaving, which bits of meaning go with which others – awr els we meit looz owr wai.

And now to the third point, which is the most important of all, and which is the reason we are looking at spelling in the chapter on international English. Spelling reformers want English words to be written as they are pronounced – pronounced by whom? In Southern England *one* is pronounced to rhyme with *fun*, in Northern England it rhymes with *on*. In England *metal* has a different consonant in the middle from *medal*; in large parts of America they are the same. Native speakers of English can usually recognise American, Australian, South African and Caribbean accents, and can often tell if a speaker is from India or Japan. The range of pronunciation is enormous; which version are we to choose to base our spelling on?

Before you answer 'Standard English, of course', think of the implications. The country with the largest number of native speakers of English is of course the United States; so if there was a referendum, they would win easily. But can we imagine the British accepting a reformed spelling based on American pronunciation? Or would even the Americans be outvoted by the millions of English speakers in India and China? When discussing Standard English in Chapter 4, I suggested that we should use that term for written English, and another term, such as Received Pronunciation (often shortened to RP), for the English spoken by educated people in the Home Counties of England. And now we can see why. How many of the billion or more English speakers use RP? Not an easy question to answer, and further complicated by the rise of what's often nowadays called 'Estuary English'. This is the English spoken by Londoners and inhabitants of the south-east of England, and it is a blend of RP and cockney. If we include those with only a slight touch of cockney in their Estuary English, then there may be twenty million speakers of RP; if we are stricter in our definition, and insist on the vowels of what used to be called 'BBC English' or 'The Queen's English', it might be half that number. But certainly it will be a minority of the sixty million or so who live in Britain, and a very small minority indeed of the world's English speakers.

The social implication of this is, surely, plain. Standard English as a written form is socially unifying: it enables people of very different

cultures, backgrounds, and education, spread all over the world, to communicate with one another. It emphasises unity, not difference, and increases communication (and, one hopes, mutual understanding). RP does no harm if regarded as one of the many variants of English, and will no doubt always enjoy high prestige, but to insist that it is the 'only correct' form of spoken English is socially divisive. And if English spelling were reformed, and made to indicate the pronunciation of RP, that would be a very divisive act. We are in the fortunate position that we can let a thousand flowers bloom when we speak, and enjoy the benefits of a common language when we write. In a world where so much goes wrong, is this not something that has gone right?

Index

This is a book to be read, rather than a reference book: to look words up one really needs a dictionary, or a guide to usage arranged like a dictionary. But since this book does discuss many of the controversial issues in the use of English today, you might want to be able to check whether a particular word or problem is dealt with. So here is an index. Topics and names are in Roman, examples and book titles in *italics*.

231